"Noyses, sounds, and sweet aires"

"Noyses, sounds, and sweet aires":

Music in Early Modern England

Compiled and Edited by Jessie Ann Owens

The Folger Shakespeare Library
Washington, DC, 2006

This volume has been published in conjunction with the exhibition *"Noyses, sounds, and sweet aires": Music in Early Modern England* presented at The Folger Shakespeare Library®, Washington, DC, from June 2 through September 9, 2006.

Gail Kern Paster, Director

Richard Kuhta, Eric Weinmann Librarian

Rachel Doggett, Andrew W. Mellon Curator of Books and Exhibitions

This exhibition and the catalogue have been funded by The Winton and Carolyn Blount Exhibition Fund and The Andrew W. Mellon Publication Fund of The Folger Shakespeare Library.

Printed in the United States.

Distributed by University of Washington Press,
Seattle and London.
ISBN 10: 0-295-98656-5
ISBN 13: 978-0-205-98656-2

Photographs by Julie Ainsworth.

Cover: Detail from *Nieuwen ieucht spieghel . . .*, 1620.

· a eulogistic oration/writing ; formal/elaborate praise
· an aggressive attack/refutation/disputation/controversy

Contents

Acknowledgments

This catalogue is a collaborative endeavor, in the best spirit of the Folger Shakespeare Library. I received so many different kinds of assistance from so many people that it would be impossible to enumerate them all. I do, however, want to signal my appreciation for particular contributions.

Peter Clark, Gerard Kilroy, Steven May, H. Colin Slim, Warwick Edwards, Susan Boynton, Leofranc Holford-Strevens, and David Klausner provided prompt answers to questions. Ellen Harris, Judith Maltby, Craig Monson, and Sarah Weiner read portions of the catalogue and essays and offered valuable comments. Ian Harwood, Kerry McCarthy, John Milsom, Eric Rice, Samuel Schmitt, and Pamela Starr wrote entries and gave crucial advice. Stacey Jocoy Houck, Nicholas Temperley, and Andrew Walkling all wrote descriptions for an entire case. Ross Duffin, Stacey Jocoy Houck, Craig Monson, Bruce Smith, Jeremy Smith, and Nicholas Temperley contributed essays, made valuable suggestions about objects to include, and helped in countless other ways. Nicholas Temperley provided new editions of psalm settings, which, thanks to Eric Rice, have been recorded by *Exsultemus*, the Boston-based period vocal ensemble.

This catalogue is also tangible evidence of the unrivaled collaboration between scholars who are Library readers and scholars who are members of the Library staff. Georgianna Ziegler, Louis B. Thalheimer Head of Reference, answered countless questions and took me into the vault to show me objects she thought might be included. Other suggestions came from Curator of Manuscripts Heather Wolfe, Curator of Manuscripts Emerita Laetitia Yeandle, Curator of Art and Special Collections Erin Blake, Andrew W. Mellon Curator of Books and Exhibitions Rachel Doggett, and Exhibitions Coordinator Leigh Anne Palmer. Erin Blake, Rachel Doggett, Leigh Anne Palmer, Heather Wolfe, and Georgianna Ziegler all contributed catalogue entries, and Heather Wolfe and Erin Blake reviewed and revised the entries for their respective areas. Head of Conservation Frank Mowery and the other conservators helped with the final choices of objects for display and the virtual reconstruction of a dismembered manuscript. Head of Reader Services Betsy Walsh and the good-natured and efficient staff of the Reading Room worked very hard to keep me supplied with books and manuscripts. Leigh Anne Palmer helped with every phase of the project; her blend of sense, efficiency, and good cheer made her a pleasure to work with. My greatest debt is to Rachel Doggett, who helped me shape the conception of the exhibition and shared her deep knowledge of the collection. Her encouragement and advice have been invaluable.

The Folger is more than a great library; it is also an unparalleled center for research in early modern studies. My work on this catalogue in some sense dates from the very happy and productive year I spent as a long-term fellow in 1998–1999. The other fellows—Susan Lanser, Patricia Fortini Brown, Ann Rosalind Jones, Peter Stallybrass, and "honorary fellow" Jo Radner—have taught me a great deal and remain close friends. Anne Hoffmann, who joined this fellowship two years ago, has shared her own passion for early music.

If this catalogue were to bear a dedication, it would read: "to tea at the Folger," in gratitude for those countless "Folger moments." There was always someone who knew something about anything I wanted to know about early modern England.

Jessie Ann Owens
Brandeis University

Soundscapes of Early Modern England

Jessie Ann Owens

Detail, cat. 27.

Ben Jonson gives the chaos and din of London a central role in his 1609 comedy *Epicoene, or the Silent Woman.*[1] Morose, "a gent that loues no noise," tries to disinherit his nephew by marrying and producing an heir; however, the only kind of woman he could bear to marry is a silent one. He even wears "a huge Turbant of Night-caps on his head, buckled ouer his eares" to block out the blare of the city. The sounds that drive him mad are the street cries of the "Fish-wiues," "Orenge-women," "Chimney-sweepers," "Broome-men," and the "Costard monger." Trve-Wit and Clerimont, the nephew's friends, describe Morose's phobia in clamorous detail:

> *Trv.* Me thinkes, a Smith should be ominous.
>
> *Cle.* Or any Hammer-man. A Brasier is not suffer'd to dwell in the Parish, nor an Armorer. He would haue hang'd a Pewterers' prentice once vpon a Shroue-tuesdayes Ryot, for being o' that Trade, when the rest were quit.
>
> *Trv.* A Trumpet should fright him terribly, or the Hau'-boyes?
>
> *Cle.* Out of his senses. The Waights of the Citie haue a Pension of him, not to come neere that Ward. This Youth practis'd on him, one night, like the Bell-man; and neuer left till hee had brought him downe to the doore, with a Long-Sword: and there left him fliourishing with the Ayre. (Act I, scene 1)

These sounds of the city—bells, cries of street vendors, the civic music of the town band (the "waits"), the noise of tradesmen—are part of the "acoustic world" of early modern England, a world, as Bruce Smith has shown, far different from ours. His book inspired me to organize this exhibition and portray the sounds of early modern England as a series of soundscapes, to hear what drove Morose mad.[2]

The term "soundscape," which the "widget" dictionary on my Mac (the term has not yet made it into the OED) defines as "the sounds heard in a particular location, considered as a whole," has been used at least since the late 1960s, when it was introduced by R. Murray Schafer for an interdisciplinary project on the sonic environment.[3] Now widely used in ethnomusicological circles, the term became part of my own working vocabulary when I taught from Kay Kaufman Shelemay's world music textbook, *Soundscapes: Exploring Music in a Changing World* (New York, 2001). For Shelemay, soundscapes "arise from the distinctive setting, sound, and significance of music"; she is particularly concerned with "music's ability both to stay in place and to move in the world today."[4] Bruce Smith brings the listener into the picture as well: "A soundscape consists, therefore, not just of the environment that the listener attends to but of the listener-*in*-the-environment. It constitutes an ecological system, and like other such systems it can be balanced or

/ the sounds of bells, the cacophony of street criers, the scraping of fiddlers in taverns

unbalanced, viable or dysfunctional."[5] Smith's perspective reminds us that we need to be thinking not only of *who* was making the sounds (and in music, that can be composer as well as performer), where, and for what purpose, but also who was listening.

In focusing on the soundscapes of early modern England rather than on the famous and mighty—the "master" composers who people our histories of music and the patrons who helped finance music—the exhibition invites the viewer to hear the wide range of sounds that Caliban described as ". . . noyses,/ Sounds, and sweet aires, that giue delight and hurt not" (*Tempest* 3.2.148–49).[6]

"NOYSES, SOUNDS . . ."

The exhibition begins with "noyses" and "sounds"—the sounds of bells, the cacophony of street criers, the scraping of fiddlers in taverns, the songs that were an essential part of plays, and the ballads heard on the street and in taverns and on stage. Imagine the sounds of bells marking the passage of time and the raucous cries of street vendors advertising goods for sale. Plays are filled with the same kinds of music—songs, snippets of ballads, catches—that you would hear in taverns and on the street; in "'What means this noise?'" Bruce Smith captures the sound world produced by comedians such as Kemp and Armin, who "move freely around the circle, from speech through music through ambient sound through exclamations back to speech through music through ambient sound . . . and so on."

And everywhere, ballads. Ballads for sale—Holmes's catch, "Will you buy a new merry Book, or a doleful Ditty" (cat. 10); ballads being sold—Savage's engraving of Laroon's "A Merry new Song," capturing the image of a ballad singer and seller (cat. 11); ballads on walls and in cases (cat. 19–23). In "Ballads in Shakespeare's World," Ross Duffin makes clear just how popular ballads were—there were probably four thousand in print by 1600—and how pervasive in Shakespeare's plays.[7] Even the ubiquitous complaints about ballads attest to their popularity. Hannah Woolley, author of *The Gentlewoman's Companion* (cat. 72), a conduct book, warns against taking "delight in an idle vain Song" and then proceeds to give quite a detailed description of "the multiplicity of vanity and trumpery which stuff these Ballads": "how an amorous or rather foolishly fond Virgin forsook Kindred and Country, to run after a stranger and her Lover. In another you find how craftily two Lovers had plotted their private meetings to prosecute their unlawful enjoyments . . . " Clearly she, too, had more than a passing acquaintance with the genre!

The sounds of the streets and taverns and theaters are captured in the very music most often heard there. Catches are rounds, familiar to us from music like "Row, row, row your boat," typically written for three or four voices of the same range, usually to humorous and even scurrilous texts. These catches (the term may derive from the Italian word for hunt, as successive parts follow or "hunt" one another, or possibly from the French word for a chase) bring to life the sounds of bells—"The great bels of Oesney" (cat. 1) and "Jak boy ho boy newis" (cat. 3); street cries—"Broomes for old shooes" (cat. 8) and "Will you buy a new merry Book" (cat. 10); the joys of sack and tobacco—"If any so wise is that Sack he despises" (cat. 15) and "Tobacco fumes away all nastie rheumes" (cat. 17).

"SWEET AIRES"

This exhibition is also about "sweet aires," the composed music, vocal and instrumental, preserved in written form in manuscripts and printed books (the sounds themselves have long since vanished). This is high-brow music, typically performed indoors, in casual settings by amateur music-lovers or in more elaborate performances by professional musicians, such as those described by Jeremy Smith in "Music and the Cult of Elizabeth: The Politics of Panegyric and Sound."

We are so accustomed to being able to "play" music by turning on a machine that it is easy to forget that not too long ago people who wanted music either had to "play" (perform) it themselves or find a live performance. Music was something special, not ubiquitous as it is today. When Randolph Helsby took a boat trip on the Thames (cat. 71), the music came not from boom boxes or iPods but from his companions: "Wee had good voyces & singinge of maddrigalls & others all the waye to Hampton & back againe."

Music literacy was probably considerably more widespread in early modern times than it is today. Indeed, being able to sing was regarded as obligatory for the well-born, as Peacham advises in *The Compleat Gentleman*: "I desire no more in you than to sing your part sure, and at the first sight, withal, to play the same vpon your Violl, or the exercise of the Lute, priuately to your selfe" (cat. 69). Peacham's recommendation, of course, must be taken with a grain of salt. Pasarello, in Marston's *The Malcontent* (1604), describes his own skills in response to the question from Malevole:

> *Mal.* Foole most happily incountred, canst sing foole?
> *Pas.* Yes I can sing foole, if youle beare the burden, and I can play vpon instruments, scurvily, as gentlemen do.[8]

Amateurs tended to play instruments that did not require lengthy training or a high degree of skill.

Evidence of amateur music-making is found throughout this exhibition, but especially in the materials that document musical instruction. Amateurs could buy textbooks, such as Morley's *A Plaine and Easie Introduction to Practicall Musicke* (cat. 31) or Dowland's translation of the early sixteenth-century treatise of Ornithoparchus (cat. 32) or Butler's *The Principles of Musik* (cat. 33); or they could buy collections of

/ *Sol, fa, mi, la.—Mi, mi mi.—Precious!*

music that contained brief didactic prefaces like Greeting's music for the flageolet, *The Pleasant Companion* (cat. 35). But they typically learned from private teachers.

A lesson on the lute is enacted in Cyril Tourneur's *The Atheist's Tragedie* (1611). In act 4, scene 1, Sebastian and Cataplasma while the time away, waiting for the arrival of Lady Levidulcia.

> *Cata.* Her purpose promis'd vs her companie ere this. *Lirie!* your Lute and your Booke.
> *Seba.* Well said. A lesson o'th'Lute to entertaine the time with till she comes.
> *Cata.* Sol, fa, mi, la.—Mi, mi mi.—Precious! Doest not see *mi* betweene the two Crochets? Strike mee full there.——So——forward.——This is a sweet straine, and thou finger'st it beastly. *Mi* is a laerg there; and the prick that stands before *mi*, a long; alwaies halfe your note. ——Now——Runne your diuision pleasingly with those quauers. Obserue all your graces i'the touch. —— Heere's a sweet cloze—strike it full, it sets off your musicke delicately.

This passage is full of technical musical terminology that every beginner would need to learn: the durations of notes (large [two times a long], long [two times a double whole note], crochet [quarter note], quaver [eighth note], prick [dot that adds half again the value to a note]), straine [a section of a composition], division [variation, typically with quick running notes], grace [ornamentation], cloze [cadence]. And of course the names of the notes, given in syllables similar to our "do re mi." That Tourneur could expect his audience to know these terms speaks volumes about the level of their musical knowledge.[9] Of course, this lesson is not about music at all, especially given the widespread association of the lute as a metaphor for sex.[10] Traces of actual lute instruction are preserved in one of the treasures of the Folger Shakespeare Library (cat. 34), which contains music in the hand of composer and lutenist John Dowland.

A very substantial record of amateur interest is found in manuscripts and especially in the printed books used for the transmission of music.[11] The Catholic Edward Paston (1550–1630) employed several scribes to create a vast collection of music in over forty sets of manuscripts and lutebooks, one of which is on exhibit (cat. 95). Printed music books can also provide a snapshot of the market for amateur music-making, as Stacey Houck demonstrates in "John Playford and the English Musical Market."

The tastes of particular owners can be seen in the titles they assembled into sets and bound together. Of the many examples in the exhibition of "binder's copies," we can only infrequently identify the name of the owner. Thus Rachel Doggett's discovery that two binder's copies (cat. 39, 74), whose handsome bindings include the initials "C. S.," can not only be traced to Sir Charles Somerset (ca. 1588–1665) but also be found in a 1622 inventory of his possessions, is particularly welcome.[12] Somerset, the third son of

a long enveloping ecclesiastical vestment
one of a band of public musicians in England employed to play for processions/public entertainment
a religious house

/ *all the bells ringing in every church*

Edward (ca. 1550–1628), fourth earl of Worcester, was a Catholic and a close associate of Henry, prince of Wales; he is best known today for the diaries of his Continental travels in 1611 and 1612. His music library, kept at Worcester House on the Strand, where William Byrd was provided a room, consists of English secular music (ballets, madrigals, canzonets), Italian vocal music published in Antwerp and Venice, and sacred music by both English and Continental composers. This discovery should spur further research into the whereabouts of the rest of his library.

"THEY HAUE LAYD IERUSALEM ON HEAPES"

The final section of the exhibition explores the sounds of religious and devotional practice. In just over a century—from Henry VIII's Act of Supremacy in 1534 to the restoration of Charles II as king in 1660—England witnessed unprecedented religious strife that had a profound impact on the institutions that supported professional music and on the kinds of music that was heard.[13]

The English Church under Henry VIII, despite its substitution of papal supremacy with royal supremacy, retained many traditional practices and customs, as this description of the celebrations at the birth of his son Edward in 1537 makes clear:

> And the same day, at eight of the clock in the morning, *Te Deum* was sung in every parish church throughout London, with all the bells ringing in every church, and great fires made in every street. And at nine of the clock there was assembled at [St] Pauls' all the orders of friars, monks, canons, priests and clerks about London, standing all about [St] Paul's in rich copes with the best crosses and candlesticks of every parish church in London. . . . and after [. . . St] Paul's choir sang an anthem [=antiphon] of the Trinity, with *Te Deum*, and the ninth respond [at matins] of the Trinity [*Summe Trinitati*], with the collect of the same. Then the king's waits and the waits of London played with the shawms; and after that a great peal of guns were shot at the Tower of London, all which solemnity was done to give laud and praise to God for the joy of our prince.[14]

The sound world represented in this description was forever altered by Henry's appropriation of church lands and monies; between 1536 and 1540, he ordered dissolved some eight hundred monasteries, priories, and other institutions, small as well as large.[15] Perhaps the most significant consequence of Henry's Act of Supremacy was that the direction of religious reform would be shaped by both the personal religious beliefs of the monarch and the balance of power in Parliament.

of a vow/wish/desire

/ *Gloria in excelsis, the Creede, Sanctus, Benedictus, and the Agnus were all songen in Englishe*

The accession of Henry's nine-year-old son Edward VI (1537–1553) marked a time of radical Protestant reform.[16] In 1547, he completed the dismantling of the great institutions that had supported the performance of complex choral polyphony by dissolving the chantries, endowments to support the commemoration of the dead. In the same year, the first public service in the vernacular was held at Westminster:

> afore the masse of the Holie Ghost there was a sermon made before the King by Doctor Ridley, Bishopp of Rochester; and after that the masse beganne, Gloria in excelsis, the Creede, Sanctus, Benedictus, and the Agnus were all songen in Englishe.[17]

The 1549 Act of Uniformity banned the Latin rite and mandated the use of *The Book of Common Prayer*, a single volume containing all the services for the Church of England. There was a sharp reduction in the number of services: the Mass and eight offices were transformed into Holy Communion, Morning Prayer, and Evening Prayer, while liturgies devoted to the saints, including the Virgin Mary, were eliminated.[18] The exhibition records both the remains of Catholic worship in the fragments of destroyed liturgical manuscripts (cat. 82, 84) and a defaced Book of Hours (cat. 83), as well as music composed for the new Edwardian liturgies in *The mornyng and evenyng prayer and communion, set forthe in foure partes* (cat. 88).

Harder to capture, but fundamental to the soundscapes of religious observance, is the impact of institutional change: the dissolution of the ecclesiastical foundations that had supported the singing of sophisticated polyphony by highly trained ensembles of boys and men throughout England, in many different institutions, large and small, meant a permanent change in the employment and training of musicians and in the role of music in the liturgy. As Roger Bowers explains, "The liturgical Reformation of 1547–9 . . . transformed the cathedral choir from a body of participating tonsured clergy enacting the Catholic liturgy to a body of static performers merely witnessing and commenting upon its Protestant successor."[19]

Edward's death in 1553 sent England from one extreme to the other, with the accession of his older half-sister, the staunch Catholic Mary I (1516–1558). Mary reinstituted Catholic liturgy and practices, ordering the printing of liturgical books, including, for example, the *Manuale* (cat. 85) that functioned as a handbook for priests, and the restoration of the means for the complex votive polyphony that had existed in Henry's time.[20]

Mary's death in 1558 without an heir brought her half-sister Elizabeth I (1533–1603) to the throne. Her reign, for forty-five years, brought at least a measure of continuity in the conduct of religion and politics, if not peace or stability. The 1559 Acts of Supremacy and Allegiance once again ended papal jurisdiction in England and made the queen the Supreme Governor of the Church. A revised version of the 1552 *Book of*

governed by bishops

From among the throng was heard the threatening cry, "Downe with the Altar, downe with the Altar"

Common Prayer was instituted in 1559. Diarmaid MacCulloch describes Elizabeth's brand of Protestantism as "peculiarly conservative, including a liking for some church imagery and elaborate choral music in worship," and reminiscent of the "idiosyncratic 'third way' religious policies of various rulers of the 1540s. . . ."[21] Many of the visitors she invited to attend "divine services" in the royal chapel commented on the music and ritual, with clergy in sumptuous regalia and the altar adorned with candles and even (in some accounts) a crucifix.[22]

The Elizabethan Settlement left significant dissatisfaction; the ensuing conflicts would play a significant role in the Civil War and continue in various guises for two more centuries. While music in the cathedrals could provide some continuity with traditional practices (though much diminished in quality), in the parishes the only music was what the congregation could provide, primarily the singing of psalms; organs that had survived the periods of iconoclasm were allowed to fall into disrepair.[23]

The irreconcilable conflict of these two practices turned into yet another "cultural revolution" during the 1640s and 1650s, a scant century after the Henrician and Edwardian reforms. The political divide between royalists and parliamentarians was mirrored in matters of religion: the royalist Cavaliers were adherents of the Church of England, with its episcopal governance and *Book of Common Prayer* liturgy; the parliamentarian Roundheads were Puritans, adherents of a form of worship centered on sermons, biblical readings, and the singing of metrical psalms.

Imagine the sounds of these two worlds in collision, represented by events that took place at Canterbury Cathedral. The cathedral chapter decreed that the sermon service would be held in the choir of the cathedral rather than in the "sermon house" (the former chapter house), thus juxtaposing the congregation gathered to hear the sermon with the congregation accustomed to services from the *Book of Common Prayer*.

> On the feast of Epiphany (January 6) 1641, the sermon congregation, thus constrained to remain also for Evensong, perceived an insupportable degree of provocation in the clergy's practice of bowing the knee in reverence of the high altar: the service was seriously disrupted with cries of "This is idolatry. . . leave your idolatry." On the Sunday following, mere barracking became mass defiance. The preacher completed his sermon, and a metrical psalm was begun; the organist chose the first section of Psalm 119, and the three officiants processed to the altar, 'ducking, ducking, ducking like wild-geese, head to tail' to commence the liturgy of Evensong. The people would have none of this popery; Psalm 119 has not one section but twenty-two, and spontaneously the congregation took it into its collective head to frustrate the start of the Office by launching precipitately into section two, and thus defiantly to keep on singing. From among the throng was heard the threatening cry, "Downe with the Altar, downe with the Altar."[24]

• (See p. 5.)
• an English R.C. of the time from about 1570 to 1791 who refused to attend services of the Church of England and thereby committed a statutory (of a statute) offense
• (archaic) bookseller/publisher; one that sells stationery
• having many values, meanings, appeals

On 26 August 1642, parliamentarian forces ransacked the Cathedral: "The high altar was overturned and the altar rails destroyed; images and tapestries were violated and defaced. Bibles and Prayer Books suffered without distinction; the great lectern of bronze was tumbled down. The organ was despoiled; the music books were rent in pieces and scattered about the floor, or looted for use in a burlesque horseback parody of the Cathedral service."[25] In 1642 Parliament closed the theaters. In 1645 the *Book of Common Prayer* was outlawed and replaced by the *Directory for the Publique Worship of God*, which mandated a service based on readings from the Bible, psalms, and a sermon, thus effectively putting an end to cathedral music, and Archbishop Laud was executed. In 1646 the episcopate was abolished.[26]

Craig Monson, in "Reading Between the Lines: Catholic and Protestant Polemic in Elizabethan and Jacobean Sacred Music," shows how successive generations of those suffering religious persecution would lay claim to "Jerusalem"—for example, the Protestant bishop Nicholas Ridley just before his execution (cat. 92) or the Catholic recusant composer William Byrd (cat. 91). It is no surprise, therefore, that William Child, a composer who lost his job as organist when the chapel at Windsor was closed, chose as the text for the anthem written "on the occasion of the abolishing of the Common Prayer": "O Lord God, the heathen are come into thine inheritance: thy holy temple have they defiled, and made Jerusalem a heap of stones" (Ps. 79).[27]

"LOST SOUND WORLDS"

Documents, manuscripts, printed books, images, and musical instruments—the material remains of musical culture—are all we have left to help us re-envision the sounds of early modern England. This exhibition brings together a selection of the precious legacy preserved in the Folger Shakespeare Library. But the objects make sense only when seen in context. We can be particularly grateful, therefore, to the authors of the essays in this volume for bringing some of these soundscapes into sharper focus. Bruce Smith reflects on the meaning of noise, especially the noises found in theatrical performances. Ross Duffin shows the pervasiveness of ballads in the early modern world (and it's not every editor who has a ballad composed in her honor). Stacey Houck explores the Playford phenomenon—the ways in which an enterprising stationer could develop a market for musical amateurs. Jeremy Smith teases out the complexity of Queen Elizabeth's patronage and its reflections in music. Craig Monson reveals the multivalent * significance of biblical texts as religious polemic. And Nicholas Temperley sketches the astonishing development of "psalm culture," tracing the roles of psalms in public and private devotion. This exhibition invites us to recapture the sounds of a distant past, to hear what drove Morose mad.

* məl-tí-və-lənt

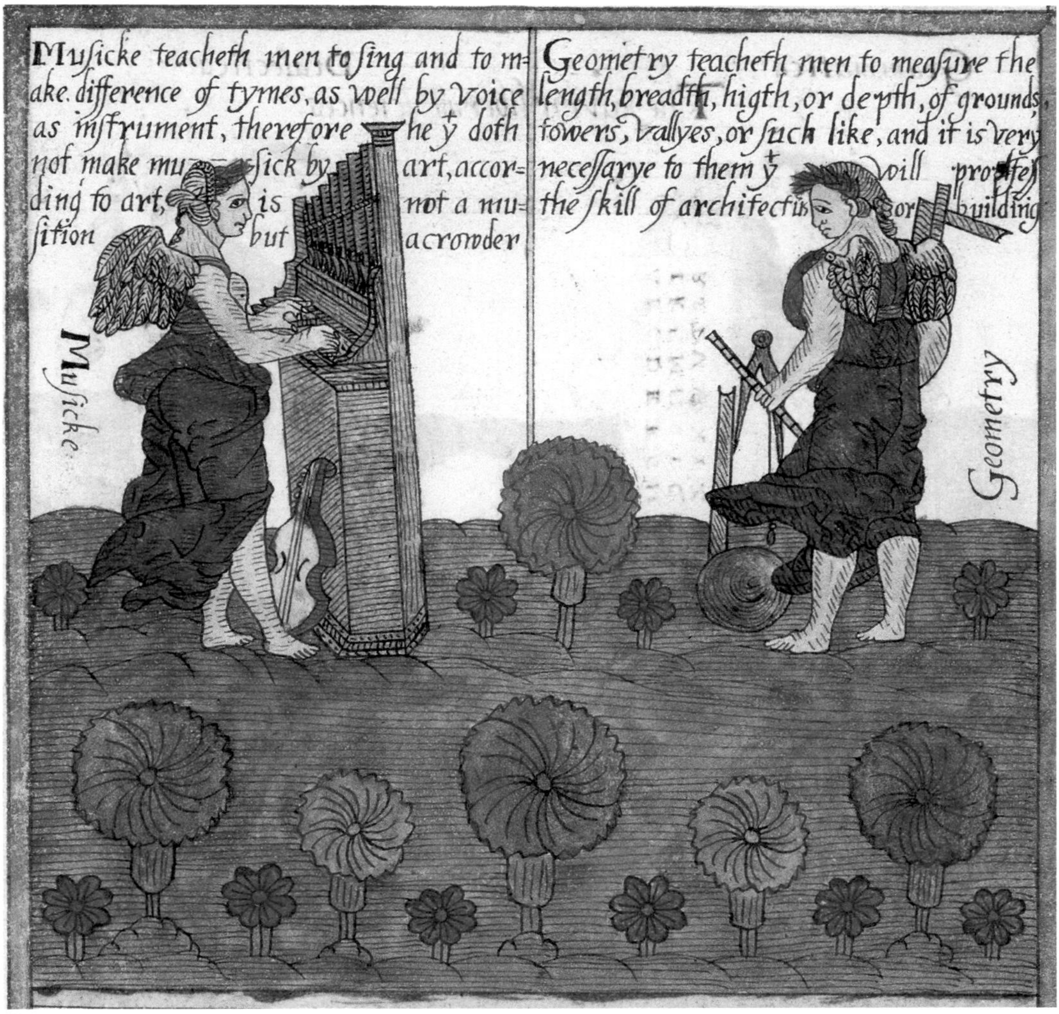
Musicke teacheth men to sing and to m=
ake difference of tymes, as well by voice
as instrument, therefore he ẏ doth
not make musick by art, accor=
ding to art, is not a mu=
sition but a crowder
Geometry teacheth men to measure the
length, breadth, higth, or depth, of grounds,
towers, vallyes, or such like, and it is very
necessarye to them ẏ will profess
the skill of architectu or building
Musicke
Geometry

Detail, cat. 50.

1 Ben Jonson, *Epicoene, or the silent woman A comedie. Acted in the yeare 1609. By the children of her majesties revels* (London, 1620), sig. B4.

2 Bruce R. Smith, *The Acoustic World of Early Modern England: Attending to the O-Factor* (Chicago, 1999), especially ch. 3, "The Soundscapes of Early Modern England: City, Country, Court." John Milsom's imaginative account of the sounds of early modern England from the perspective of actions—singing, playing instruments, composing and authorship, owning music, listening—has also shaped my thinking about the exhibition; see "Music, Politics, Society," in *A Companion to Tudor Britain*, ed. Robert Tittler and Norman Jones (Malden, 2004).

3 The term occurs in Schafer's 1969 pamphlet *The New Soundscape: A Handbook for the Modern Music Teacher.* He expanded the meaning of soundscape to "the sonic environment. Technically, any portion of the sonic environment regarded as a field for study" and founded the World Soundscape Project in 1971. Perhaps the most influential of the publications from this project is his *The Tuning of the World* (New York, 1977), reissued in 1994 under the title *The Soundscape: Our Sonic Environ-ment and the Tuning of the World* (the definition is given on p. 274 in the 1994 edition). For continuations and expansions of the project see the World Forum for Acoustic Ecology (http://interact.uoregon.edu/medialit/wfae/home/index.html), the Acoustic Ecology Research Group (http://webapps1.ucalgary.ca/~acoustic/links.html), and the World Soundscape Project (http:// www.sfu.ca/~truax/wsp.html).

4 This definition, kindly provided by Shelemay, will appear in the forthcoming second edition.

5 Smith, *The Acoustic World*, 44.

6 For several useful histories of music that are organized by genre or by composer biography, see "Suggestions for Further Reading."

7 See as well Smith, *The Acoustic World*, ch. 7; Tessa Watt, *Cheap Print and Popular Piety 1550–1640* (Cambridge, 1991).

8 Act I, sc. 8. Cited by Craig Monson, "Elizabethan London," in *The Renaissance from the 1470s to the End of the 16th Century*, ed. Iain Fenlon (Englewood Cliffs, 1989), 336.

9 John Milsom considers an early sixteenth-century text replete with musical terminology in "Songs and Society in Early Tudor London," *Early Music History* 16 (1997): 280.

10 sig. H2. Katharine Eisaman Maus, ed., *Four Revenge Tragedies* (Oxford, 1995), 300–301, with an explication of the *double entendres* on 415. See also Julia Craig-McFeely, "The Signifying Serpent: Seduction by Cultural Stereotype in Seventeenth-Century England," in *Music, Sensation, and Sensuality*, ed. Linda Phyllis Austern (New York, 2002).

11 For an overview of English music books, both manuscripts and prints, see the essays by John Milsom and Mary Chan in vols. 3 and 4 of *The Cambridge History of the Book in Britain* (Cambridge, 1999).

12 Michael G. Brennan, "Sir Charles Somerset's Music Books (1622)," *Music & Letters* 74 (1993): 501–18.

13 This section is partly drawn from the more extended discussion in Jessie Ann Owens, "La musica inglese dalla Riforma alla Restaurazione," in *Enciclopedia della Musica*, ed. Jean-Jacques Nattiez, vol. 4 (Turin, 2004).

14 As cited by John Milsom, "Sacred Songs in the Chamber," in *English Choral Practice 1400–1650*, ed. John Morehen (Cambridge, 1995), 161. I use historiographically problematic terms such as "Catholic" or "Puritan" merely as a convenient shorthand, hoping that readers will remember to put in their own mental "scare quotes." For a salutary warning about the complicated meanings of "Catholic" during this period of rapid change, see Peter Marshall, "Is the Pope Catholic? Henry VIII and the Semantics of Schism," in *Catholics and the 'Protestant Nation'*, ed. Ethan Shagan (Manchester, 2005).

15 Peter le Huray, *Music and the Reformation in England 1549–1660* (Cambridge, 1978; 1st ed., 1967), 2.

16 Eamon Duffy, *The Stripping of the Altars: Traditional Religion in England 1400–1580* (New Haven, 1992); Diarmaid MacCulloch, *The Boy King: Edward VI and the Protestant Reformation* (Berkeley, 2002).

17 As cited in *The Wanley Manuscripts*, ed. James Wrightson (Madison, 1995), 1:xi.

18 John Harper, *The Forms and Orders of Western Liturgy* (Oxford, 1991); Roger Bray, ed., *The Sixteenth Century*, The Blackwell History of Music in Britain (Oxford, 1995); Le Huray, *Music and the Reformation.*

19 Roger Bowers, *English Church Polyphony: Singers and Sources from the 14th to the 17th Century* (Aldershot, 1999), 6:62.

20 Daniel B. Page, *Uniform and Catholic: Church Music in the Reign of Mary Tudor (1553–1558)*, (Ph.D. diss., Brandeis University, 1996).

21 Diarmaid MacCulloch, *Reformation: Europe's House Divided 1490–1700* (London, 2003), 288–91.

22 Monson, "Elizabethan England," 307–10.

23 Nicholas Temperley, *Music in the English Parish Church* (Oxford, 1979), 49–53. On the state of cathedral music, see James Saunders, "Music and Moonlighting: The Cathedral Choirmen of Early Modern England, 1558–1649," in *Music and Musicians in Renaissance Cities and Towns*, ed. Fiona Kisby (Cambridge, 2001).

24 Bowers, *English Church Polyphony*, 4:449.

25 Ibid., 4:450.

26 Temperley, *The English Parish Church*, 77–78; Stanford E. Lehmberg, *Cathedrals Under Siege* (Exeter, 1996).

27 Le Huray, *Music and the Reformation*, 55.

“What means this noise?”

Bruce R. Smith

Detail, cat. 24.

噪音, रव, ψόφος, *strepitus*, ضوضاء, *rumore, ruido, ruído, Geräusch, lawaai, bruit*: every culture recognizes noise, but each culture's noise is different. For a start, the sounds that are out there to be heard are *different.* The roar of jet engines, the rumble of automobile motors, the hum of electrical equipment, the blinging of cell phones, the thud of hyper-powered stereo systems: none of these now ubiquitous urban noises were present in Shakespeare's London. Instead, a patron making his way through the city streets, down to a ferry-landing along the Thames, across the water, up the bank, past bearbaiting pits, and through the doors of the Globe Theatre would have heard cart wheels rumbling over cobble stones, peddlers hawking their wares, ferrymen yelling out for passengers, waves slapping boat sides, church bells bonging in the distance, and dogs yelping—two hundred of them, according to one foreign visitor[1]—in kennels that served the South Bank's bearbaiting pits. The soundscape of London in 1606 was nothing like the soundscape of London in 2006. It may not be accurate, in fact, to refer to these aural events as noises. All of the sounds, even the barking dogs, figured in meaningful patterns—meaningful, that is, to the human beings who passed through those sounds in the course of their everyday lives.[2] (The barks were, of course, meaningful in their own right to the dogs that produced them.) In 1606, as in 2006, noises provided the raw material out of which heard meanings were made.

Once inside the theater's cylindrical surround, patrons of the Globe in Shakespeare's day may have heard intermittent sounds from outside: bells, yells, yelps. Today the intermittent sounds most likely to be noted by someone taking in a performance in the rebuilt Shakespeare's Globe are jet planes whining their way toward Heathrow Airport, eighteen miles to the west. The *scale* of noise has changed no less than the sounds themselves. What has *not* changed across the four centuries is the way performances of Shakespeare's plays emerge out of noise. In the case of the original Globe, that aural matrix was provided by the ambient sounds of London and, at closer range, by the rustles, thuds, thumps, coughs, sneezes, and conversational buzz of the audience.

However different the outside noises may have been, a gathering audience still makes the same kinds of sounds. In modern indoor theaters the sign that the performance is about to begin is visual: the house lights dim, and the audience quiets down. Sometimes a recorded track of music and/or environmental sounds ushers the audience into the fictional world they are about to inhabit—a device that live theater has taken over from film. At the original Globe the cues were all aural. Three trumpet blasts overpowered the audience's fidgeting and murmuring. Then came the play's first scripted words, often spoken by a single booming male voice. Sometimes, according to the scripts, that voice belongs to a prologue: "Two households, both alike in dignity/ In fair Verona, where we lay our scene,/ From ancient grudge break to new mutiny" (*Romeo and Juliet*, Pro. 1–3); "Open your ears; for which of you will stop/ The vent of hearing

• an officer on a ship in charge of equipment/maintenance

/ *A tempestuous noise of thunder and lightening heard*

• martial sounds — used as a stage sound in Elizabethan drama

when loud Rumour speaks?" (*2 Henry IV*, Pro. 1–2); "O, for a muse of fire,/ That would ascend the brightest heaven of invention!" (*Henry V*, Pro. 1–2).[3] Sometimes the voice is that of a male authority figure within the fiction: "Now is the winter of our discontent/ Made glorious summer by this son of York" (Richard, Duke of Gloucester, in *Richard III*, 1.1.1–2); "Now, fair Hippolyta, our nuptial hour/ Draws on apace" (Theseus in *A Midsummer Night's Dream*, 1.1.1–2); "So shaken as we are, so wan with care,/ Find we a time for frighted peace to pant" (King Henry in *1 Henry IV*, 1.1.1–2). More often, though, Shakespeare directs several voices to speak, and frequently those voices belong to minor characters: "As I remember, Adam, it was upon this fashion bequeathed me, by will but poor a thousand crowns" (Orlando to Adam in *As You Like It*, 1.1.1–2); "Who's there?" (Bernardo to Francisco in *Hamlet* 1.1.1); "Tush, never tell me! I take it much unkindly/ That thou, Iago, . . . should'st know of this" (Roderigo to Iago in *Othello*, 1.1.1–3); "Nay, but this dotage of our General's/ O'erflows the measure" (Philo to Demetrius in *Antony and Cleopatra*, 1.1.1–2). "As I remember," "Tush," "Nay": these exclamations are markers of conversations already in progress, as if the voices have emerged out of the audience's din.

On occasion Shakespeare's plays begin when scripted noise overwhelms the audience's noise: "*Thunder and lightning*" inaugurate *Macbeth* (SD before 1.1), Coriolanus erupts onto the stage in "*a company of mutinous Citizens with staves, clubs, and other weapons*" who clamor all at once to speak (SD before 1.1), the opening stage direction to *The Tempest*—"*A tempestuous noise of thunder and lightening heard*" (SD before 1.1)—gives way to the cries of a sinking ship's master, boatswain, and passengers. On at least one occasion, what the silenced audience is scripted to hear first is music. "If music be the food of love, play on," sighs Orsino in *Twelfth Night* (1.1.1). The music that precedes this opening line drafts into the fiction something that usually happened outside the fiction. Patrons of London's indoor theaters (Shakespeare's company had outfitted the indoor Blackfriars Theatre in 1596–97 but were prevented from using it themselves until 1609) fully expected for the price of admission not only a play but a pre-play musical concert. In 1602, the very year *Twelfth Night* premiered at the Middle Temple and the Globe, a foreign visitor recorded in his journal a performance by boy actors at the Blackfriars and noted, "For a whole hour before, a delightful performance of *musicum instrumentalem* is given on organs, lutes, bandores, mandolins, violins, and flutes."[4] The published script of John Marston's tragedy *Sophonisba*, written for boy actors playing in the same venue three or four years later, calls for music, vocal as well as instrumental, during and between the play's five acts.[5] The three songs that Feste sings in *Twelfth Night* blur the boundaries between musical concert and dramatic fiction. Beyond music, Shakespeare's scripts call for other sound effects: brass "flourishes" to mark royal entries and exits ("*Flourish. Enter Claudius King of Denmark* . . ." reads the SD before *Hamlet* 1.2.1); drums and/or "alarums" to signal battles ("A flourish, trumpets! Strike alarums,

- a person who wears a mask
- Someone gullible
- young man of fashion; ladies' man / suitor / paramour
- cry weakly
- Sound / utter raucously; proclaim flamboyantly

drums," commands King Richard in *Richard III*, 4.4.149); volleys from guns and/or a small cannon to amplify public events ("*a peal of ordnance are shot off*" to accompany the removal of Hamlet's body in *Hamlet* 5.2.357; the stage direction "*Chambers discharged*" announces the arrival of Henry VIII and his fellow maskers at Cardinal Wolsey's banquet in *Henry VIII* 1.4.50). It was partly "the noise of drums and trumpets" that prompted neighbors of the Blackfriars Theatre to prevent Shakespeare's company from using the space until 1609.[6]

No less present in performance at the Globe would have been unscripted sounds like the actors' footfalls on the platform's planks, the swish of velvet breeches as they made their entrances and exits, the clink of swords within scabbards as they walked about. Some of these sounds might signify within the fiction—the scrape of metal on metal during sword fights, for example—but others could be heard as noise. Add to these on-stage noises the rumble of sounds from outside the theater and the stirrings of a mostly standing audience within, and it is easy to appreciate how scripted words were always being spoken above an undercurrent of noise. Sometimes that noise could interrupt a performance in progress. The audience in London's theaters, according to Michael Drayton, would break out into "Shouts and claps at every little pause,/ When the proud round on every side hath rung." If displeased, the audience's response might be even louder. Thomas Dekker in his guide to bad behavior, *The Gull's Hornbook*, advises his would-be gallant to secure a seat on the stage itself and to "mew at passionate speeches, blare at merry, find fault with the music, whew at children's action, whistle at the songs."[7] N.B.

The idea of a play as a contest or *agon* goes back to ancient Greece, when tragedians like Sophocles competed for prizes during the festival of Dionysius.[8] We still use that model when we speak of a play as having "protagonists" and "antagonists." The contests of rhyming wit among the four courting couples in *Love's Labour's Lost* demonstrate how actors compete for "air time" in their speeches no less than they compete for stage space in their movements. The Princess of France and her three ladies set out to foil the King of Navarre and his three lords. "The effect of my intent is to cross theirs," the Princess tells her ladies. "They do it but in mockery-merriment,/ And mock for mock is only my intent" (5.2.137–39). If Drayton and Dekker are right, the contest in Shakespeare's theater may have been less actor against actor than actors against audience. Actors then and now are noise-control specialists. Only at the end do actors yield power back to the people who are supposed to sit there and listen. Don't keep me a prisoner on this island, the actor who has played Prospero begs the audience at the end of *The Tempest.* "But release me from my bands/ With the help of your good hands." It is not just the audience's applause he wants but their shouts: "Gentle breath of yours my sails/ Must fill, or else my project fails" (Ep. 9–12). At play's end Shakespeare's plays devolve back into the noise out of which they emerged in the beginning. At the Globe,

/ A jig shall be clapped at, and every rhyme/ Praised and applauded by a clamorous chime

at least through the 1590s, the aural space between speech and noise was bridged by music and dancing. A Swiss traveler, Thomas Platter, saw *Julius Caesar* at the Globe in 1599 and noted in his journal that when the play proper was over, "they danced very marvelously and gracefully together, as is their wont, two dressed as men and two as women."[9] The romps of successful tricksters and adulterous lovers in the surviving jigs suggest that hands clapping in rhythm and perhaps not so gentle breaths yelling in approval were just what the singing and the dancing invited.[10] The Prologue to Beaumont and Fletcher's comedy *The Fair Maid of the Inn* observes, "A jig shall be clapped at, and every rhyme/ Praised and applauded by a clamorous chime."[11]

Before the discovery of electricity, before the invention of recording devices, amplification, and radio, sound was place-specific. You could see where sounds were coming from. It was sounds, as much as sights, that made *this* place different from *that* place. The *Oxford English Dictionary* recognizes this place-specific quality in the oldest definition of "noise," with citations going back to the thirteenth century. "Noise" in this most basic sense is "the aggregate of sounds occurring in a particular place or at a particular time."[12] To hear all there was to *here* in the Globe and the Blackfriars we need to attend, then, not just to speech but to music, to exclamations like "tush," "nay," "oh," and to non-verbal sounds. We can map these sounds as a circle:

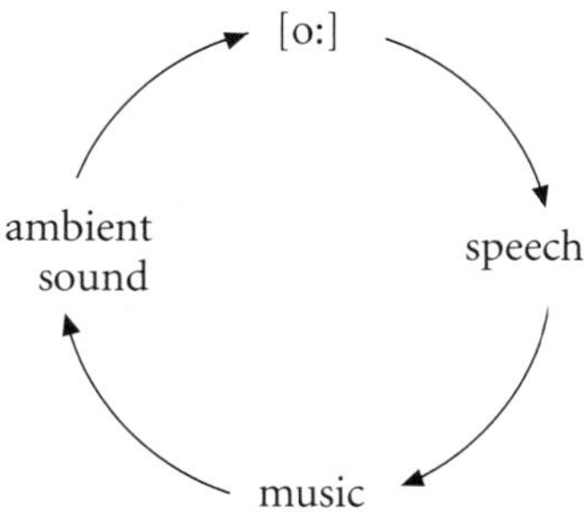

The course of a performance at the Globe moves us clockwise around the circle, beginning with the ambient sounds of London outside the theater and the rustle of the audience within. Depending on the venue, music may be folded into that ambient sound. Next an exclamation—"nay," "tush," "oh"—gives us our bearings in a world of speech, a world with tightly controlled structures of meaning. Music in the course of the performance or at the play's end immerses us in sound structures of a different sort. Words can contribute to that structure, but music also communicates with the more abstract world of ambient sounds. Those sounds imply structures of hearing, even though they have little or nothing to do with words. Cartwheels over cobbles, church bells, ferrymen calling for customers, dogs barking in kennels: aural markers like these defined the soundscape of early modern London. People used those sounds to structure their movements through space. Thumping footsteps, rustling velvet, clinking swords: actors and audiences likewise used non-verbal sounds to structure the time and space of performance. Through it all, around it all, was the constant crackle of noise.

In the English spoken by Shakespeare and his contemporaries one word for a band of musicians was "a noise" (OED, "noise, *n.*," I.3.b). The music they made could likewise be called "noise." "Make a joyful noise unto the Lord, all ye lands," begins Psalm 100 in the King James translation of the Bible. "Serve the Lord with gladness: come before his presence with singing." "Noise" in early modern English might also refer to strife or quarreling (OED II.5) or to rumor (OED II.6.a) and the reputation that rumor sustains (OED II.6.b). All of these varying meanings are invoked—sometimes this one, sometimes that one—in the verbal tags for "noise" catalogued at the beginning of this essay. Chinese, Sanskrit, Classical Greek, Latin, Arabic, Italian, Spanish and Portuguese, German, Dutch, French: it is surprising how few cognates there are among the words for noise in these languages, even among the Romance languages derived from Latin. *Strepitus* in Latin becomes the murmuring voices of *rumore* in Italian, the onomatopoeia of *ruido* in Spanish and *ruído* in Portuguese, the barbarity of *bruit* in French. The growling [r] in German *Geräusch* and the broad [a] in Dutch *lawaai* seem to catch what noise sounds like. The origin for all these [r] sounds is probably to be traced to the Sanskrit रव, *táva*. What noise *feels* like is registered in the Arabic ضوضاء and the English *noise*, both of them cognates of the Latin word *nausea*, literally sea-sickness.[13]

What, then, *is* noise?[14] The definitions that have been proposed fall into three sorts: physical, psychological, and social. The definition of noise in modern physics is precise enough: noise is random frequencies across a broad band of sound waves.[15] Onomatopoeic words like *ruido* and *Geräusch* register this randomness. In psychological terms, noise is what a person *hears* as noise. The Arabic and the English words recognize this subjective quality. Noise is also a social construction: noise is what a given culture chooses to *call* noise. As such, noise haunts the border where physical sound becomes human meaning. Hamlet articulates the situation precisely when he excoriates loud, wildly gesticulating actors who rip through speeches "to split the ears of the groundlings, who for the most part are capable of nothing but inexplicable dumb shows and noise" (*Hamlet* 3.2.10–13).

An electronic search of Shakespeare's digitized works turns up eighty-six iterations of the word "noise."[16] One group of quotations represents noise as loud, harsh, unpleasant sounds (OED I.2.b). Thus

• a section of the theatre reserved for the actors used esp. for dressing for stage entrance

/ *the sounds of bells, the cacophony of street criers, the scraping of fiddlers in taverns*

• writing according to standard usage

Bolingbroke first uses a "brazen trumpet" to challenge the besieged Richard II, then decides on less aggressive measures: "Let's march without the noise of threat'ning drum" (*Richard II*, 3.3.32, 50). Another group of passages hears noise in rumor or report (OED II.6.a). "Open your ears," commands the Prologue to *2 Henry IV*; "for which of you will stop/ The vent of hearing when loud Rumour speaks?" Taking on the identity of Rumor, the Prologue comes onstage "to noise abroad," signaling the victory of Prince Harry over Henry Monmouth (Pro. 1–2, 29). By far the largest group, however—thirty-two instances in all—invokes noise in the form of a question: what's that noise? The knocking at the gate in *Macbeth* offers a good example. "*Knock within*" goes the stage direction, cuing a banging inside the tiring house located to Macbeth's rear. "Whence is that knocking?" Macbeth exclaims. "How is't with me when every noise appals me?" (2.2.55–56). Modern research in the psychology of hearing has demonstrated that, if a listener cannot see the source of a sound, he or she tends to imagine that sound as coming from behind. And so in *Macbeth* with the knock "within." In fact, Macbeth never finds out, in this scene at least, that the knocking at the gate is Macduff and Lennox's. That discovery is left to the Porter after Macbeth and Lady Macbeth have exited. More often, however, the question "What's that noise?" is given an answer. When a messenger runs onstage in *2 Henry VI* crying "A miracle!" the Duke of Gloucester responds, "What means this noise?/ Fellow, what miracle dost thou proclaim?" (2.1.62–63). The news concerns a man supposedly cured of his blindness at the Shrine of St. Albans—a hoax that King Henry shortly exposes. To label Gloucester's speech a question is perhaps to miss a curious slippage between questions and exclamations. In early modern orthography there was as yet no separate punctuation mark for exclamations: question marks did service for both.[17] Every instance of "What's that noise?" was—and still is—both a question and an exclamation.

In his instructions to the players Hamlet has words not only for the principal actors, warning them not to "tear a passion to tatters," but for "those that play your clowns." Hamlet is concerned that they stick to the text: clowns should "speak no more than is set down for them; for there be of them that will themselves laugh to set on some quantity of barren spectators to laugh too, though in the mean time some necessary question of the play be then to be considered" (3.2.10, 39–44). Commentators have usually taken this to be a reference to extemporized jokes and added dialogue, but what Hamlet is distinguishing between here is two kinds of sounds: words on the one hand versus laughter on the other. Words come from the head (or feel as if they do); laughter comes from the belly. Unlike words, laughter doesn't mean anything. More than principal actors like Richard Burbage, who played most of Shakespeare's male leads, it is clowns who invite us to hear the full panoply of sounds in Shakespeare's plays. Clowns are, in a word, *noisy*. Every clown makes noise (even mimes, if you listen hard enough to the movement of air), but each

/ *all to the accompaniment of a pipe's piping and a tabor's tappings*

clown's noise is different. Certainly that was the case with Shakespeare's clowns. Scholars usually make a distinction between the two main comedians who worked with the Lord Chamberlain's Men and the King's Men in the course of Shakespeare's career.[18] While Will Kemp stayed with the company, through 1599, Shakespeare tailored clown-roles to Kemp's skills as a physical comedian. Lancelot Gobbo's opening schtick in *The Merchant of Venice* is typical of Kemp's style. Debating whether to leave his stingy master Shylock and take up service with generous Bassanio, Lancelot in his first speech gets to play three parts at once: himself in the middle, "the fiend . . . at mine elbow," and "my conscience hanging about the neck of my heart" (2.2.2, 12). First "the fiend" advises him to run; then his conscience says "Budge not" (2.2.18); and all the while Kemp gets to leap from one subject position to another. Lancelot's blind old father arrives, and the two of them play out a physical parody of Isaac blessing Esau (Genesis 27). When Kemp left the company in 1599, he staged a self-promoting publicity stunt by *dancing* the hundred miles from London to Norwich, all to the accompaniment of a pipe's piping and a tabor's tapping. A write-up of the affair appeared in 1600 entitled *Kemp's Nine Days' Wonder*. Meanwhile, Kemp's replacement, Robert Armin, brought to the Lord Chamberlain's Men singing talents that inspired such roles as Feste in *Twelfth Night* (1602), the Fool in *King Lear* (1606), and possibly Autolychus in *The Winter's Tale* (1611). (See cat. 24.)

As different as their talents may have been, Kemp and Armin were alike in their flirtations with noise. In the sounds they are scripted to make, both comedians move freely around the circle, from speech through music through ambient sound through exclamations back to speech through music through ambient sound . . . and so on. At every point on the circle the energy they create is centrifugal: it flies away from the specificity of words. More obviously is this the case with Kemp. As Peter in *Romeo and Juliet*, Kemp keeps getting the right words in the wrong places. Peter is supposed to be delivering invitations to the Capulet's ball. The trouble is, he can't read. "Find out whose names are written here?" Peter asks himself. "It is written that the shoemaker should meddle with his yard [think 'penis'] and the tailor with his last [hear 'lass'?], the fisher with his pencil and the painter with his nets, but I am sent to find those persons whose names are here writ, and can never find what names the writing person hath here writ" (1.2.36–42). Solipsistic semantics (a shoemaker uses a last, a tailor a yard, a fisher a net, and a painter a pencil) reached their apotheosis in Kemp's Dogberry in *Much Ado About Nothing*. To Conrad's insult, "Away, you are an ass," Constable Dogberry indignantly replies, "Dost thou not suspect my place? Dost thou not suspect my years?" (4.2.71–73). As the star performer in post-play jigs, Kemp propelled sound even more energetically in the direction of noise. As "Singing Simpkin," Kemp fended off rivals in seducing a Wife:

/ *But I know a man can help you at need. With a fa la, la, la, la, la, la, la, la, la, la, la*

Wife: Blind Cupid hath made my heart for to bleed,
Fa la, la, la, la, la, la, la, la.
Simpkin: But I know a man can help you at need.
With a fa la, la, la, la, la, la, la, la, la, la, la.[19]

Fa *la*: with that iamb, the singing dancers run away with the words.

By comparison with Kemp's jigs, Robert Armin's songs in *Twelfth Night* might seem to be located solidly along the sector of semantic sound. After all, his solo songs have words:

When that I was and a little tiny boy,
With hey, ho, the wind and the rain,
A foolish thing was but a toy,
For the rain it raineth every day. (5.1.385–88)

"Hey, ho," however, moves away from words towards voiced passion. And what about that "and a"? Why not "when I was a little tiny boy"? Because the musical rhythm will have it so. In Robert Armin's singing, dactylic rhythm (/ x x / x x) trumps logical syntax. So, too, with Feste's other set-piece songs in *Twelfth Night*. "O mistress mine, where are you roaming?" (2.3.38 ff) and "Come away, come away death" (2.4.50 ff) transport listeners into a state of passion that both is, and is not, a matter of words. Gary Tomlinson has devoted an entire book to this musical state-of-passion and has given it a series of local habitations in seven operas as well as a name that embraces them all: "fascination." In Tomlinson's description, "The effect of operatic singing constitutes one subspecies within a huge family of human experiences brought about by heightened utterance—chanting, shouting, singing, incantation, whatever. . . . In them, voice, employed in exceptional ways and in special, carefully demarcated circumstances, opens to perception invisible realms. Voice connects its bearers and hearers to ordinarily supersensible realities."[20] The ballads and rounds that Feste plunges into along with Sir Toby, Sir Andrew, and Maria amid the midnight revels of act two, scene three, slide along the circle even further. Full verbal texts for Feste's free-standing songs are provided in the printing of *Twelfth Night* in the 1623 folio text of *Mr. William Shakespeare's Comedies, Histories, and Tragedies.* The ballads and rounds, by contrast, are cued through first-line tags ("Let our catch be 'Thou Knave,'" Sir Andrew cries out at 2.3.63 or "There dwelt a man in Babylon, lady, lady," sings Sir Toby at 2.3.77, cat. 23) and one explicit stage direction ("*They sing the catch,*" SD after 3.2.68). Each of the drunken foursome's popular songs trails off into laughter. To the ears of the steward Malvolio, trying

/ Save thee, friend, and thy music

/ ye squeak out your coziers' catches without any mitigation or remorse of voice

to sleep upstairs, it all sounds like noise. "My masters, are you mad?" Malvolio asks as he breaks up the party. "Or what are you? Have you no wit, no manners, nor honesty, but to gabble like tinkers at this time of night? Do ye make an alehouse of my lady's house, that ye squeak out your coziers' catches without any mitigation or remorse of voice?" (2.3.83–88). In "O mistress mine," Feste sings that "Journeys end in lovers meeting" (2.3.42). In the ballads and rounds of Sir Toby and crew, singing ends in gabbling and squeaking —that is to say, in noise.

Feste's way with unsung words is no less slippery. The role capitalizes on Robert Armin's famous ability to take a phrase from someone's speech and turn it into something else again. In his jest book *Quips upon Questions, or A Clown's Conceit on Occasion Offered* (1600), Armin takes phrases thrown at him by the audience and blows them up like so many bubbles—until they pop. When Viola, disguised as "Cesario," first encounters Feste in *Twelfth Night*, her words imply that she has found him with a tabor, or small drum, like Kemp's:

> *Viola:* Save thee, friend, and thy music. Dost thou live by thy tabor?
> *Feste:* No, sir, I live by the church.
> *Viola:* Art thou a churchman?
> *Feste:* No such matter, sir. I do live by the church for I do live at my house, and my house doth stand by the church.
> *Viola:* So thou mayst say the king lies by a beggar if a beggar dwell near him, or the church stands by tabor if thy tabor stand by the church.
> *Feste:* You have said, sir. To see this age!—A sentence is but a cheverel glove to a good wit, how quickly the wrong side may be turned outward. (3.1.1–13)

And that is exactly what Robert Amin did with other people's words: he turned them inside out. Neither Kemp nor Armin (nor Shakespeare, for that matter) had read Jacques Derrida, but both of Shakespeare's clowns in effect *deconstruct* language. In their distinctly different ways, they disconnect sound from sense and in so doing force us to hear sound as *sound.* In both clowns we confront a refusal to take words at face value. Instead, we find ourselves on a happy romp across the open border where meaning gives way to noise.

What means this noise? That sounded meanings are contingent.

1 Frederic Gershow, "Diary of the Journey of Philip Julius, Duke of Stettin-Pomerania, through England in the Year 1602," ed. Gottfried von Bülow, *Transactions of the Royal Historical Society*, new series vol. 6 (1892): 169–70.

2 "Soundscape" is a notion put on the map, so to speak, by R. Murray Schafer in *The Tuning of the World* (New York, 1977), 3–67, and explored more fully in Barry Truax, *Acoustic Communication* (Norwood, NJ, 1984), 42–56. In *The Acoustic World of Early Modern England* (Chicago, 1999), 52–71, I attempt to chart three specific soundscapes: one in the City of London, one in the country at Kenilworth Castle, and one at court in Whitehall Palace. On patterns of circulation within cities as acts of meaning-making, see Michel de Certeau, *The Practice of Everyday Life*, trans. Steven Rendall (Berkeley, 1984). De Certeau's model is visual and spatial; the model I am suggesting is aural.

3 Quotations from Shakespeare's plays are taken from William Shakespeare, *The Complete Works*, ed. Stanley Wells and Gary Taylor (Oxford, 1988), and are cited in the text by act, scene, and line numbers.

4 Gershow, "Diary," 29, spelling modernized. On music in early modern London's theaters, see Ross W. Duffin, *Shakespeare's Songbook* (New York, 2004), 15–41; Mary Chan, *Music in the Theatre of Ben Jonson* (Oxford, 1980), 14–15; John H. Long, *Shakespeare's Use of Music*, 3 vols. (Gainesville, 1963–1971); Peter J. Seng, *The Vocal Songs in the Plays of Shakespeare: A Critical History* (Cambridge, MA, 1967); and F. W. Sternfeld, *Music in Shakespearean Tragedy* (London, 1963), 14–20. Seng's book has not been superseded by Duffin's and deserves to be better known.

5 Smith, *Acoustic World*, 221.

6 Quoted in Andrew Gurr, *The Shakespearian Playing Companies* (New York, 1996), 283, spelling modernized.

7 Quoted in Andrew Gurr, *The Shakespearean Stage 1574–1642*, 3rd ed. (Cambridge, 1992), 226, 228, spelling modernized.

8 On the etymology of *agon* and its English cognates *agony, agonistic, antagonist, antagonistic,* and *protagonist*, see *OED*, "agony," etymology. The classic critical treatment of the idea of drama as *agon* is to be found in Northrop Frye, *The Anatomy of Criticism* (Princeton, 1957), 186–92. Frye regards *agon* as particular to the genre of romance.

9 Thomas Platter, *Travels in England*, trans. Clare Williams (London, 1937), 166.

10 Jigs as a phenomenon are studied, and surviving scripts anthologized, in Charles Read Baskervill, *The Elizabethan Jig and Related Song Drama* (Chicago, 1929). See also Smith, *Acoustic World*, 157–63.

11 Pro. 9–10 in Francis Beaumont and John Fletcher, *The Dramatic Works in the Beaumont and Fletcher Canon*, ed. Fredson Bowers and others, 10 vols. (Cambridge, 1966–1996), 10:559, spelling modernized.

12 *Oxford English Dictionary Online*, 2003 draft revision (http://dictionary.oed.com, accessed 25 September 2005), "noise, *n.*", I.1.a. Further references to the *OED* are cited in the text by word and definition number.

13 *OED*, "noise, *n.*," provides a full etymology of the English word "noise," via Anglo-Norman *noice* and Old French *noise*. The Arabic cognate with Latin *nausea* is specified in Hani Lubbadeh, ed., *Al-Nibras English-Arabic Dictionary* (Cairo, 1993), "noise."

14 Intersections of noise with culture, especially literary culture, have been suggestively studied by Brigitte Cazelles, *The Soundscape of Early French Literature*, Medieval and Renaissance Texts and Studies (Phoenix, 2006); Kenneth Gross, *Shakespeare's Noise* (Chicago, 2001); Wai Chee Dimock, "A Theory of Resonance," *Publications of the Modern Language Association of America* 112 (1997): 1060–71; Michel Serres, *Genesis*, trans. Geneviève James and James Nielson (Ann Arbor, 1995); and William R. Paulson, *The Noise of Culture: Literary Texts in a World of Information* (Ithaca, NY, 1988).

15 Stephen Handel, *Listening: An Introduction to the Perception of Auditory Events* (Cambridge, MA, 1989), 553, where "noise" is defined as "A random oscillation that is not periodic. At any point in time all frequencies have an equal probability of occurring."

16 "The Works of the Bard," http://www.it.usyd.edu.au/~matty/Shakespeare/test.html, accessed 25 September 2005.

17 M. B. Parkes, *Pause and Effect: An Introduction to the History of Punctuation in the West* (Berkeley, 1993), 41–61, dates the first appearance of the *punctus exclamatatus* to the fifteenth century, but printers through the early seventeenth century continued to use [?] where we would use [!].

18 There are three fine accounts of Shakespeare's fools/tricksters/clowns: Nora Johnson, *The Actor as Playwright in Early Modern Drama* (Cambridge, 2003); Bente A. Videbaek, *The Stage Clown in Shakespeare's Theatre* (Westport, CT, 1996); and David Wiles, *Shakespeare's Clown: Actor and Text in the Elizabethan Playhouse* (Cambridge, 1987).

19 Anonymous, "Singing Simpkin," rpt. in Baskervill, *Elizabethan Jig*, 444, spelling modernized.

20 Gary Tomlinson, *Metaphysical Song: An Essay on Opera* (Princeton, 1999), 4.

Ballads in Shakespeare's World

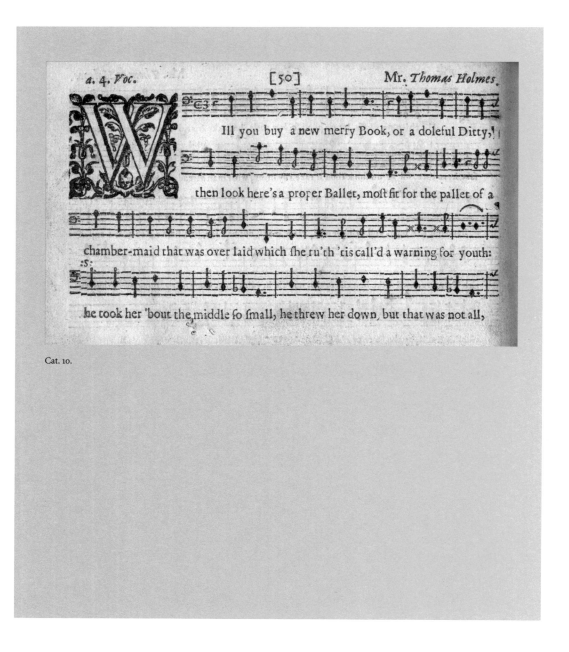

Ross W. Duffin

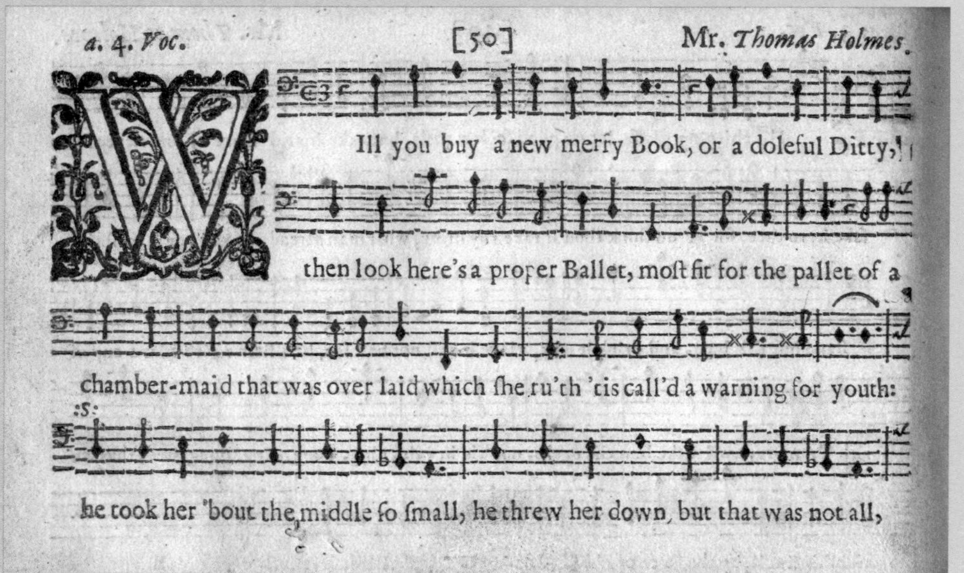

Cat. 10.

• dark stain; smudge
• printed on a sizable sheet of paper on one side or on both sides and folded
• a distance/interval

/ *The music like fingernails scraping on glass—*

A brave new ballad, very pitiful, and as true;
to the tune of Packington's Pound

Jessie Ann Owens, a scholar by trade,
commissioned an essay on ballads and such,
But little suspected the blunder she'd made,
or how such an essay her volume could smutch!
The subject was crass,
The writer an ass;
The music like fingernails scraping on glass—
Don't tell her, I beg you, don't tell her, I pray,
for ballads are not simply useless, my dear,
But part of the fabric of life in that day:
the age of our poet, th'immortal Shakespeare.

Topical, sensationalizing, exploitive of the misfortunes of others, straining credulity, moralizing . . . What? Ballads? I was actually talking about reactions to the 2005 Hurricane Katrina disaster. But there were similar elements to be seen in the Elizabethan broadside ballad and parallels amid the enormous audience for both, including those genuinely sympathetic, as well as morbidly curious, and even doomsayers. Ballads (or "ballets") had a huge entertainment value, as well—a potential not lost in the presentation of the news today—and while ballads rarely reached the poetic sublime, they were often pithy, amusing, and catchy. They were also pervasive in Shakespeare's day and, as we shall see, familiar to an enormous number of Elizabethans from all walks of life.

There is an oft-cited distinction between ballad poetry of oral tradition and the so-called street ballad, or broadside ballad. This may be traced in particular to the work of the nineteenth-century American scholar Francis J. Child, who viewed the ballad in oral tradition as superior morally and poetically to the printed form.[1] While crude verses do lurk among the broadsides, enough early printed versions of "Child Ballads"—supposedly from oral tradition—have been found to suggest that the distinction was not nearly so clear in the sixteenth century. Moreover, we are frequently unable to tell at this remove whether a ballad originated in print or in oral tradition.

Certainly, the telling of stories through musical or poetical performance can be dated in Britain at least back to the Anglo-Saxon *Beowulf* epic (and probably to the beginning of language). The term "ballad" itself seems to come from "ballade," a French poetic form especially prevalent in the fourteenth century, and the earliest English usage dates from that time. By the early fifteenth century, ballads were no longer just oral, but were circulating as single manuscript sheets—like broadsides except for the hand-copying. The printing of ballads seems to have begun around 1500 and proceeded to such an extent that by 1520, the Oxford bookseller John Dorne logged 193 "ballets" sold in the space of a year.[2] Yet from this early period, even up to 1540, only four fragments and one complete sheet survive today.[3]

By Edward's reign, ballads were being printed at an ever-quickening rate, and over the next few decades, they became no less than the primary publications of the London presses. We refer to them as "broadside" ballads because they were generally printed on a single side of a large piece of paper, as was also done for proclamations. By 1557, before the end of Mary's reign, it became necessary in the eyes of the authorities to exercise some control over this burgeoning enterprise and, from that year, all broadside ballads had to be licensed by the Stationers' Company (a sort of guild of printers and booksellers) before they could be printed. Licensing meant passing the censors of the Company, and yet there are plenty of lewd ballads that managed to survive that scrutiny, so either the censors weren't very vigilant, or they were more concerned about sedition and religious unorthodoxy than with indecency. In more modern terms, *Lay, lady, lay* might have squeaked through, but *The times they are a-changin'* had no chance.

By 1600, about two thousand ballads had been licensed, but we know that unlicensed ballads were issued as well: perhaps another two thousand, or more.[4] We know, for example, that there were forty printers registered to print broadsides in the first ten years of Elizabeth's reign, but in spite of the small number of surviving copies, an additional thirty unregistered printers' names are found on extant broadsides before 1580.[5] By 1603, when King James reorganized the Stationers' Company, "Ballad Stock" was one of the five newly-created divisions, along with "Bible Stock," "Irish Stock," "Latin Stock," and "English Stock."[6] Such legitimacy recognizes that printing broadside ballads was big business.

Early in the sixteenth century, ballads had sold for a halfpenny apiece, but by mid-century they had risen to a penny, at which price they remained until the late seventeenth century.[7] For comparison, an unskilled laborer's daily wage was about sixpence (also the cost of a play quarto), so the cost of a ballad might be expressed as about ten dollars in today's money—about the same as first-run movie admission—and therefore within the budget of even working class people, at least on an occasional basis. It cost the printers fourpence to register a ballad with the Stationers' Company and probably about forty shillings to buy or commission a new one from a ballad writer. Nonetheless, the potential volume of sale was large and the income great, so the Company was frequently called upon to discipline printers who violated "copyright" in an attempt to avoid the fourpence fee and perhaps even to defraud the rightful copyright

a folded sheet pasted flat against the inside of the front/back of a book

holder. When a printer didn't have to pay an author, profits were even greater. And with an estimated fifty percent literacy rate in Elizabethan England—including country maids like Mopsa and Dorcas—the potential market was in the range of 1.5 to 2 million readers.

In spite of the quantities printed, a good many broadsides, registered or unregistered, have been lost. Of the total number of broadsides issued in the sixteenth century, only about 260 English sheets survive to this day, many as fragments preserved because of their use as endpapers or hingepads in the bindings of later books.[8] A single sheet of printed paper was a fragile thing compared to a bound book, and most broadsides, it appears from the few surviving copies, found alternative, more prosaic uses, once the sheets had been "fingered to death" or the ballads were out of date. One common fate for ballads was to be pasted near the hearth, much as we today attach favorite cartoons to our refrigerators. In Ben Jonson's *Bartholomew Fair* (3.5.49–50) of 1614, for example, Cokes says: "O sister, do you remember the ballads over the nursery-chimney at home o' my pasting up?"

In some inns and taverns, ballads pasted on the wall became a sort of semi-permanent "entertainment wallpaper." As Joseph Addison wrote in the *Spectator* in 1711: "I can't, for my Heart, leave a Room before I have thoroughly studied the Walls of it, and examined the several printed Papers which are usually pasted upon them."[9] Imagine if dentists today didn't keep magazines in their waiting rooms, and hotels neglected to provide television sets, but proprietors managed to keep their patrons amused by pasting things all over the walls. At my own home, in a little bathroom under the stairs, we inherited actual wallpaper that reproduces newspaper clippings dating back to the late nineteenth century, and it has provided no end of fun for guests who, for whatever reason, happen to be spending time in that room. It also provided early incentive for our kids to learn to read, so I can imagine that pasted ballads did the same for generations of early modern English children.

Something that made broadsides more visually appealing was their customary use of woodcuts for decoration. Not that the woodcuts often had much to do with the subject of the ballad; they were typically whatever the printer had available, and the same woodcut got used again and again for a variety of different ballads. If a woman happened to be featured in the ballad, for example, then a gentlewoman with a fan might appear at the head, regardless of its suitability to the actual text. Also, since woodcuts got used over and over, they deteriorated in quality through repeated pressings, some even developing apparent wormholes in the woodblock. Once in a while, however, a special effort was made, and the woodcut created was more than just a generic graphic to catch the eye.

Who wrote all those sixteenth-century ballads? We know the names of about two hundred ballad writers from the Elizabethan period, and some of them were "professionals":[10] William Elderton (d. ca. 1592),

/ *every poore Milk maid can chant and chirpe it under her Cow*

36 Thomas Deloney (ca. 1543–1600), Samuel Rowlands (ca. 1570–ca. 1630), and Richard Johnson (1573–ca. 1659) are names that appear again and again in connection with ballads. It is not always clear whether someone like Deloney, for example, actually wrote a certain ballad or simply edited or perhaps expanded an anonymous one. Consequently, it is very difficult to discover when a ballad actually appeared, since anonymous ballads may have circulated orally for some time before making it into print. Indeed, the oral transmission of ballads continued long after the broadside industry was in full swing, and it has been estimated that for every broadside sold, hundreds of people heard one sung.

This reinforces the point that ballads were part of both oral and written culture. They were the "hums" of the lowest rank of society, where "every poore Milk maid can chant and chirpe it under her Cow, which she useth as a harmlesse charme to make her let downe her milke."[11] The gravedigger in *Hamlet* (5.1.69–72, etc.) sings not just a broadside, but a respectable song from *Tottel's Miscellany* of 1557.[12] This, too, would no doubt have been commonly referred to as a ballad; even the biblical "Song of Songs" was rendered as "Ballet of Ballets" in the 1568 "Bishop's Bible," overseen by Archbishop Matthew Parker.[13] Farther up the social ladder from milkmaids and gravediggers, Shakespearean parsons like Sir Hugh absentmindedly sing ballads, gentleman-merchants like Petruchio sing snatches, petty nobility like Falstaff and Sir Toby liberally sprinkle their speech with sung lines from ballads. Even the Prince of Denmark teases Polonius about not knowing the next line to a "pious chanson" (or "godly ballet," as it is called in one of the Quartos).

In the real world, foreign ambassadors took note of ballads and sent back reports of them to their respective governments.[14] And according to Henry Wheatley, editor of *Percy's Reliques*, a ballad singer named Mat Nash, whose specialty was border ballads like *Chevy Chase*, delighted Lord Burghley to such an extent and was so generously rewarded by the Principal Secretary, that he was able to retire. Wheatley gives also the story of a woman who, as we might say today, "played the palace": having sung her way to London, the "gypsy," Alice Boyce, was allowed to sing *O the Broom* and *Lady Green Sleeves* before Queen Elizabeth.[15] There is no corner of society in Elizabethan England that escaped reading, singing, or hearing ballads.

How many ballads might one of these singers have known? It is difficult to say for certain, but in Cleveland, Ohio, I know an Irish balladeer named Dermot Somerville who in the 1980s and '90s sang in various pubs around town. On more than one occasion I watched as patrons would approach him between songs and request this or that favorite. He received all such requests with equanimity and, though I never once saw him consult a book of lyrics, he would forthwith favor us with a performance of the request. After witnessing this yet one more time, I was finally moved to ask: "Dermot, exactly how many songs do you know?" "I'm not quite sure," he replied, "but I think it's about five hundred and fifty."

Like many other free-lance musicians, Dermot held a "day job" in the computer industry, so from his astonishing ability in what amounted to a sideline, we can begin to imagine the repertoire of a full-time ballad singer in the Elizabethan period.

Taken together, the contents of surviving ballads provide a glimpse of popular culture in Shakespeare's day that is quite remarkable. They were the entertainment of the time: the Elizabethan equivalent of television sitcoms and mini-series, and even feature movies. They reflect the society at the same time as they affect it. Just as more people today probably know about Queen Elizabeth through Shekar Kapur's 1998 movie *ELIZABETH*, most Elizabethans knew about Dido, Diana, and Daphne through ballads, rather than through Virgil and Ovid. The ballads may have simplified or distorted the original stories, but like feature films today their primary purpose was to entertain, not educate, even though their versions must have acquired a kind of common-knowledge truth.

Countless moralizations of ballads—parodies with a moral and religious message—were issued in the Renaissance, as well. A ballad might be registered on a certain day, and its popularity can be gauged by the fact that a moralization (or imitation, answer, or attack) was registered within a few days in an attempt to capitalize on that success. It is interesting that Shakespeare almost never seems to cite moralizations *per se*. Perhaps he viewed them as derivative artworks, or maybe they just never achieved the popularity of the original ballads and therefore were not worth mentioning. Similarly, except for the ballad-mongering of Autolycus, Shakespeare avoids reference to what might be termed the "tabloid" equivalent among broadside ballads—the stories of monstrous fishes, apocalyptic predictions, etc.—even though we suspect such ballads sold well or there would not have been so many of them.

It is hard to condemn Elizabethans for indulging in such things. After all, a search of actual tabloid headlines[16] over the year prior to this writing in 2005 turned up such curious selections as:

> LOUD ROCK SHOW MAKES TEEN'S HEAD EXPLODE!
>
> GIANT PIGEON TERRORIZES NEW YORK
>
> MASSIVE LOCH NESS MONSTER FART SWAMPS TOURIST BOAT

And where does this tendency to swallow the incredible come from? Here is a ballad title given in Jonson's *Bartholomew Fair* (2.4.18):

> WIND-MILL BLOWNE DOWNE BY THE WITCHES FART

Could tabloid writers be reading Jonson? Do they have a stash of old broadsides in a newsroom closet? Or is it just a case of the constancy of human nature—a fact of life that has kept Shakespeare fresh for four hundred years as well? Besides, some of those "tabloid" ballad stories from the sixteenth century found their way into legitimate historical chronicles like those of Holinshed and Stowe, which just goes to show how much authority naturally resides in anything printed, regardless of how unbelievable it may seem to most of us. As Mopsa says, "I love a ballad in print a-life, for then we are sure they are true."[17] This also emphasizes just how dangerous ballads could be as propaganda. *Monty Python* fans will remember Brave Sir Robin's trusty balladeer truthfully recording—to Robin's great chagrin and utter helplessness—how his master "ran away." Perhaps unintentionally, this modern example captures both the power of the ballad and the vulnerability of the person balladized, and also explains how Falstaff could threaten Hal with having ballads made up about him:[18] whether or not the ballads were true, they would be "sung to filthy tunes" for the sheer fun of it, and somebody would believe them. As Andrew Fletcher remarked in 1704: "If a man were permitted to make all the ballads, he need not care who should make the laws of a nation."[19]

Aside from their existence as broadsides, ballads were occasionally collected and published in volumes. There are some cases where we have a Stationers' Register entry for a ballad but no surviving copy except in collections such as Clement Robinson's *A Handefull of Pleasant Delites*, issued first in 1566 but with the earliest, nearly-complete copy coming from 1584.[20] Besides getting more mileage out of old material, this was a way of legitimizing the poetry, for in spite of the title-page characterization of the contents as "Sonets and delectable histories," these were mostly street ballads with lipstick. Other ballad collections aspiring to "poetic miscellanies" include Richard Johnson's *Golden Garland of Princely Pleasures* (1620)[21] and Thomas Deloney's *Garland of Good Will* (ca. 1592).[22] William Cavendish, first duke of Newcastle (and a soldier, horseman, and poet), is said to have committed Deloney's book, consisting of two dozen long ballads, entirely to memory,[23] and Deloney's second poem from that collection, *Shore's Wife*, alluded to by Shakespeare in *Richard III*, was so popular that it was reprinted for three hundred years.

Another important source for ballads is manuscript commonplace books: volumes in which individuals copied poems, sayings, etc., that they wanted to remember or carry with them. Many "lost" ballads—whether originally printed or from oral tradition—survive only because someone took the trouble to copy them into such personal collections. In some cases, the manuscript versions pre-date the broadside by some decades and confirm an earlier existence than might be suggested by the surviving print. One of the most important text manuscripts for Shakespeare's period is the Shirburn ballad manuscript,[24] an anthology compiled ca. 1585 to ca. 1616 and containing eighty ballads, no less than twelve of which were

- book of memorabilia (1578)
- a leaf, leaf number, case of loose papers

alluded to by Shakespeare in one way or another. The Folger Shakespeare Library contains several manuscript commonplace books, including Folger MS V.a.399 (cat. 25) which preserves one of the earliest versions of the song *Walsingham*, excerpted by Ophelia beginning with the first line of the second stanza: "How should I your true love know" (*Hamlet* 4.5.23).

This somewhat notorious commonplace book (also known as the Hall Commonplace Book) was once owned by the antiquarian and scholar, John Payne Collier. Even during Collier's lifetime, it was alleged that he had forged things in various early books, including a copy of the Second Folio (1632).[25] Former Folger Manuscript Curator Giles Dawson,[26] along with Carole Rose Livingston,[27] proved that eighty-three of the ballads in this particular manuscript were forged by Collier, perhaps to make it more valuable for sale, perhaps to garner the glory of publishing them (which he did in many cases), perhaps in a romantic attempt to re-create ballads registered but apparently lost forever, or perhaps just to prove he could do it. He was pretty good at both the versifying and the handwriting, but not good enough to remain undetected.[28]

So how does Shakespeare use the ballads that were all around him?[29] In *The Second Part of Henry IV* (2.4.36–38), to give one example, Falstaff says:

> *When Arthur first in court* (empty the Jordan) *and*
> *was a worthy king*: how now Mistris *Doll?*

Scholars have long recognized that he is interspersing his commands and questions with the lines from a ballad entitled, *The Noble Acts Newly Found, of Arthur of the Table Round*,[30] which begins:

> When Arthur first in court began,
> and was approved king:
>
> By force of arms great victories won
> and conquest home did bring.

Falstaff starts the first line, then switches to a command—"empty the Jordan" (a "jordan" is a chamber pot)—returns to a misremembered second line of the ballad, and finally breaks off to address Mistress Doll. The ballad is actually about Sir Lancelot rather than King Arthur, and it seems to fit Falstaff's self-image as a brave knight with a romantic flair in a way that must have been obvious as well as comical to the audience.

• a person who stood in the pit of an Elizabethan theatre; a person of unsophisticated tastes

There are several other instances where Shakespeare has a character quote an actual line or two from a ballad. *Come o'er the burn, Bessy*, for example, was begun by Edgar in *King Lear* (3.5.27) and answered in parody fashion by Lear's Fool. The poem, an allegorical dialogue by William Birch, concerns the divine right of the monarch to rule, a concept that certainly resonates in *King Lear. O' the Twelfth Day of December* is quoted (among many other songs) by Sir Toby in *Twelfth Night* (2.3.91). It recounts the Battle of Musselburgh Field, or Pinkie Cleugh as it is known in military history. In his previous speech (2.3.84), Toby quotes *There dwelt a man in Babylon* (cat. 23), a ballad that is actually used twice by Shakespeare—the other time by Sir Hugh in Quartos of *Merry Wives of Windsor* (3.1.24). It is interesting that Folger MS V.a.438 contains what seems to be the earliest version of this ballad in a book of medical recipes from the 1560s. In the First Folio, Sir Hugh's quotation is replaced by the similarly sited *Whenas we sat in Babylon*, a ballad-meter version of Psalm 137 from the Sternhold and Hopkins metrical psalter. *The God of love*, a ballad by William Elderton pleading for divine help in love, is cited twice in *Much Ado about Nothing*, first by Hero (3.1) and then by Benedick (5.2.26–29). Its poem was lost for centuries and only came to light in 1958. *The Friar and the Nun* is an old ballad, probably dating back to the fifteenth century, and is begun by Petruchio in *Taming of the Shrew* (4.1.148–49) as "It was the friar of orders grey." *Jepha, Judge of Israel* is the ballad Hamlet uses to tease Polonius (2.2.403–420). The connection to the play seems to be that, like Jeptha, Polonius has "one fair daughter and no more" who will soon die, perhaps due to the actions of her father. The list goes on.

Not all ballad references in the plays are documented quotes of a line or two from the song, spoken or perhaps sung by a character. Indeed, sometimes the naming of a character is itself sufficient to make a connection with a ballad. And sometimes, only the tune title is cited, inviting the audience to make a connection between the scene of the play and some popular ballad set to the tune. Such a connection may seem tenuous at first, but it is important to remember that *everyone* knew the tune titles. In almost no printed ballad is the music given on the page. Instead, the title of the ballad is followed by "to the tune of *Greensleeves*," or some such directive. The tunes and their titles were so well known that it was not necessary to use precious space on the broadside to print the music again and again. Besides, music notation was understood by only a miniscule percentage of the population, so it would have been wasted on most people. The same tunes, furthermore, were the musical currency of stage jigs, which were the "half time shows" of Elizabethan theater: farcical song and dance playlets in which the entire dialogue was sung to one or more ballad tunes.[31] Lastly, we know the tunes were heard in court circles as well, since many of them survive only in arrangements for lute or keyboard by composers like William Byrd and John Dowland.[32] There is no question that Shakespeare's audience, from the lowliest groundling to the highest

* What percentage of congregants today can sing from music notation?

noble, knew not only the texts to the ballads, but also the tunes, both by name and by melody. What then for us may seem like obscure allusions were for them clear, obvious references to universally recognized artifacts of popular culture.

One humorous window into that familiarity comes in the following passage from Thomas Tomkis's play, *Lingua,* published in 1607:[33]

> *Common Sense:* Memory, do you hear the harmony of the spheres?
>
> *Memoria:* Not now, my lord, but I remember some 4000 years ago when the sky was first made, we heard very perfectly.
>
> *Anamnestes [page to Memoria]:* By the same token, the first tune the planets played . . . was *Sellenger's Round,* in memory whereof ever since, it hath been called *The Beginning of the World.*
>
> *Common Sense:* How comes it we hear it not now?
>
> *Memoria:* Our ears are so well acquainted with the sound that we never mark it.

The implication is that tunes like *Sellenger's Round* were so familiar that, like Muzak, they faded into the background. So why does Shakespeare cite these popular songs in his plays? It is my contention that there is frequently some extra layer of meaning or expectation created for his audience through the use of these references. A few examples will help to illustrate the point.

In *The Winter's Tale* (5.2.21–25), a character says, "The news, Rogero?" This is Shakespeare's only naming of this gentleman and, in fact, his only use of the name or word Rogero in his entire *œuvre.* The answer to the question even draws attention to the fact that *Rogero* is a ballad tune:

> *[Rogero]:* Nothing but bonfires. The oracle is fulfilled; the King's daughter is found. Such a deal of wonder is broken out within this hour that ballad-makers cannot be able to express it.

It happens that there is a ballad set to *Rogero* about an irrationally jealous husband, who ultimately kills his innocent wife and her supposed lover. There are clear parallels between this and the plot of *The Winter's Tale* where, at this point in the play, Leontes' ill-founded jealousy of Hermione and Polixines has already created a desperate situation. Reminding the audience of the ballad at this point, before the resolution of the difficulties, would surely invite them to expect an unhappy end to the play, in parallel with the ballad.

Another example comes from *The Taming of the Shrew* (3.2.122). Petruchio says, "I should bid good morrow to my bride." One of the most popular ballads set to the tune, *The Bride's Good Morrow* was the *Ballad of Patient Grissel*, detailing the treatment of Griselda by her husband, and the extraordinary patience and obedience she showed in the face of countless trials and indignities. From this allusion, then, the audience would probably guess that Petruchio was about to subject Kate to a series of such tests of her own mettle and, given the portrait of Kate's character to that point, they might well expect a cataclysm of some sort! Shakespeare had earlier reminded the audience of this story by having Petruchio say—ironically and, as it turned out, prophetically—"for patience she will prove a second Grissell" (2.1.295).

These two examples show how a tune title alone can constitute Shakespeare's reference. One of my favorite examples of a connection involving a ballad title comes from *Hamlet* (4.5.42) when Ophelia says, "They say the owl was a Baker's daughter." At this point in the play, Ophelia is already quite distracted, and that line has mostly been seen as a non-sequitur from a mad character. In the late eighteenth century, however, reports began circulating of a West Country legend that a baker's daughter who refused to give bread to Jesus was transformed by him into an owl.[34] Granted, legends are not bound by reality—or religious orthodoxy, for that matter—but the report of a legend hundreds of miles from London and nearly two hundred years after Shakespeare seemed somewhat tenuous to me. I found a reference to an Elizabethan song title that mentioned a "Baker's daughter" but it did not appear to be related: *The Merry Miller's Wooing of the Baker's Daughter of Manchester.*[35] The more I thought about it, however, the more I realized that a far more likely explanation for Ophelia's line was that Shakespeare was making a ridiculous pun on the homophones "wooing" and "whooing" (that is, "courting" and "hooting," respectively). The "wooing of the baker's daughter" can be construed to mean that the baker's daughter is making a "whooing" sound; if she makes a whooing sound, she must be an owl. Hamlet himself uses puns to help *feign* madness, so it wouldn't be surprising to find Ophelia doing it authentically. Indeed, this kind of free-association seemed to me both likely and significant for Ophelia (more so than the legend), especially since this particular ballad is about a seduction, and perhaps lends support to the theory that Hamlet had earlier seduced her. Indeed, this line immediately precedes her *Tomorrow is St. Valentine's Day* song (4.5.48–55, 58–66), with its condemnation of young men for seducing maidens.

In some cases, there is no doubt that Shakespeare is alluding to a song. He quotes a line or more and thus makes an explicit connection, often revealing something about the character's thought processes at the same time. In other cases, it is more questionable. One of the admittedly more tenuous citations in my *Shakespeare's Songbook* comes from the following speech by Theseus in *A Midsummer Night's Dream* (4.1.124–27):

- [Daedalus] legendary builder of the Cretan labyrinth [maze] who makes wings to enable himself and his Icarus to escape imprisonment
- (See above)... falls into the sea/drown when the wax of his wings melts as he flies too near the sun
- Son of Zeus/Europa, King of Crete who for his just rule is made supreme judge in the underworld after his death
- a group performing together

A cry more tuneable was
never holla'd to, or cheer'd with horn,
In *Crete*, in *Sparta*, nor in *Thessaly*.
Judge when you hear.

Theseus is actually speaking about his hunting dogs, but in the play he is just on the point of discovering his daughter and her three friends asleep in the forest after their nocturnal elopement. It happens that *In Crete* is the name of a not-so-serious ballad about Dedalus, Icarus, and their escape from King Minos. This ballad actually achieved a certain celebrity in literary circles in 1596 when Thomas Nashe wrote jokingly that it was "food from heaven" for his archrival, Gabriel Harvey.[36] The earliest source for its tune, by the way, is Folger MS V.a.159, the so-called Lodge Commonplace Book (cat. 61). At any rate, in both quarto and folio editions of *A Midsummer Night's Dream*, "In Crete" appears with the first letter capitalized, so it even *looks* like the ballad title as much as it *sounds* like it. The ballad ends with a plea to the poet's lady to fly securely with him to some secret trysting place. So, though there is no guarantee that Shakespeare was playing on the connection to the flight of the lovers, it seems to be a significant juxtaposition.

A modern play that included, in passing, such disparate and even fragmentary lines as "Stormy weather," or "Hey Jude," or "You can get anything you want," (I'm dating myself, I know) would easily be recognized as containing allusions to popular songs. People would immediately think of the tunes and, to some extent, the rest of the lyrics of those songs, and would realize that those members of the audience who didn't recognize the song references and the associations they conjured up were missing part of the message. So it is with Shakespeare and ballads. He does cite other types of music: his extensive use of rounds like those from the Lant Roll, Melvill's Book of Roundels (cat. 3), and Ravenscroft's three collections (cat. 1) would be worth a study unto itself.[37] And occasionally, he shows awareness of more elevated genres like accompanied lute songs and consort songs. Nevertheless, the references to ballads are everywhere in Shakespeare's plays and, in countless ways, woven more intricately into the fabric of his world.

Detail, cat. 14.

1 See Child's monumental edition (from whence the term "Child Ballads" comes), *The English and Scottish Popular Ballads*, 5 vols. (Boston, 1883–1898).

2 F. Madan, ed., "The Daily Ledger of John Dorne, 1520," in *Collectanea. First Series*, ed. Charles Robert Leslie Fletcher, Oxford Historical Society Series, vol. 5 (Oxford, 1885), 71–77.

3 Carole Rose Livingston, *British Broadside Ballads of the Sixteenth Century: A Catalogue of the Extant Sheets and an Essay* (New York, 1991), 31.

4 Ibid., 32.

5 Hyder E. Rollins, "The Black-letter Broadside Ballad," *PMLA* 34 (1919): 260. This article remains one of the best introductions to the subject by someone who devoted his life to ballad scholarship.

6 Natascha Würzbach, *The Rise of the English Street Ballad, 1550–1650*, trans. Gayna Walls (Cambridge, 1990), 19.

7 Rollins, "The Black-letter Broadside Ballad," 296, 304.

8 Livingston, *British Broadside Ballads*, 32.

9 *The Spectator* 2, no. 85 (7 June 1711): 23.

10 Rollins, "The Black-letter Broadside Ballad," 260.

11 Richard Brathwaite, *Whimzies: or, a new cast of characters* (London, 1631), 12.

12 The song, *I Loathe That I Did Love*—somewhat garbled and much shortened in the grave-digger's version—is by Thomas, Lord Vaux.

13 *The. holie. Bible. conteyning the olde Testament and the newe* (London, [1568]). STC 2099.

14 See, for example, *CSP Venetian* for 21 March 1559.

15 Henry B. Wheatley, ed., *Reliques of Ancient English Poetry, Consisting of Old Heroic Ballads, Songs, and Other Pieces of our Earlier Poets, Together with Some Few of Later Date, by Thomas Percy* (London, 1876), 1:xxxiv. Bishop Percy was an early ballad scholar and owner of the "Percy Folio Manuscript" (London, British Library, Additional MS 27879), an important ballad anthology compiled ca. 1643.

16 See, for example, the collected headlines at http://www.citynewsstand.com/TopTen.htm.

17 *The Winter's Tale* 4.4.252–53.

18 *1 Hen. IV* 2.1.43–46.

19 Andrew Fletcher, *Account of a conversation concerning a right regulation of government . . . from London the 1st of December, 1703* (Edinburgh, 1704), 10.

20 *A handefull of pleasant delites containing sundrie new sonets and delectable histories, in diuers kinds of meeter* (London, 1584). STC 21105.

21 *The golden garden of princely pleasures and delicate delights wherein is conteined the histories of many of the kings, queenes, princes, lords, ladies, knights, and gentlewomen of this kingdome* (London, 1620). STC 14674.

22 *The garland of good vvill. Diuided into three parts: containing many pleasant songs, and pretty poems, to sundry new notes* (London, 1628). STC 6553.5.

23 See Rollins, "Black-letter Broadside Ballads," 337n.

24 Shirburn Castle, North Library 119 D 44. It was edited by Andrew Clark as *The Shirburn Ballads 1585–1616* (Oxford, 1907).

25 *Mr. VVilliam Shakespeares Comedies, Histories, and Tragedies* (London, 1632). STC 22274. This so-called "Perkins Folio" now resides in the Huntington Library.

26 Giles E. Dawson, "John Payne Collier's Great Forgery," *Studies in Bibliography* 24 (1971): 1–26.

27 Carole Rose Livingston, "The Pervasive Pattern of Fraud and Forgery in the Ballad Scholarship of John Payne Collier," in "Extant English and Scottish Broadside Ballads of the Sixteenth Century" (Ph.D. diss., New York University), pt. 2, ch. 5, 950–1000. Dawson's and Livingston's evidence is summarized (and the whole corpus of Collier's forgeries discussed throughout) in Arthur Freeman and Janet Ing Freeman, *John Payne Collier: Scholarship and Forgery in the Nineteenth Century*, 2 vols. (New Haven, 2004), 1:502–7.

28 As recently as 1982, one Collier biographer was still not acknowledging his deception. See Dewey Ganzel, *Fortune and Men's Eyes: the Career of John Payne Collier* (New York, 1982).

29 All of the items discussed here from the plays of Shakespeare appear with tunes and complete lyrics in Ross W. Duffin, *Shakespeare's Songbook* (New York, 2004). This essay is based on the discussion in that book. Further discussion, especially on the history of many of the songs over the centuries, can be found in Peter J. Seng, *The Vocal Songs in the Plays of Shakespeare: A Critical History* (Cambridge, MA, 1967).

30 This ballad was registered by Thomas Deloney on 8 June 1603 but had already appeared ca. 1592 in his *Garland of Good Will.* It may also be the same ballad that was registered in 1565–1566 as *A Pleasaunte History of an Adventurous Knyghte of Kynges Arthurs Couurte.* See Hyder E. Rollins, *An Analytical Index to the Ballad-Entries (1557–1709) in the Registers of the Company of Stationers of London* (Chapel Hill, 1924; reprint Hatboro, PA, 1967), entries 1951, 2107.

31 On the stage jig, see Charles Read Baskervill, *The Elizabethan Jig and Related Song Drama* (Chicago, 1929; reprint New York, 1965).

32 For a comprehensive study of tunes for ballads, see Claude M. Simpson, *The British Broadside Ballad and its Music* (New Brunswick, NJ, 1966). This has antecedents in the work of earlier scholars, such as William Chappell, *The Ballad Literature and Popular Music of the Olden Time: A History of the Ancient Songs, Ballads, and of the Dance Tunes of England, with Numerous Anecdotes and Entire Ballads; also a short Account of Minstrels*, 2 vols. (London, 1855–1859; reprint New York, 1965).

33 *Lingua: or the combat of the tongue, and the fiue senses for superiority. A pleasant comœdie* (London, 1607). STC 24104.

34 Douce communicated the most fully developed form of this story to Edmond Malone sometime before the latter's death in 1812, and it was included in the notes to Malone's posthumous *The Plays and Poems of William Shakspeare* (London, 1821), 7:426. Douce's note is as follows: "This is a common story among the vulgar in Gloucestershire, and is thus related: 'Our Saviour went into a baker's shop where they were baking, and asked for some bread to eat. The mistress of the shop immediately put a piece of dough into the oven to bake for him; but was reprimanded by her daughter, who insisting that the piece of dough was too large, reduced it to a very small size. The dough, however, immediately afterwards began to swell, and presently became of a most enormous size. Whereupon, the baker's daughter cried out "Heugh, heugh, heugh," which owl-like noise probably induced our Saviour for her wickedness to transform her into that bird.' This story is often related to children, in order to deter them from such illiberal behaviour to poor people." George Steevens had already noted the story in his 1778 edition: "a legendary story, which both Dr. Johnson and myself have read, yet in what book at least I cannot recollect. —Our Saviour being refused bread by the *daughter of a baker*, is described as punishing her by turning her into an *owl*." See *The Plays of William Shakspeare*, ed. George Steevens and Samuel Johnson (London, 1778), 10:346.

35 The ballad was registered on 2 March 1581 and survives uniquely in the Shirburn ballad manuscript. See Rollins, *Analytical Index*, entry 1785.

36 See Thomas Nashe, *Have With You to Saffron Walden* (London, 1596), 33.

37 On the Lant Roll (ca. 1580), see Jill Vlasto, "An Elizabethan Anthology of Rounds," *Musical Quarterly* 40 (1954): 222–34. On David Melvill's *Ane Buik off Roundells*, compiled in Aberdeen in 1612, see Granville Bantock and H. Orsmond Anderton, eds., *The Melvill Book of Roundels* (London, 1916; reprint New York, 1972). See also Thomas Ravenscroft, *Pammelia, Deuteromelia, Melismata* (London, 1609, 1611; reprint Philadelphia, 1961; 3 vols. New York, [1998]). STC 20757–59.

John Playford and the English Musical Market

Stacey Houck

Cat. 47.

Regarded by modern scholars as the "Father of English music printing," John Playford (1623–1686/7) was almost solely responsible for the revival of the English music market in the middle of the seventeenth century. He then proceeded to dominate this market for the next thirty-five years with an extensive series of musical collections. Indeed, Playford's musical primer, *An Introduction to the Skill of Musick* (originally *A Breefe Introduction to the Skill of Musick*, 1654), continued in successive editions until 1730; later musical treatises excerpted theoretical sections of the *Introduction* throughout the eighteenth century. Interestingly, however, early music historians of the eighteenth century tarred Playford with the same brush as other publishers, characterizing him as merely an opportunistic tradesman. It was not until twentieth-century historians began to explore his connections to music that his importance was rediscovered.[1]

The rediscovery of Playford happened to coincide with a revival of interest in English country dance and English folk tunes. Playford's *The English Dancing Master* (1651) proved to be essential to research in both areas and further spurred interest in Playford and his sources.[2] Several theories about Playford developed, and it became clear that he was intimately connected to the musical communities of his day as a singer, performer, copyist, and collector, as well as publisher. Playford himself gives his readers much of this information in his introductions and editorial notes that describe his musical pursuits and reflect his shrewd business sense, respect for tradition, and devotion to the improvement of music. With his publications, he sought not only to fill a musical and cultural need, but also to create new markets, particularly among musical amateurs. This latter function of Playford's music has led some to view his works primarily as *Gebrauchtsmusik*, that is, as useful but simple works with little importance beyond their function as amateur entertainment. A more recent reassessment of Playford's output, however, also considers his place within the larger sociopolitical context of his period.[3] In these studies, Playford's ardently royalist political stance is seen as a factor in his musical choices; his music becomes an important resource for what it can reveal of its time.

When he left his hometown of Norwich in 1640 to become an apprentice to the London stationer John Benson, Playford found himself in the chaotic world of London at the beginning of the Civil War. During the early years of the conflict, large numbers of apprentices were regularly active in street riots. One such riot threatened the king's palace and was a motivating factor in the monarchy's departure from London; King Charles I was not to return until the time of his trial and execution in 1649. Witnessing his king's retreat and later his execution was surely traumatic for a young royalist such as Playford. After finishing his apprenticeship in 1647,* Playford opened his own shop in the Inner Temple Churchyard and began an active publishing campaign. Within a four-year period, from 1647 to 1650, he published over twenty-seven titles, twenty-five of which were political in nature and revealed a strong royalist bias.[4]

* Age 24.

/ *a tour de force of country dance tunes*

However, the publishing freedoms that had been granted in 1643 with the beginning of Parliamentary rule were rapidly being curtailed in the later 1640s. Playford's last purely political tract nearly led to his imprisonment and a possible death sentence. At this point early in 1649, Playford disappears from sight and may have been in prison or in hiding. When he reemerges, he is busily refashioning himself as a music publisher.

As both a stationer and a musician Playford was in an ideal position to collect and promote music. Possessing some training and a genuine interest in music, he seems to have been accepted into London's musical circles,[5] and he could easily copy music—and was probably encouraged to do so during informal meetings at taverns and in private homes. An instance of Playford's musical copying can be found in Folger Library MS V.a.411 (cat. 45).[6] This manuscript is a clean copy of pieces in separate parts that Playford used for singing and playing with his musical club. He thanked his friends at the beginning of a later printed version for their "Excellent Musical performances, when it [the music] was thrown before you in loose Papers."[7] The fact that these fragmentary sheets contain works by Robert Johnson (1583–1633) probably written for a Jacobean staging of Shakespeare's *Tempest* means that Playford may have gathered this repertory near the beginning of his time in London. With a collection of such manuscripts "laying by," possibly gathered in part during his apprenticeship, Playford was positioning himself to change the focus of his publishing to music. Since music publication previously had proven so unpromising for stationers, there had been virtually no music published in England in over twenty-five years.[8] Clearly a new marketing scheme would be required.

Playford moved gingerly at first, testing public response. Although it is generally assumed that the *English Dancing Master* (1651), a *tour de force* of country dance tunes and choreography, was his first music publication, the first piece he published was actually a reprint of psalms by William Child.[9] Playford's decision to republish Child's psalms may have been a calculated risk to see if their settings "after the New Italian Way" would elicit negative responses from various social and religious quarters. It is likely that in choosing to publish psalms, Playford was hoping to achieve the same kind of success as the 1648 publication *Choice Psalmes* (cat. 102) that had been composed and collected by Henry Lawes and published by Humphrey Moseley.[10] Lawes's *Choice Psalmes* were unabashed in their open dedication to King Charles and served to connect the death of Lawes's brother William with the plight of the then imprisoned monarch. Playford did not dedicate his publication of the psalms to the late king or to his son, but he took pains to mention "his Majesty" on the title page. Since Child was not a member of the Royal Chapel as Lawes had been, his full title, "organist of his Maties free Chappell of Windsor" was given. Playford may have hoped to appeal to the same kind of audience that Moseley attracted while still publishing in a safe genre. The *Psalmes* apparently attracted buyers as they merited a second edition in 1657, when they reappeared as *Choise*

/ Musick and Mirth: a Choice Collection of Rounds or Catches for three Voyces

Musick to the Psalmes.[11] But while the *Psalmes* were Playford's first musical publication, and thus mark his move into the world of music publishing, they also mark the continuation of his older royalist biases. It seems plausible that in Lawes's *Psalmes*, not to mention other royalist cultural publications (mostly products of Moseley's publishing), Playford saw a means to promote his political agenda, albeit more subtly, by prefacing seemingly apolitical material with royalist codes and innuendo.

Having achieved success with the *Psalmes*, Playford was determined to explore further the possibilities of music publishing. His second, and arguably most popular, musical publication was the aforementioned *English Dancing Master*. This collection, with significant additions, continued into eighteen editions, the last dated 1721.[12] The first edition contained 105 dances with their titles, tunes, and dancing instructions. With no evidence to the contrary, scholars have maintained that Playford's collection of dances was the product of his own interest and compilation of tunes. However, Keith Whitlock has recently argued that Playford's tunes, their titles, and their choreography came from rough copies of Stuart masques.[13] While this is a controversial suggestion requiring more investigation, it does account for the highly detailed and polished look of this early publication. Furthermore, a subtle effort to revive music from the court of the deceased king through the medium of print and to label it "English" in a proto-nationalist way would have been a cultural act of defiance against the English Republican government.

The success of these two books gave Playford the confidence to launch a more ambitious marketing plan to reach all of the potential music market through both repertory and instruction. Earlier English attempts at music publishing had been almost exclusively directed toward a skilled, or at least highly adept, musical audience. In contrast, Playford attempted to supply music to both professionals and novices, while paying special attention to the latter—a clever, long-term policy. With his third publication, *A Musicall Banquet* (1651), Playford launched his new strategy. This collection is comprised of four parts: "Some Rules for Voice and Viol"; "Excellent new Lessons for the Lyra Viol"; "Musica Harmonia: or, Choice Almans, Corants, and Sarabands, for one Treble and Bass [viol]"; and "Musick and Mirth: a Choice Collection of Rounds or Catches for three Voyces." Looking back on this volume some three years later, Playford remarked:

> That little Booke finding such acceptance among all Lovers and Practitioners in Musick. I resolved to inlarge each of these Tracts, and to Print them in severall Books, which I have now (through Gods permission) accomplish'd. Whereby you have a much larger Banquet than you had before.[14]

- the whole series of musical notes recognized
- the act of measuring; measurement
- adherant of a king or monarchical government
- different from the violin family in having a deep body, flat back, sloping shoulders, usu. six strings, a fretted fingerboard, and a low-arched bridge; of the 16th/17th centuries; in treble/alto/tenor/bass sizes

Seeing that his assessment of the market had been correct, Playford enlarged each section to stand alone, a decision which spawned some of the most important and long-running series in his entire output.

But what had dictated the original make-up of *A Musicall Banquet*? This may seem an irrelevant question given the later popularity of the separate volumes. However, Playford, as he says so often in his introductions, had many pieces "laying by him" and could have chosen any number of different arrangements for this early volume. The collection begins with a unifying prefatory set of "Directions." Here, in what amounts to Playford's first printed pedagogic text, the length is modest and the directions almost tentative, explaining only the basics of tunings, the gamut, mensuration, and note-values with their related symbols. The first two sections after the brief rules contain mainly instrumental music for viols. This was a prudent choice considering Parliament's general approbation of domestic music-making, as long as it was, as the outspoken religious reformer William Prynne stated, "music in and of itselfe."[15] It was more daring to include the third section of vocal music because of potentially offensive lyrics. But catches and rounds had enjoyed currency as far back as Queen Elizabeth's time, and as such were not newcomers to the social music scene. On the surface, *A Musicall Banquet* appears to be simply a retrospective look at mostly pre-war music.

Closer inspection reveals that this seemingly innocuous music hides many possible royalist messages. First, by including music for viols—with which Playford catered to the aristocratic taste for the viol and viol consort music—he asserted his support for the former king. Charles was renowned as an *aficionado* of the viol and its music, and as an enthusiastic amateur on the bass viol. A more interesting political message, however, lies in the instrumental repertory, mainly drawn from popular broadside ballads. With some boldness, Playford printed the popularly recognizable ballad titles, although some in abbreviated forms, for these instrumental pieces. The piece, "A la Mode de France," is a good example: it had a prominent ballad text that discussed Queen Henrietta Maria's attempts to raise Continental support for Charles.[16] "When the K. enjoyes &c." is the boldest inclusion. It is, of course, the very famous royalist ballad, Martin Parker's "When the King enjoyes his owne again." This ballad, reportedly written in 1643, enjoyed constant favor with royalists and had many alternate texts including "The World is turned Upside Down" and "A Review of a Rebellion."[17] Playford audaciously prints a musical mirroring of the king's trial in the last piece of the first section, "Colonel Gerard's Tune," also known as "Colonel Gerard's Mistresse." Several of the texts connected to this tune, for example "The King's last Speech at his Time of Execution" and "The Weeping Widow," refer to the king's execution and his grieving queen. Over half of the tunes in this section reveal royalist affiliations. While some readers may not have recognized these tunes, royalist sympathizers certainly did.

(1574) an instrumental notation indicating the string, fret, key, or finger to be used instead of the tone to be sounded

Parliament's attitude toward ballads—the performance, printing, sale, and even the mere possession of them after 1649—was unequivocally negative. As of the 1643 Printing Act, ballad sellers, if caught selling their wares, were to have their sheets confiscated and were to be whipped as "common rogues."[18] If the printers and publishers could be identified, they were also held accountable. Playford, therefore, took some degree of risk in publishing both *The English Dancing Master* and *A Musicall Banquet*. In the absence of any evidence to the contrary, we must assume that he escaped all censure. The royalist associations of these pieces seem to have passed by the censors, who perhaps did not understand the "new" tablature notation or merely discounted untexted music's ability to convey meaning.[19]

The next section of *A Musicall Banquet*, "Musica Harmonia," also has strong royalist leanings made only more explicit in 1655 when the section was expanded and retitled *Court Ayres*. As with *The English Dancing Master*, these pieces are dance music, many of which could probably be related to the pre-war Stuart masque or to Charles himself, who was known, even to the common people, as a great dancer—a point that many detractors used to criticize his excesses.[20] In addition to possible royal associations with dance music, Playford emphasizes the music of William Lawes, asserting a striking royalist preference. Lawes is described here as "that Rare and accomplished Master in Musick" and his name is spaced and centered on the frontispiece of the section, followed by the word "Deceased"—almost as much an accusation as a statement. William Lawes was one of Charles's favorite musicians, so much so that when he joined the king's army, Charles tried to keep him in the commissary, a position of relative safety.[21] Nevertheless, Lawes was killed in the battle of Chester in 1645. One biographer has argued that his death, for musicians and poets, had "become a symbol of the excesses of the Puritan Rebellion."[22] Clearly all was not as harmonious as the title might imply.

The last section of the *Banquet* is "Musick and Mirth." These are vocal pieces, which were probably more dangerous for Playford to print. Though Puritan apologists rightly insist that many Puritans accepted secular music, the official party line was one of mistrust. However, any Puritan seriously considering, even for a moment, some of these jovial pieces, published for "all Lovers of MUSICK," could not help but notice that, as Playford himself says in the introduction, "though they be Ancient, the method is true, and much matter couched in a few words."[23] The matter that is couched in these catches for the "understanding reader" is royalist rhetoric, the same rhetoric evinced by their textual cousins, miscellanies and drolleries. It is distinguished by a pronounced anti-Puritan aesthetic that values drinking, carefree entertainment, and a certain degree of sexual looseness.

When these pieces are compared with the contents of the later *Catch that Catch Can* (1652), it seems clear that Playford was careful to choose pieces with more abstruse references for *The Musicall Banquet*—

• a lively 16th century court dance; a Canary Islands usu. sweet wine similar to Madeira
• a young girl; female servant; lewd woman

/ *learne to sing, or to play on the viol*

literally the first book of its type to be printed in England since Thomas Ravenscroft's books of rounds, published from 1609 to 1613 (cat. 1).[24] But despite Playford's caution, the rowdy carousing of the "Boyes" can hardly be missed. Their loose ideal is exemplified in pieces like "Let's cast away care," composed by William Lawes. Aside from its status as the unofficial slogan of the Interregnum cavalier, the piece's title must have been particularly obnoxious to Puritans because the order of their workweek and even the veneration of the Sabbath are flouted in the lyrics:

> he that plays at his work, & works in his play, keeps neither working, nor yet holyday
> set businesse aside then if you'l be merry, and drown your dry thoughts in canary and sherry.[25]

Being "merry" or a "poet" in this language means to be a cavalier, shaking off Puritan "gloom" by throwing back a glass of sherry or canary—both liquors were highly taxed at the time due to Parliamentary efforts at social reform. Such carousing also included wenches and bawdy references, especially since sexual licentiousness was understood to be anti-Puritan and thus proper cavalier behavior.

Four series of books grew from the four sections of *A Musicall Banquet*: *The Introduction to the Skill of Musick*, *Musicks Recreation*, *Court Ayres*, and *Catch that Catch Can*. The humble "few rules and directions for such as learne to sing, or to play on the viol" announced in the title of *A Musicall Banquet* developed first into the 1654 publication the *Breefe Introduction to the Skill of Musick*, and then into the 1655 *Introduction to the Skill of Musick* (nineteen editions between 1655 and 1730; cat. 30, 44, 98). The structure of the first few editions shifted as Playford jostled his borrowed materials, the music, and his contributing authors' sections, but the main division into instructions for voice and viol remained consistent.

Looking at Playford's attempts at pedagogy from a larger cultural perspective, we can see that his *Introduction* fits into the genre of the instruction book flooding the Commonwealth book market. The most prevalent of these were books for instruction in rhetoric and etiquette, also called compliment or courtesy books, in the tradition if not the style of Henry Peacham's 1622 *Compleat Gentleman* (cat. 69).[26] These books, through "profit and delight," promised to open a door to the world of refinement; the cover of one of the most popular compliment books, *The Academy of Complements*, reads:

> Wherein Ladies, Gentlewomen Schollers, and strangers may accommodate their Courtly practice with gentile Ceremonies, Complementall amorous high expressions, and forms of speaking or writing of Letters most in fashion.[27]

A historian of these texts describes them as "products of bundling together of writing from diverse sources altered to suit the envisioned purposes of readers, set in an educative, Royalist frame, and offered as an emblem and exemplar of elite, usually courtly, life."[28] Although there is clearly tension in the idea of making that which is elite and privileged into a common commodity, another goal (beyond that of financial gain) was to improve and, to a degree, refine the lower classes. But the intention was not altruistic so much as curative, in the sense that royalists hoped that by raising the lower classes' understanding of quality, they might come to better respect tradition and hierarchy. These same objectives are at work in Playford's musical pedagogy.

Throughout the *Introduction*, the concepts of musical and social improvement balance each other, with a marked royalist slant. Playford's language concerning technical matters is dry, matter-of-fact, and useful in its practicality. Like other royalist stationers' productions, however, the body of material needs to be placed against its extra-textual framework including prefatory notes, repertory choices, and editorial comments to understand its full message. In the preface to the 1655 edition, Playford opens with a clear statement of social improvement:

> There is nothing that more conduceth to the prosperity and happinesse of Nation, then the good education of youth and children . . . and therefore the rudest swains of all Nations, doe make this double use of their articulate Voyces: but to speake well, and to sing well, are of Art. . . . necessary thereof in the breeding of children, partly from its naturall delight, and partly from the efficacy it hath in moving affections and vertues.[29]

After stating this goal of aiding the nation, and delivering the promised musical knowledge, Playford offers practice pieces to help solidify that new knowledge. Typically, these repertory choices, labeled as "necessary" to the basics of voice training, are cavalier texts that celebrate either mirth or sexuality.

The 1658 edition contains the same introduction concerning education for the good of the nation, but the character of the volume is noticeably different. The lusty secular tunes from the 1655 edition are exchanged for psalms. However, the most prominently placed psalms—again for the "necessary" practice of the voice—are those by George Sandys and Henry Lawes, the favorites of King Charles I. Playford's literal change of tune indicates his growing interest in the psalms, which would see its culmination in his *Whole Book of Psalms* (1677; cat. 43).[30] Later editions of the *Introduction* continued to add new sections and delete older outdated material. The eighth edition of 1679 further exhibits Playford's growing concern for sacred music by including a section on "The Order of Singing Divine Service in Cathedrals & Collegiate

Chapels."[31] After Playford's death, the most significant alteration to the *Introduction* was the replacement of older composition manuals in 1694 with "The Art of Descant" written by Henry Purcell. Beyond serving Playford's own needs as a tradesman, musician, and royalist, the *Introduction* increased both the size and the understanding of the amateur music audience for the next century.

Instrumental music was highlighted in two series: *Musicks Recreation* and *Court Ayres. Musicks Recreation* (1652, 1661, 1669, and 1682) was a series of viol music expanded from *A Musicall Banquet*'s "New Lessons for the Lyra Viol." For the 1652 edition, Playford increased the original 27 pieces to 102, keeping most of the earlier works and adding several royalist tunes: "Glory of the North," "Cavaliers Horn-pipe," "Simon the King," and "Gather your Rosebuds," among others. Like *A Musicall Banquet, Musicks Recreation* contained a mixture of songs (mostly without text), dances, and instrumental works; the majority of new pieces were dance-oriented. The prominence of dance music can also be seen in *Court Ayres*, the expansion of *A Musicall Banquet*'s "Musica Harmonia."[32] *Court Ayres* was published in 1655 and later expanded again to *Courtly Masquing Ayres* in 1662. Dance and instrumental works may have posed few problems for contemporary audiences since Cromwell himself danced and held official state masques; however, Playford's title choice—highlighting the word "Court"—must have raised a few eyebrows in a period when the monarchical court was in exile.

Catch that Catch Can (cat. 10, 15, 47) with its sacred counterpart *Sacred Hymns and Canons* (1652 and 1658) was an expansion of "Musick and Mirth," the fourth section of *A Musicall Banquet.*[33] From the original twenty pieces, the catch and round collection grew to one hundred secular and forty-three sacred pieces. The first and largest part of the book is the collection of jovial secular songs. As was mentioned in the earlier discussion of "Musick and Mirth," these pieces evince anti-Puritan and, to some extent, anti-Parliamentary rhetoric through their emphasis on leisure pursuits such as carousing, gambling, and wenching.

Going beyond this happier side of cavalier life, the collection also contains songs that show its hardships, particularly imprisonment as seen in "Down in a Dungeon Deep" and "A pox on the Jaylor." Many royalists found themselves in debtors' prisons throughout the period as new taxes, fines, and excises were levied in Parliament's attempts to improve the finances of the country. But despite and because of such hardships and the changing social landscape around them, cavaliers clung even more tightly to their merriments. Though John Hilton, the original compiler of *Catch that Catch Can* (1652) died in 1658, a new expanded edition of his collection was released that year (cat. 10).[34] In this new edition, Playford added a significant number of works, several of which were culled from early catch books, likely in an effort to exploit their inherent nostalgia for both financial and political reasons. After the Restoration, this collection

• adjective for "Charles", esp. Charles I and Charles II

/ *he then harmonized these tunes in three voices to create the sweetest harmony*

grew and changed in several more editions (see cat. 15, 46).[35] These publications expanded until 1726, by which time the practice of catch singing had become a popular pastime that would continue to thrive throughout the eighteenth century.

Other vocal collections were divided primarily into two series: those collected by Playford, and those collected by Henry Lawes and published by Playford. The collection *Select Ayres and Dialogues* (cat. 48) appeared three times during the Interregnum (1652, 1653, and 1659). It grew in size—1652 with 68 pieces, 1653 with 80 pieces, and 1659 with 121 pieces—and was a constantly changing collection of pieces by various composers.[36] Playford seems to have initiated the series without having first conferred with the composers involved. Lawes makes this clear in the introduction to his first book of *Ayres and Dialogues* (1653) noting that "now the Question is not, whether or no my Compositions shall be Publick, but whether they shall come forth from me or from some other hand."[37] However, any animosity Lawes felt seems to have been quickly dispelled since Playford published Lawes's series. These collections were aimed at upper-middle class to aristocratic audiences or those aspiring to such status. Unlike catches with their explicit coarseness and debauchery, these songs, dialogues, and part songs are holdovers from the late Caroline court in both their refined style and sentiment. Many pieces actually dated from the 1630s, though others were written in a similar style throughout the 1640s and early 1650s. With this great variety of music for differing tastes and skill levels, Playford served his musical audience and reinscribed a cultural aesthetic that helped pave the way for the Restoration.

Upon the return of the king, Playford finally was promoted within the Stationers' Company and emboldened to attempt his first major improvements to psalmody. With the Restoration, Playford's loyal efforts seem to have been recognized and some royal pressures brought to bear on his behalf, raising his professional status.[38] The return of monarchy also brought back the Church of England and an opportunity to revise, among other things, the book of psalms. That Playford had been anticipating such an opportunity is attested to in his *Introduction* (1658), and he seems to have prepared a revised version in short order to be published in 1661.[39] This version of the psalms, however, was only the beginning for Playford. Subsequently he tried different methods of harmonizing tunes in an effort to improve the practice of the divine service, finally devising a workable solution with his 1677 *Whole Book of Psalms* (cat. 43).[40] Unlike earlier compilers of harmonized psalm books, Playford attempted to use the best tunes in contemporary common practice together with some tunes salvaged from older versions; he then harmonized these tunes in three voices to create the sweetest harmony without taxing the parish clerks' musical resources beyond practicality. Finally, not wanting to leave such decisions to chance, he tried to set psalms to tunes appropriate both in meter and in sense, so serious texts would have suitably grave music. Though

58 Playford was not able to witness the lasting effects of his edition, his version of the psalms inspired the formation of church choirs and the general resuscitation of English psalmody.[41]

Though Playford does not seem to have won the affections of his fellow publishers, his efforts were appreciated in contemporary artistic circles. Several elegies were written upon his death. The most famous of these, written by the future poet laureate Nahum Tate and set by Henry Purcell, is also the most apropos (cat. 49).[42] Set in a pastoral style that was a commonplace for the period, Tate's elegy exhorts the shepherds to weep for the lost Theron. The ancient Mediterranean King Theron (488–472 BCE) was a great patron of the arts.[43] Perhaps even more interesting than the name itself is Tate's decision to use classical allegory to mourn Playford's death. This style of eulogy was generally reserved for artists or aristocrats, not for common tradesmen. This poetic treatment is legitimized if one considers Playford's loyalist efforts to keep a genteel rhetoric alive in English society through music.

The revival of music printing by John Playford in the mid-seventeenth century is of enormous importance to both the history of English music and our understanding of the cultural politics of early modern England. Playford knew this market from the inside, and his publications not only taught and supplied customers with music, but also encouraged the early formation of concert series and music clubs.[44] Within the larger cultural atmosphere of Civil War and Restoration society, music was one piece in a complex design. Nevertheless, printed music, along with plays and poetry, powerfully asserted a royalist message. Music could be even more effective than its textual counterparts, however, since literary works were often censored—their seditious messages all too clear in the black and white of the printed page. Possibly due to its technical complexities or simply because the graphics on the page made it harder for censors to pick out offensive lyrics, music could carry similar texts unnoticed. Beyond the written word, music, through the medium of print, could communicate evocative tunes to the far corners of the nation reminding audiences of the pleasures—holidays, festivals, and playhouses—supported by royalist, and later Tory, leadership. This power to communicate, both with and without lyrics, made music a considerable force in the war for public opinion. Playford continued his loyalist stance throughout the Restoration, championing the traditional values of the Caroline court. Although his nostalgic approach eventually caused his music to fall out of step with fashion, his efforts to improve music were still felt as they continued to shape the English musical landscape for the next century.

1 The reconsideration of Playford began with Frank Kidson, "John Playford and 17th Century Music Publishing," *Music Quarterly* 4 (1918): 516–34, and continued through the work of Margaret Dean-Smith, Russell C. Nelson, Nicholas Temperley, and P. A. Munstedt. Some notable publications include, Dean-Smith, ed., *Playford's English Dancing Master 1651* (London, 1957); Nelson, *John Playford and the English Amateur Musician* (Ph.D. diss., University of Iowa, 1966); Temperley, "John Playford and the Metrical Psalms," *Journal of the American Musicological Society* 25 (1972): 331–78 and "John Playford and the Stationers' Company," *Music & Letters* 54 (1973): 203–12; Munstedt, *John Playford, Music Publisher: A Bibliographic Catalogue* (Ph.D. diss., University of Kentucky, 1983).

2 Evidence suggests that of the 105 tunes in the 1651 edition at least sixty were already associated with ballads by the mid-seventeenth century. See Evelyn Kendrick Wells, "Playford Tunes and Broadside Ballads [three parts]," *Folk Dance and Song Journal* 3, no. 2 (1937): 81–99; 3, no. 3 (1938): 195–202; 3, no. 4 (1939): 259–80.

3 Stacey Jocoy Houck, *Decoding Music Resistance: Vocal Music in the Service of the King (1625–1660)* (Ph.D. diss., University of Illinois, 2005).

4 See Munstedt for a complete listing of Playford's musical publications, both registered and otherwise.

5 It has been conjectured that Playford was educated at the almonry or choir school attached to Norwich Cathedral. See Temperley, "John Playford and the Metrical Psalms," 343.

6 Folger Library MS V.a.411, fol. 11r Johnson, "Full fathom five" (*Tempest* 1.2).

7 *Catch that catch can: or the musical companion. Containing catches and rounds for three and four voyces* (London: W. Godbid for John Playford, 1667), i.

8 For a discussion of the few music publications from this period, see John Caldwell, *Oxford History of English Music*, 2 vols. (London, 1991–1999), 1:503–60.

9 William Child, *The first set of psalmes of .III. voyces fitt for private chappell or other private meetings with a continuall bass either for the organ or theorbo newly composed after the Italian way* (London: for John Playford, 1650).

10 Henry Lawes and William Lawes, *Choice psalmes put into musicke, for three voices* (London: James Young for Humphrey Moseley and Richard Wodenothe, 1648). Folger Library call number L640. As a publisher, Moseley specialized in plays and poetry; he generally did not print music. However, he is also known for his staunch royalist publishing efforts. For more information, see Warren Chernaik, "Books as Memorials: The Politics of Consolation," *Yearbook of English Studies* 21 (1991): 207–17.

11 William Child, *Choise musick to the Psalmes of David, for three voices with a continuall base either for the organ or theorbo* (London: for John Playford, 1657).

12 The eighteenth edition is undated, but it has been suggested that it postdates 1728; Dean-Smith, *Playford's English Dancing Master 1651*, xxviii.

13 Keith Whitlock, "John Playford's *The English Dancing Master* 1650/1 as Cultural Politics," *Folk Music Journal* 7 (1999): 548–78.

14 *Court-ayers: or, pavins, almains, corant's, and sarabands, of two parts* (London: for John Playford, 1655), preface.

15 William Prynne, *Histrio-Matrix* (London: E. A. and W. I. for Michael Sparke, 1633), 274.

16 Claude Simpson, *The British Broadside Ballad and its Music* (New Brunswick, NJ, 1966), 516.

17 Although it was common for ballad tunes to be appropriated by opposing sides in the conflict, this tune was unshakably royalist. The ballad scholar William Chappell reports that it adhered so strongly to the Stuart monarchy that upon the Glorious Revolution of 1688, the tune remained attached to James II and his exiled court. Chappell, *Popular Music of Olden Time*, 2 vols. (New York, NY, 1965), 2:434.

18 C. H. Firth and R. S. Rait, *Acts and Ordinances of the Interregnum, 1642–1660*, 3 vols. (London, 1911), 1:1022.

19 On Playford's use of the term "new" to describe this tablature, see Frank Traficante, "Lyra Viol Tunings: 'All Ways have been Tried to do It,'" *Acta Musicologica* 42 (1970): 183–205 at 187–88.

20 For a discussion of the king's public image, see R. Malcolm Smuts, "Public ceremony and royal charisma: the English royal entry in London, 1485–1642," in *The First Modern Society, Essays in English History in Honour of Lawrence Stone*, ed. A. L. Beier, David Cannadine, and James M. Rosenheim (Cambridge, 1989), 90–92.

21 Willa McClung Evans, *Henry Lawes, Musician and Friend of Poets* (New York, 1941).

22 Murray Lefkowitz, *William Lawes* (London, 1960), 37.

23 *A Musicall Banquet* (London: T. H. for John Benson and John Playford, 1651), preface.

24 Thomas Ravenscroft, *Deuteromelia* (London: [T. Snodham] for Thomas Adams, 1609). Folger Library call number STC 20757.

25 *A Musicall Banquet*, 3:11.

26 Henry Peacham, *The Compleat Gentleman* ([London]: [John Legat] for Francis Constable, [1622]). Folger Library call number STC 19502 c. 1.

27 *The Academy of Complements* (London: T. Badger, for H[umphrey] Moseley, 1645).

28 Adam Smyth, "Printed Miscellanies in England, 1640–1682: 'store-house[s] of wit,'" *Criticism* (2000): 1–36.

29 John Playford, *Introduction to the Skill of Musick* (London: for John Playford, 1655), preface.

30 *The whole book of Psalms* (London: W. Godbid for the Company of Stationers and are sold by John Playford, 1677). Folger Library call number 167– 105q.

31 Playford, *Introduction to the Skill of Musick* (London: for John Playford, 1679). Folger Library call number P2481.

32 Expanded from an original 30 pieces to 245 in *Courtly Ayres* (1655).

33 John Hilton, *Catch that catch can, or, a choice collection of catches, rounds & canons for 3 or 4 voyces* (London: for John Benson and John Playford, 1652). Folger Library call number H2036.

34 Hilton, *Catch that catch can, or, a choice collection of catches, rounds and canons* (London: W. G. for John Benson and John Playford, 1658). Folger Library call number H2037.

35 Playford, *The Musical Companion* (London: W. Godbid for John Playford, 1673). Folger Library call number P2490.

36 *Select ayres and dialogues for one, two, and three voyces* (London: W. Godbid for John Playford, 1659). Folger Library call number W2909.

37 Henry Lawes, *Ayres and dialogues, for one, two, and three voyces* (London: T. H. for John Playford, 1653), preface.

38 Temperley, "John Playford and the Stationers' Company," 204.

39 Temperley, "John Playford and the Metrical Psalms," 347.

40 *The whole book of Psalms* (London: W. Godbid, for the Company of Stationers, sold by John Playford, 1677). Folger Library call number 167– 105q.

41 Temperley, "John Playford and the Metrical Psalms," 375–77.

42 Nahum Tate, *A pastoral elegy on the death of Mr. John Playford* (London: for Henry Playford, 1687). Folger Library call number T203.

43 A second, although less likely, possibility concerning the name Theron is that since it is Greek for "hunter," there may be a humorous reference to Playford's constant search for new materials to publish.

44 Singing and catch clubs had been an informal part of English society since the Elizabethan period, but the continued popularity of catch singing encouraged Playford's son to suggest in 1701 that such clubs should become a permanent fixture. Thus the title page of *The Second Book of the Pleasant Musical Companion* (1701) states that it was "Published chiefly for the encouragement of the Musical Societies, which will be speedily set up in all of the chief cities and towns in England." Many towns answered the call and social singing clubs flourished throughout the long eighteenth century.

• a eulogistic oration/writing; formal/elaborate praise

Music and the Cult of Elizabeth: The Politics of Panegyric and Sound

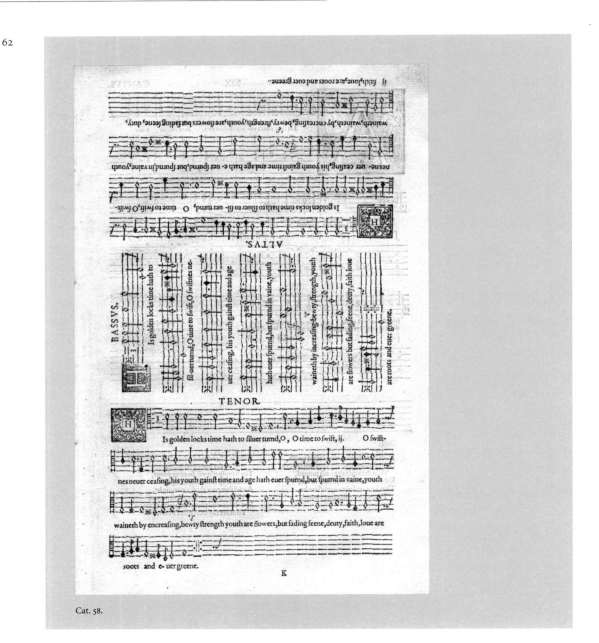

Jeremy Smith

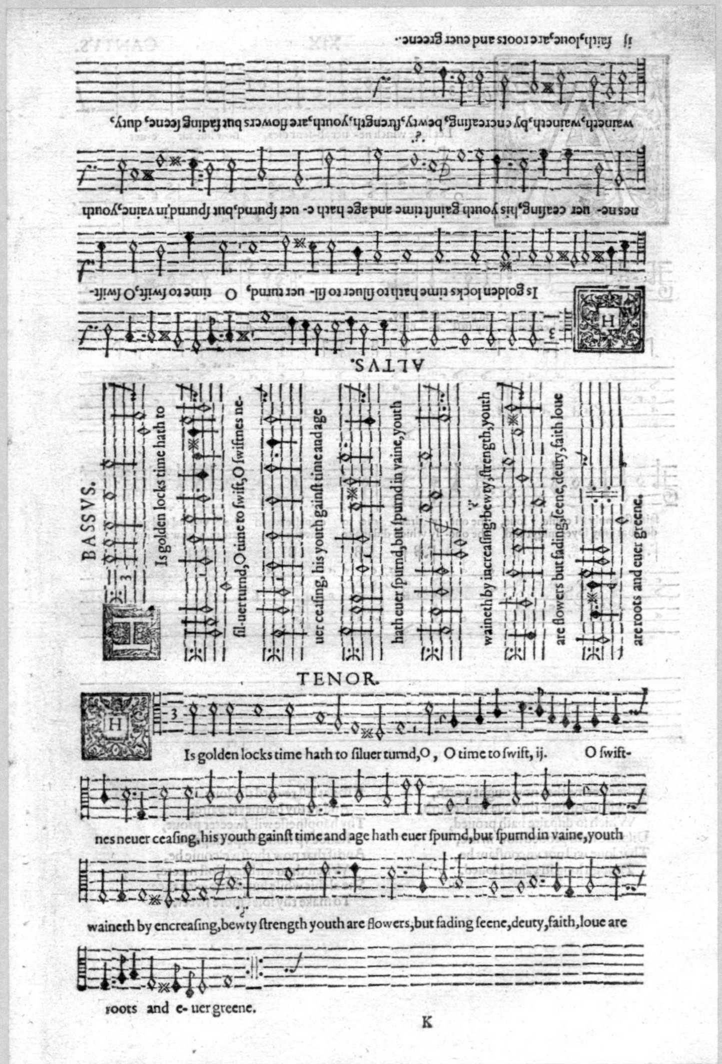

Cat. 58.

Throughout her reign, Elizabeth I was extravagantly exalted both as a virginal goddess and as an object of youthful desire. Once treated as spontaneous outpourings of loyal affection and subservience, or as mere sycophantic irrelevancies, the fantastic sounds, images, and texts of this cult of Elizabeth now seem to have been designed to reflect neither a "golden relationship" of monarch and subject nor mere flattery of a capacious royal ego. From the queen's point of view the cult fostered an alternative to religious structures that established order in pre-reformation England, often serving to redirect Catholic rites centered on the Virgin Mary.[1]

Less obviously, but no less powerfully, the cult provided a means for others to advance their political positions, especially through a process that Richard McCoy has recently dubbed "chivalric compromise."[2] The quintessential forum for these exchanges was the tiltyard, a field often adjoining a royal castle that was equipped with barriers for jousting. Here, in honor of their ruler, elaborately armored Elizabethan courtiers competed in an antiquated form of ritualistic violence before foreign dignitaries and members of the English public at large, many of whom had paid standard theater fees (from 12d to a shilling) to see the spectacle. Flattering their queen with various "devices" before taking up their lances, these courtiers idealized their ruler but also cleverly conveyed self-serving agendas meant to pressure her to help them satisfy their personal ambitions. Eventually these rituals were used by some to express political viewpoints opposing the queen, although the opposition was usually couched in the Petrarchan conventions of unrequited love.

By the mid-1570s, the cult of Elizabeth was so entrenched in English political life, and so effective in communicating its messages, that it had begun to obscure some of the actual problems of the reign. As the revisionist historian Christopher Haigh has noted, the cult began to function more and more like a carefully managed propaganda machine: with elaborate tilts, visitations, entertainments, epideictic literature of all sorts, paintings, music, etc., produced and consumed under the auspices of the queen's appointed officers at court.[3] Flattery and symbolism were permeating features of the mature cult. The queen's persona was creatively fused with those of such famous imperial virgins as Astraea and Gloriana to explain and sustain her right to rule, and with virgins of mythological love like Cynthia, Diana, and Belphoebe to enhance her status as a match for, and source of inspiration to, men of power and influence.[4]

In the last decades of the twentieth century, scholars seeking traces of England's political and social worlds in fictional texts of the Elizabethan era have moved from producing new views of individual works representing the cult, such as Edmund Spenser's *Faerie Queene,* toward consideration of entire literary genres, such as the Elizabethan pastoral (which they have shown to have close relations with this royalist propaganda machine).[5] Music's role in the cult has not been studied with the same zeal shown by literary

/ *music is indispensable to the state*

historians. But, scholarly neglect notwithstanding, music played an integral part in the queen's cult. Some of the most important composers of the era—Thomas Tallis, William Byrd, and Thomas Morley—were directly involved in its production. And there is a theme in many of the poems set by John Dowland for lute and voice that has a definite relationship with the phenomenon.

The Triumphes of Oriana (1601; cat. 57), a collection of English madrigals, has long captured the popular imagination as the era's most enduring musical tribute to Elizabeth. But *The Triumphes*, discussed below, had purposes much more complex than a simple panegyric for Elizabeth. Rather, it was Thomas Tallis and William Byrd's *Cantiones, quae ab argumento sacrae vocantur* of 1575 (cat. 36, 60) that was at the time the clearest musical counterpart to Spenser's *Faerie Queene*, at least in the way it was presented to its audiences. In his "letter of the authors," Spenser stated explicitly his purpose to use both allegory and the epic to honor Elizabeth. He also used the opportunity to cast himself as the Virgilian poet uniquely capable of serving such a Casear in this way.[6] Similarly the authors of the *Cantiones* promulgated an argument that benefited themselves as much as their queen.

The two most prominent members of the queen's Chapel Royal, Tallis and Byrd, stood as equals to any of the greatest musical composers on the Continent. This was the explicit premise of the *Cantiones*. There was also an implicit message: that the motet genre would best demonstrate their compositional acumen. With the device of a poetic *quid pro quo*, the famous Elizabethan educator Richard Mulcaster pronounced in his dedicatory poem that in return for England's appreciation of foreign music, the *Cantiones* would be "borne through foreign lands to be appraised by the judgment of artists."[7] If any answer was needed about how it would fare, it was provided in a short patriotic section entitled, "On Music of the English," which maintained that the music should "fear neither the boundaries nor the reproach of any nation."

For the queen's sake, an insistent note of patriotism and royalist flattery rings through the Latin words in the opening pages of the *Cantiones*, but there one also finds something in "plain" English: an excerpt from the patent of monopoly for music printing, music paper, and music importation that the queen had granted the composers that year (cat. 60). Obviously they had lobbied to obtain this favor from the queen, and they drew as much from the rhetorical sphere as they did from Elizabethan realpolitik. On the theoretical side, they discussed the usefulness of music to a queen, asserting pointedly that "music is indispensable to the state." More practically they enlisted the services of Ferdinando Heybourne *alias* Richardson, who wrote a commendatory poem in the preface. Only a teenager at the time, Heybourne had already established musical qualifications of note, although these were no doubt secondary to his close association with the queen, who favored him enough to allow him to play keyboard for her in her Privy Chamber.[8]

/ *the phrase "Rex Gloria" is repeated some forty times*

There is also evidence to suggest that the *Cantiones* was to function as part of a uniquely Elizabethan holiday. The year it was published, 1575, was also the seventeenth year of Elizabeth's reign, and the commemoration of her accession was celebrated that year, as it would be every year of her long reign, on November 17th. Apparently to reflect this happy numerological coincidence, each composer contributed seventeen motets to the collection (later study has revealed that some of their multi-part works were divided up to reach the desired total of thirty-four).[9]

The numerological tricks make it seem likely that the works were performed on the November 17 holiday. If so, how would they have been received? The *Cantiones* music itself, described as *argumento* and cast not so much in the Latin of Catholic ritual as in the Latin of international humanists, seems designed to support the lofty premise that Byrd and Tallis ranked with the finest Continental composers. The prevalence of elaborate canonic settings, works employing *cantus firmus* scaffoldings, and motets in seven and eight parts showed that the two composers could produce works that would stand comfortably among those of their Continental rivals at the very pinnacle of compositional virtuosity.[10] However, the music and texts also served broader political purposes.

Performances by the exclusively English ensemble of the Chapel Royal—featuring Tallis and Byrd as the most prominent musicians among their membership—were of special interest to the queen's foreign visitors. Judging by extant accounts, those that heard this group perform were not only sincerely impressed by the sounds themselves but were also acutely aware of the political undertones. As Craig Monson has demonstrated, the sound of glorious music in Latin could mollify fears of the immoderate influence of radical Protestantism and help the queen maintain her famous middle way between extremist religious factions.[11] In Byrd's "Attollite portas," the phrase "Rex Gloria" is repeated some forty times (and rather often at the very top of the singers' ranges) before the doxology begins dramatically with the phrase "Gloria patri."[12] It seems that Byrd picked this text purposely to emphasize the Latin wording "Gloria," perhaps to underline the majesty as well as the open-mindedness of Elizabeth's rule.

Byrd was willing to celebrate his "Glorianna," but both composers were also staunch Catholics with other political goals in mind. They enjoyed the comfort of her protection and her sanctuary as members of her Chapel, but they took advantage of the opportunity to publish to make a plea for their tormented coreligionists. In 1575 it had been only five years since Pope Pius V had issued his notorious bull, *Regnans in Excelsis*, excommunicating the followers of Elizabeth. Already by 1571 the English Parliament had retaliated with a set of harsh laws directed against the nation's Catholics. Monetary fines and property confiscation were imposed on those who failed to attend Church of England services. The penalty for refusing to take the Oath of Supremacy was life imprisonment; for missionaries or Catholic priests, who were now considered traitors, the penalty was death.

This religious issue was the one on which Byrd and Tallis struck their "chivalric compromise." Interspersed with texts in the *Cantiones* that generally exhorted all to "love your neighbor as yourself" (as in Byrd's "Diliges Dominum") were others, like Byrd's expressive opening motet, "Emendemus in melius," which almost seemed to put the queen herself on notice:

> Emendemus in melius quae ignoranter peccavimus, ne subito praeoccupati die mortis quaeramus spatium poenitentiae et invenire non possumus. . . .
> (Let us amend what we have transgressed through ignorance, lest, should the day of death suddenly overtake us, we seek time for repentance and cannot find it. . . .)

Tallis's "In ieiunio et fletu" is less aggressive. Here there are no suggestions about the dire consequences of choosing one faith over another, but the work takes on particular significance in view of the penalties imposed on Catholic priests in 1571:

> In ieiunio et fletu orabant sacerdotes: parce Domine populo tuo, et ne des hereditatem tuam in perditionem. Inter vestibulum et altare plorabant sacerdotes dicentes: Parce populo tuo.
> (Fasting and weeping, the priests shall pray: Spare thy people, Lord, and give not thy heritage over to destruction. Between the porch and altar, the priests shall pray: Spare thy people.)

Tallis's musical treatment, usually temperate with potentially expressive texts, in this case is as evocative as the words he set. To represent the "fasting priests," he scored the work with an appropriately thin texture; but he then moved to an expansive treatment for the reiterated plea "Spare thy people," with the full choir intoning the phrase in affective homophony. Tallis's music emphasizes the specific issue at hand. Even though Parliament had declared priests of Tallis's religion to be traitors, the composer seems to remind the queen that, as Englishmen, they are still her "people," her subjects.

Did these messages come across too forcefully? Unfortunately, no documentation of the royal reception survives. In the next year, however, the queen dipped into her own coffers to compensate the two composers for their losses when sales of the *Cantiones* failed to cover expenses.[13] Perhaps the very act of singing the texts rather than speaking them aloud reduced the work's seditious impact, keeping the composers in their monarch's favor. The Latin language may also have functioned as a kind of safeguard.

/ *the Knights Tilters rode slowly into the tilt-yard, to the sound of sweet music*

Their title carefully made the point that the songs were sacred only by their "argument," thus assuring religious authorities that the music was not meant for the purpose of worship. While some texts were indeed drawn from Catholic liturgy, the emphasis was on Christian biblical and exegetical sources that were shared and admired by Catholics and Protestants alike. Since the work apparently escaped censorship of any kind, Tallis and Byrd might be commended for taking all the precautions necessary to enjoy a certain kind of free speech under the auspices of royal panegyric. But one cannot ignore the potentially neutralizing impact of all the "back and forth" here—the gestures of subservience that were countered by acts of assertive entreaty (and *vice versa*). In the end, we must accept that there was an implicit cultural agreement at work: certain controversial political positions were both permitted and contained as they were filtered through the queen's cult.

The performance fate of the *Cantiones* is not known. Let us imagine the not unreasonable case, however, that the Chapel Royal performed some, if not all, of the *Cantiones* before the queen and a select group of foreign dignitaries in her chapel on 17 November 1575. We then may suppose that the queen, her foreign guests, all her courtiers, and the crowds, too, would assemble at the barriers outside Winchester castle to watch, or participate in, an elaborate jousting tournament that would top off a most auspicious Queen's Day. Here Elizabeth would likely hear more music with potentially political texts, as courtiers exploited the spectacular setting of a chivalric device to make protected yet provocative points to their queen. This time, however, the main topic would be unrequited love.

Describing the most famous tilts of the 1580s and 1590s, Roy Strong noted that these "were an integral part of the aesthetic milieu. . . . Everyone knew about them, everyone had seen them." But he also remarked that surviving descriptions of the devices, at least those with any detail, have proven rather elusive (numerous score cards with tallies of broken lances, however, are still extant). One exception, "virtually the only one," as Strong notes, was the Accession Day Tilt of 1590.[14] On this day the official Queen's Champion, Sir Henry Lee, who was said to have started the whole business of tilting for the queen, had come to the field to joust and then to retire from his lofty position. The event was described with satisfying detail. It was also richly adorned with music, as the following excerpt shows:

> The resignation was conducted with all due ceremony. The queen being seated in the gallery, with Viscount Turenne, the French ambassador, as the Knights Tilters rode slowly into the tilt-yard, to the sound of sweet music. Then, as if sprung out of the earth, appeared a pavilion of white silk, representing the sacred temple of Vesta. In this temple was an altar, covered with a cloth of gold, on which burned wax candles, in rich candlesticks. Certain princely presents

• virgins consecrated to the service of the Roman goddess Vesta

/ *I'll teach my swains this carol for a song*

• one who prays for another (13c)

were also on the altar, which were handed to the queen by three young ladies, in the character of vestals. Then the royal choir, under the leadership of Mr. Hales, sang the following verses, as Sir Henry Lee's farewell to the court:

My golden locks, time hath to silver turned
(Oh time too swift, and swiftness never ceasing),
My youth 'gainst age, and age at youth have spurned;
But spurned in vain, youth waneth by increasing.
Beauty, strength, and youth, flowers fading seen,
Duty, faith, and love, are roots and ever green.

My helmet, now, shall make a hive for bees,
And lover's songs shall turn to holy psalms:
And feed on prayers, that are old age's alms.
And so, from court to cottage, I depart,
My saint is sure of mine unspotted heart.

And when I sadly sit in homely cell,
I'll teach my swains this carol for a song,
Blest be the hearts, that think my sovereign well,
Cursed be the souls, that think to do her wrong.
Goddess, vouchsafe this aged man his right,
To be your beadsman, now, that was your knight.

After this had been sung, Sir Henry took off his armour, placing it at the foot of a crowned pillar, bearing the initials E. R. Then kneeling, he presented the Earl of Cumberland to the queen, beseeching that she would accept that nobleman for her knight. Her majesty consenting, Sir Henry armed the earl and mounted him on horseback; he then arrayed himself in a peaceful garb of black velvet, covering his head with a common buttoned cap of country fashion.[15]

Clearly nothing was spared that might add to the elaborateness of this spectacle. Indeed, the Chapel Royal itself—now without Tallis (d. 1585) and probably without Byrd (whose religious politics had contest of two on horses; joust (Also, p. 63.)

already begun to affect his career adversely)—was enlisted to sing a "prayer" of sorts for their queen, who was represented as the "Goddess" Vesta. The setting is rich with romantic play-acting (with Catholic trappings *and* pagan rituals, no less). But the event portrayed was not purely fictional. Although Lee appeared on the tilts in various guises after this—once as the "Unknown Knight," for example—Cumberland did indeed take his place thereafter as the Queen's Champion.

During Cumberland's reign the tilts became even more elaborate. The courtier responsible for this development was not Cumberland himself but the queen's Master of the Horse, Robert Devereux, the second earl of Essex. Essex was the favorite in the running for the title of "champion" in 1590, but the queen apparently passed him over when she learned that he had married Francis Walsingham without first obtaining royal permission. This was only one of the many times Essex would move from a position of favor to disfavor in the eyes of the queen. As far as tilting was concerned, however, Essex was hardly deterred by the demotion. Even if Cumberland held the highest honor, Essex dominated the field thereafter and, more than any other courtier, used the tilts for his own political purposes.

"My golden locks," which was quoted in full in the description above, has survived in a beautiful musical setting for lute and voice by John Dowland. He published it in his 1597 *First Booke of Songes* (cat. 58), with a shift from third to first person as the only substantial textual change.[16] In 1600 Dowland published other verses that were performed at the 1590 Accession Day: "Time's eldest son, Old Age," "Then sit thee down, and say thy *Nunc Dimittis*," and "When others sing *Venite exultemus*." These three interconnected songs describe *inter alia* the prayers Lee had promised to say for Elizabeth during his retirement. As such, they form a rather transparent account of the cult's long-standing purpose to counter the Catholic "Cult of Mary" and restore order around another female leader. The speaker, cast as a monk, suggests to his listener that in order to worship Elizabeth properly he (and all) should substitute a few prayers for others, and, particularly, to sing a "*Vivat Eliza* for an *Ave Mari*." Lee did not forsake his poetic role as a jouster-turned-goddess-worshiper after Elizabeth's death. In "Far from the triumphing court," he bemoaned the restraining force of old age as he expressed a wish to leave his monkish retirement and return to the tiltyard in honor of Queen Anna, James I's consort. Dowland's setting of these verses was published in *A Musicall Banquet* of 1610.

Dowland's involvement with noteworthy Elizabethan tilters was not confined to his relations with Lee. In his collection of 1597, Dowland also set poems that have been attributed to Cumberland and Essex. These are filled with sentiments that fit the tiltyard personae of these figures so well that it seems immaterial whether or not the verses were actually penned by the two courtiers. The putative Cumberland text, "My thoughts are wing'd with hopes," was set by Dowland as a stately galliard:

. not returned / repaid / reciprocated

/ *And whisper this but softly in her ears,*

My thoughts are wing'd with hopes,
    my hopes with love.
Mount Love unto the moon in clearest night
And say, as she doth in heavens move,
In earth so wanes and waxeth my delight:
And whisper this but softly in her ears,
Hope oft doth hang the head, and Trust shed tears.

And you my thoughts that some mistrust do carry,
If for mistrust my mistress do you blame,
Say though you alter, you do not vary,
And she doth change, and yet remain the same:
Distrust doth enter hearts, but not infect,
And love is sweetest season'd with suspect.

If she, for this, with clouds do mask her eyes,
And make the heavens dark with her disdain,
With windy sighs, disperse them in the skies,
Or with thy tears dissolve them into rain;
Thoughts, hopes, and love return to me no more
Till Cynthia shine as she hath done before.

No extant record confirms that this poem was sung on the tiltyard, but without doubt it was intended for the queen's ears. In the second stanza, Elizabeth's personal motto, *Semper Eadem*, itself appears in the lines: "Say though you alter, you do not vary, / And she doth change, and yet remain the same." The voice we hear is that of the courtier and the theme is the standard one, unrequited love. But the love he discusses is oddly conditioned by "mistrust," engendered by the apparent inconstancy of a goddess moon that waxes and wanes. Though the doubting lover pleads that love is "sweetest" when "season'd with suspect," he fears that his momentary doubts will cause the eruption of cosmic anger in the skies.

All the anxiousness caused by such suspicions in love could hardly have appealed to the courtier seeking royal love, although it well served the queen's purposes. Intense factionalism had become a reality of courtly life in the late-Elizabethan era, or as some have lately called it "the nasty nineties."[17] Whether

· frugal to the point of being stingy

or not she deliberately encouraged it, the queen realized she could benefit from strife at court. To exacerbate the tension, she maintained a policy of parsimoniousness while keeping hopes alive. If the courtiers were suspicious of others in this turbulent environment, their anxiety would lead to more infighting, all of which would focus attention on her as the center of power and the arbiter of disputes.

Clever royal positioning and mounting cases of backbiting at court are, I believe, alluded to in "My thoughts are wing'd with hope." Its main purpose, however, may have been simply to present the goddess "Cynthia" in her best light—that is, for the moon itself to appear "in clearest night." Certainly the astronomical imagery here—"the heavens dark with her disdain"—suggests an awesome power. Complaint or no, in Dowland's majestic setting this poem seems to epitomize the way the cult was supposed to work. Courtiers were to be kept on their toes while a changeless image of an ageing queen was lovingly maintained.

Dowland's setting of the poem attributed to Essex, "Can she excuse," is also in galliard form. It too has unrequited love as its topic. Yet it presents matters from a very different point of view:

Can she excuse my wrongs with Virtue's cloak?
Shall I call her good when she proves unkind?
Are those clear fires which vanish into smoke?
Must I praise the leaves where no fruit I find?
No, no. Where shadows do for bodies stand
Thou may'st be abused if thy sight be dim;
Cold love is like to words written on sand,
Or to bubbles which on water swim.
Wilt thou be thus abused still,
Seeing that she will right thee never?
If thou canst not o'ercome her will
Thy love will be fruitless ever.

Was I so base that I might not aspire
Unto those high joys which she holds from me?
As they are high, so high is my desire.
If she this deny, what can granted be?
If she will yield to that which reason is,
It is Reason's will that love should be just.

72

Dear, make me happy still by granting this,
Or cut off delays if that die I must.
Better a thousand times to die
Than for to live thus still tormented
Dear, but remember it was I
Who did for thy sake die contented.

Essex was the most prominent of the courtiers in the last decade of Elizabeth's reign and the leader of one of the two most prominent factions at court.[18] He owed much of his power and fame to his status as the queen's favorite, but he was also notoriously frustrated with her lack of interest in and backing for his various martial exploits. In 1589 he audaciously initiated diplomatic contacts with James VI of Scotland, whom he supported as the queen's successor (Essex would not live to see James become England's next king). Accused of "upstaging the queen" on the tiltyards and ignoring her commands on the battlefield, he rather often went too far in his complaints and independent actions. During periods of royal disfavor, Essex took on the attitude of the melancholy lover, penning or commissioning obsequious poems to plead for the queen's forgiveness.

By 1600, after many swings back and forth in his relations with Elizabeth, Essex broke ranks. He had by then defied orders, burst uninvited into the queen's Privy Chamber, and even once reached for his sword after Elizabeth struck him across the head. On several occasions he was subjected to house arrest at his estate in Wanstead. Rather than languishing there, he wrote passionate letters and poems, sponsored plays, and even attempted to make a grand comeback on the Accession Day tiltyards, where presumably he would have re-established his status as the most electrifying of the courtiers who dared to woo the queen. But these plans failed and, instead, in what seems—in hindsight at least—like an act of true desperation, Essex gathered his followers together and staged an ill-fated *coup d'etat* to put James VI on the English throne, a move that led to Essex's execution.

Many of Essex's poems betray his mounting frustration with the queen and her policies toward him. Among these, "Can she excuse" stands out as an extreme example. Hardly a line is without some form of pointed criticism. Nor is anything of the "sweetness" and power of royal love suggested here. Instead the "Emperor's clothes" of royal wooing and unrequited love are finally revealed for what they seem to have been all along: ephemeral, inconstant, empty, "cold," and "fruitless."

Dowland set this restless poem with music that features syncopation and cross-rhythms and, most noticeably, a particularly unsettled part for the singer. The wide-ranging melody in the first half of the

• to ~~keep~~ protect oneself from losing by a counterbalancing transaction

/ *decidedly somber despite the cheerful nature of the music*

song is countered with the speech-like immobility in the second, at which point the lute begins a menacing step-wise ascent up the fret-board. In its melody and rhythm at least, the music depicts well the mercurial nature of Essex's personality and the intensity with which he dealt with his ruler. Of course, had he sung this to the queen on the tiltyard, Essex would have been restrained as much by the genre of unrequited love as he was by the social order of Elizabethan rule. But if we listen actively to this song, I think we can easily imagine we are hearing someone who is ready to burst all constraining bonds.

Many works by Dowland, such as the texted version of his famous "Lachrimae," "Flow my tears," have some basic form of unrequited love as their theme. Their tone fits in somewhere between the extremes represented in poems attributed to Cumberland and Essex discussed above. But Essex so dominated the scene that it is perhaps not surprising that two scholars, Lillian Ruff and Arthur Wilson, have claimed that it was Essex himself who inspired the whole melancholy trend in Dowland's *ouevre.*[19] To counter a theory as general as this with another of larger scope is only to overtax the evidence; but perhaps the tiltyard and the queen's cult in general will prove to have been the stronger motivation for the *Zeitgeist* of sadness that was epitomized in Dowland's own motto, *Semper Doland semper dolens.* And Essex did indeed play a major role in the musical world. It was in the most celebrated of all anthologies of English madrigals, *The Triumphes of Oriana* (cat. 57), I believe, that the most daring of Essex's political positions was expressed in music. Long thought to celebrate the queen and to help her mourn Essex's death, the *Triumphes* was in fact originally designed to celebrate the replacement of Elizabeth with James VI and his wife, Anna of Denmark.[20]

The *Oriana* collection includes twenty-four pieces by twenty-two composers, all English, and each one ends with some version of the text "then sang the shepherds and nymphs of Diana, long live Oriana." The common refrain has done much to sustain a theory, advanced somewhat tentatively in the eighteenth century by Sir John Hawkins, that Oriana was a metaphor for Elizabeth.[21] Hawkins noted that the set was produced very soon after Essex's execution, that the name Elizabeth was nowhere mentioned therein, and that the tone of the dedication penned by the publisher and author of two madrigals, Thomas Morley, was decidedly somber despite the cheerful nature of the music. All this gave Hawkins pause; yet he seems in the end to have relied on his historical common sense, deciding that since it was published during her reign none other than Elizabeth herself could have inspired such a grand final acclamation for royal longevity. Had Hawkins known that "one Morley" (whom scholars have unanimously seen as Thomas, the composer) had played a part in a tiltyard device for the Earl of Essex in 1595, he might have further hedged his bets.[22] Additionally, Hawkins did not consider the fact that Oriana did not fit any traits of Elizabeth that could be conceived as flattering to her. As the heroine of a vastly popular romance whose sexual activities were recounted with relish therein, Oriana was far from easily associated with a "virgin

next to the last

queen" and was instead best known as the adoring wife of a fictional knight, Amadis de Gaul. Furthermore, in the most famous madrigal in the set, Thomas Weelkes's "As Vesta," Elizabeth probably does indeed appear but surely not in the main role:

> As Vesta was from Latmos hill descending,
> She spied a maiden Queen the same ascending,
> Attended on by all the shepherds' swain,
> To whom Diana's darlings came running down amain,
> First two by two, then three by three together,
> Leaving their goddess all alone, hasted thither;
> And mingling with the shepherds of her train,
> With mirthful tunes her presence entertain.
> Then sang the shepherds and nymphs of Diana:
> Long live fair Oriana.

Here Oriana is acclaimed, as always, as queen in the end, but the madrigal begins with Vesta, the same character that had been so ceremoniously linked with Elizabeth on the tiltyards during that particularly memorable Accession Day when her "champion" retired. I think it would be difficult to argue that people had already forgotten the former association. In any case, Elizabeth would be more fittingly cast as virginal Vesta than as a married princess like Oriana; and if Elizabeth played the title role rather than that of the heroine, when Vesta "descends" from "Latmos Hill" and "spies Oriana ascending," what was figured there was a change in female rulers that Essex had wanted to see just the year before.

Weelkes was not the only one to suggest that the set was a tribute to Anna of Denmark. The Oriana composers all chose to match the "long live" acclamation with an elaborate and extensive outpouring of melismatic music. As was customary in melismatic writing, the composers chose the penultimate syllable of the last word as the place to add many time-consuming musical notes. Thus as each madrigal drew to a close a resounding flourish on the syllable "a" would finally come to rest on the last syllable of the word Oriana, "na." In this way, the name "Anna" was thus pronounced most memorably at the end of each piece.

Since it was published soon after Essex's execution, Morley took some steps to obscure the treasonous nature of the set. He never mentioned Essex or Anna herself by name. It was only after Elizabeth's death (1603) that any conflicting evidence about Oriana's true identity first appeared in print. In 1604 the poet Ben Jonson had composed a work for the new king that ended "Long liue ORIANA," which clearly referred

/ Long have the shepherds sung this song before, As prophesying what should come to pass

to Anna. But in the same year Thomas Bateson published a madrigal with a revised couplet "in heaven lies Oriana," to suggest rather clearly that Elizabeth must surely have been his honoree. Oriana (as Elizabeth) was bid farewell again in 1613 and 1619, in musical settings by two Chester Cathedral organists. Yet Jonson was not alone in establishing that Oriana could be seen as Anna in 1604. In that year Thomas Greaves published a set of five-voice madrigals that included a welcome ode to James I, which exclaimed "England, receive the rightful king." Following it, Greaves placed his setting of "Sweet nymphes" to honor James's consort:

Sweet nymphes that trip along the English lands,
    Go meet fair Oriana, beauty's queen,
Virtue invites and chastity commands.
    Your golden tresses trim with garlands green,
    For such a sight hath not before been seen.
Then sing in honour of her and Diana:
Long live in joy the fair chaste Oriana.

Long have the shepherds sung this song before,
    As prophesying what should come to pass.
The gentle nymphs henceforth lament no more,
    The times are changed, it is not as it was.
    Dian shall flower, and Venus fade like grass.
Then sing in honour of her and Diana:
Long live in joy the fair chaste Oriana

Unlike the other poems about Oriana that were published in 1604, this one links directly with Oriana madrigals of the past, which are described as "songs" that were "sung before." This relationship gives to Greaves's poet the kind of authority we need to answer the question of who Oriana had been in the recent past. Significantly this poet casts Oriana as the living Queen Anna rather than the late Queen Elizabeth.

It might fairly be seen to detract from the Elizabethan image to discover that the musical tribute so many have seen as the most compendious in the musical field came to her only as the result of a deliberate cover-up, when she was given an identity that had formerly been bestowed on her likely successor. But even this seeming slight to the queen can be construed in a complimentary way. Of course it is impossible to know Elizabeth's thoughts as she heard a Byrd motet telling her to mend her ways or Essex's thinly veiled threats in a Dowland lute song. We cannot know her response to the seditious suggestions in Weelkes's madrigal that had her "descending" from her throne as a younger woman was "ascending" to take her place. The simple fact that Elizabeth probably heard all these published pieces (or knew about them) is sufficient cause for admiration. Many subsequent rulers have been much less tolerant of freedom of expression in the arts. These musical examples show that this queen allowed quite a bit of latitude, which is yet another reason why Elizabeth's reign fascinates us today, no less for its creative efforts than for the political achievement of its ruler.

1 See Helen Hackett, *Virgin Mother, Maiden Queen: Elizabeth I and the Cult of the Virgin Mary* (New York, 1995).

2 Richard McCoy, *The Rites of Knighthood: The Literature and Politics of Elizabethan Chivalry* (Berkeley, 1989).

3 Christopher Haigh, ed., *The Reign of Elizabeth I* (Athens, GA, 1985), 9.

4 See Elkin Calhoun Wilson, *England's Eliza*, 2nd ed. (New York, 1966).

5 See Louis Adrian Montrose, "Of Gentlemen and Shepherds: The Politics of Elizabethan Pastoral Form," *English Literary History* 50 (1983): 415–59 and Arthur F. Marotti, "Love is not Love: Elizabethan Sonnet Sequences and the Social Order," *English Literary History* 49 (1982): 396–428.

6 See *Edmund Spenser's Poetry*, ed. Hugh MacLean and Anne Lake Prescott, 3rd ed. (New York, 1993), 1–2.

7 For texts and translations of the *Cantiones* cited here and below, see *Cantiones Sacrae (1575)*, ed. Craig Monson, The Byrd Edition, vol. 1 (London, 1972). Mulcaster was an Elizabethan schoolmaster and author of some repute. His students were taught to sing and performed for the queen; see William Barker, "Mulcaster, Richard (1531/2–1611)," in *Oxford Dictionary of National Biography*, ed. H. C. G. Matthew and Brian Harrison (Oxford, 2004), http://www.oxforddnb. com/view/article/ 19509 (accessed September 17, 2005).

8 See Richard Marlow, "Sir Fernando Heyborne alias Richardson," *Musical Times* 115 (1974): 736–39.

9 Joesph Kerman, "Old and New in Byrd's *Cantiones Sacrae*," in *Essays on Opera and English Music: In Honour of Sir Jack Westrup* (Oxford, 1975), 25–26.

10 See Joseph Kerman, "The Elizabethan Motet: a Study of Texts for Music," *Studies in the Renaissance* 9 (1962): 273–308.

11 Craig Monson, "Elizabethan London," in *The Renaissance: From the 1470s to the End of the 16th Century*, ed. Iain Fenlon (London, 1989), 335–36.

12 Of course on a more subtle level this all might have also been designed to remind the queen that it was the "Lord" of the Trinity who was the "true" Gloriana.

13 Monson (ed.), *Cantiones Sacrae*, viii.

14 Roy Strong, *The Cult of Elizabeth: Elizabethan Portraiture and Pageantry* (Berkeley and Los Angeles, 1977), 151.

15 R. Chambers, *The Book of Days* (London and Edinburgh, 1869), 2:590–91.

16 Thomas Clayton, "'Sir Henry Lee's Farewell to the Court': The Texts and Authorship of 'His Golden Locks Time Hath to Silver Turned,'" *English Literary Renaissance* 4 (1974): 268–75.

17 See John Guy, "The 1590s: The Second Reign of Elizabeth I?" in *The Reign of Elizabeth I: Court and Culture in the Last Decade*, ed. John Guy (Cambridge, 1995), 19.

18 Paul E. J. Hammer, "Devereux, Robert, Second Earl of Essex (1565–1601)," in *Oxford Dictionary of National Biography*, http://www.oxforddnb.com/view/article/7565 (accessed September 17, 2005).

19 Lillian M. Ruff and D. Arthur Wilson, "The Madrigal, the Lute Song and Elizabethan Politics," *Past and Present* 44 (1969): 3–51.

20 The following discussion of Oriana is drawn from my "Music and Politics in Late Elizabethan England: The Identities of Oriana and Diana," *Journal of the American Musicological Society* 58 (2005): 507–58. In his *Anna of Denmark, Queen of England: A Cultural Biography* (Philadelphia, 2001), 173, n. 1, Leeds Barroll discussed the Scottish queen's preference for the Danish spelling "Anna."

21 Sir John Hawkins, *A General History of the Science and Practice of Music . . .*, 5 vols. (London, 1776), 3:405–6.

22 Ruff and Wilson, "The Madrigal," 16.

[See p. 5.]

Reading Between the Lines:
Catholic and Protestant Polemic in Elizabethan and Jacobean Sacred Music

Craig Monson

Michael East, *The third set of bookes: vvherein are pastorals, anthemes, neopolitanes, fancies, and madrigales, to 5. and 6. parts.* London, [1610].

In 1605 a young French visitor to England named Charles de Ligny was arrested in London and locked up in Newgate Prison for having in his possession "certain books which Master William Byrd composed and dedicated to Lord Henry Howard of His Majesty's Privy Council."[1] This publication, possession of which was subversive enough to get one arrested, was Byrd's *Gradualia I*, originally published earlier that same year. *Gradualia*, Byrd's major compositional enterprise of the 1590s and early 1600s, provided systematically-ordered settings of the Propers for the major feasts of the Roman Catholic church year (i.e., the ritual texts that change with every religious occasion). It is now recognized as the most overt expression of the composer's abiding commitment to the Old Religion, under siege in Protestant England. Indeed, de Ligny's arrest confirms that the religious and political implications of Byrd's recent musical print did not escape Jacobean authorities either.

De Ligny's narration of his misadventures in England reveals that *Gradualia* was only the most obvious manifestation of Byrd's usually more covert activities in support of the Catholic cause.[2] The Frenchman related that he had also visited a house outside London where he had encountered the prominent Father Henry Garnet, for twenty years the leader of the surreptitious Jesuit mission in England. Other Jesuits and English Catholic gentlemen, engaged in music-making when de Ligny arrived, joined Garnet on that occasion, and their number included "Mr William Byrd who played the organs and many other instruments."[3]

It turns out that Byrd's affiliation with the prominent Jesuit in fact extended all the way back to Garnet's arrival in England in 1586, when another secret, festive gathering, including services and music, had been held at Hurleyford to welcome him and his Catholic colleague Robert Southwell. The only member of that welcoming committee singled out in Father William Weston's description of that meeting was, once again, William Byrd.

During the 1590s and the early 1600s, and even before, Byrd walked a fine line. As a leader of Queen Elizabeth I's Chapel Royal, he regularly performed in Anglican services, which he provided with some of their finest surviving music. In his home parish, however, he not only refused to attend Protestant church services and worked in quiet ways to aid fellow Catholics, but also employed his musical talents to support the Catholic cause, to speak to those who had ears to hear. Since vocal music can be socially constructed by its listeners and consequently can mean different things to different people at different times and places, we can rarely be absolutely sure what English composers such as Byrd may have meant their motets or anthems to say. But an Elizabethan or Jacobean audience—much less literal minded than today's listeners, familiar with a time-honored tradition of biblical allusion, and accustomed to thinking metaphorically or allegorically—could be encouraged to read and hear sacred music in particular, and sometimes symbolic, ways.

Gradualia represented Byrd's most blatant attempt to serve the needs of his local Catholic community. The choice of specific feasts for inclusion in the print—for example, affording the feasts of the Blessed Virgin Mary, much maligned by Protestants, pride of place; incorporating the Feast of Corpus Christi, a doctrine strongly opposed by Protestant reformers; and including the Mass for All Saints, commemorating those who had died in the faith—could also speak, "between the lines," to the plight of Catholics in England. The addition of certain miscellaneous motets to *Gradualia I* made similar points most openly. The clearest example would have to be the non-liturgical motet, "Unam petii a Domino," setting the very direct language of Psalm 62:4:

> Unam petii a Domino, hanc requiram: ut inhabitem in domo Domini omnibus diebus vitae meae. Ut videam voluntatem Domini, et visitem templum eius.
> (One thing I have asked of the Lord, this will I seek after: that I may dwell in the house of the Lord all the days of my life. That I may see the Lord's goodwill and visit his temple.)

The reappearance of the very same forthright words (identical even down to alteration of the Psalmist's "Ut videam *voluptatem*" to "Ut videam *voluntatem*") as an epigraph on the title page of Catholic Robert Parsons' popular and widely reprinted *The First Booke of the Christian Exercise* (p. 83) suggests just how bold Byrd's proclamation of religious freedom may have been.

While Byrd's publishing enterprise on Catholics' behalf may have seemed a good idea early in 1605, it turned out to have been singularly ill-timed. Within months of *Gradualia I*'s appearance, the discovery of the Gunpowder Plot to blow up Parliament on 5 November 1605 drove James I's security forces to red alert, prompting a new wave of anti-Catholic sentiment and restrictive measures. Byrd seems quietly to have shelved the publishing project (only a single copy from 1605 is known to survive). He waited until 1607 to issue *Gradualia II*. Only in 1610, when tensions had eased somewhat, did he re-release both volumes with new title pages (cat. 94).

Whereas *Gradualia* represented Byrd's most direct musical support for the Roman Catholic cause, his previous efforts had been considerably more furtive and circumspect, but no less useful. Between 1592 and 1595, he had separately published settings of the Ordinary of the Catholic Mass (i.e., those ritual texts that recur consistently from week to week, forming the backbone of the Mass), one each for three, four, and five voices. Significantly, these were printed in modest partbooks of just eight pages each, without title page. Consequently, there was no mention of the words "Mass" or "Ordinary." Although the date and printer's name are not mentioned, "W. Byrd" is clearly indicated (cat. 93). The simple, practical format suggests that the publications must have been intended for surreptitious services within the Catholic community, making allowances for variations in musical complexity and available forces. There was sufficient demand to prompt a second edition of the three- and four-part Masses around the turn of the century.

Somewhat earlier, during the 1580s when Jesuit activity in England intensified and persecution of English Catholics continued to escalate, Byrd seems to have spoken out in a series of motets. Most were published in his 1589 and 1591 *Cantiones Sacrae I* and *II* (cat. 91), on texts that could be heard as protests against the plight of beleaguered Catholic recusants in England. The fact that the same texts set in Byrd's motets, whether direct biblical citations or recurring turns of phrase, also turn up in some 225 books and pamphlets by Catholic apologists and Jesuit propagandists suggests that the allegory behind Byrd's "political" motets would not have escaped his audience. More than a dozen motet texts ring changes on such themes as:

> –the Egyptian captivity ("Deliver us out of the hand of the Egyptian Pharoah and out of the slavery of the Egyptians" proclaims "Domine, tu iurasti patribus nostris" [1589]);
>
> –the fall of Jerusalem ("Thy holy city is become a desert, Zion is become a desert, Jerusalem is forsaken," according to "Civitas sancti tui" [1589]; "More than Jerusalem, the chosen city, was despoiled, the joy of our heart is turned to grief and our delight into bitterness," as "Vide, Domine, afflictionem nostram" [1589] declares); and
>
> –the Babylonian captivity ("How shall we sing the Lord's song in a strange land" Byrd asks in "Quomodo cantabimus canticum Domini," composed in direct response to "Super flumina Babylonis illic sedimus et flevimus," composed and sent to him by his sympathetic Catholic colleague on the Continent, Philippe de Monte).

These same themes also reappear repeatedly in Catholic writings. During hard times in 1588 Henry Garnet wrote privately, for example:

> All our hopes turned precipitately into sorrow. All things are with us as they were with the Jewish people as they were about to go forth from Egypt. . . . Now with redoubled energy the chiefs and persecutors of Egypt have turned on us all the wrath they have conceived against Moses and Aaron.

• eviscerate/divide into four parts

/ *layinge a syde our myrth and musicke, to sitt & weepe*

 A year earlier, Robert Southwell had complained in his *Epistle of comfort, to the reverend priestes, & to the honorable, worshipful, & other of the laye sort restrayned in durance for the Catholicke fayth*:

> For upon the fluddes of *Babilon*, what cause have we, but layinge a syde our myrth and musicke, to sitt & weepe, remembering our absence, out of our heavenly *Sion*: In the vassalage and servilitye of *Egipt*, where we are so dayly oppressed with uncessante afflictions, & filthy workes.[4]

But arguably Byrd's most direct musical condemnation of Catholic persecution in a motet must be his large-scale setting of Psalm 78:1–4 (Psalm 79 in the King James version), "Deus venerunt gentes / Posuerunt morticinia / Effuderunt sanguinem / Facti sumus opprobrium" (cat. 91). This motet reads like a graphic description of the suffering and martyrdom of numerous Catholic priests, commonly hanged, drawn, and quartered, beginning with the notorious execution of Edmund Campion in 1581. Byrd responded to Campion's execution with his consort song "Why do I use paper, ink and pen?" published in his *Psalmes, Sonets, & Songs* of 1588 (cat. 107). The grim realities of the martyr's sufferings were also graphically illustrated in grisly engravings in such publications as Richard Verstegan's *Theatrum crudelitatum haereticorum nostri temporis* (cat. 89). Catholic writers' descriptions of these persecutions also echoed the psalmist's words that Byrd had set. The *secunda pars* of the composer's motet, "Posuerunt morticinia servorum tuorum escas volatilibus coeli: carnes sanctorum bestiis terrae" ("The dead bodies of thy servants have they given to be meat unto the fowls of the heavens, the flesh of thy saints unto the beasts of the earth"), for example, was treated poetically in a "Complainte of a Catholicke for the death of M. Edmund Campion," printed in Alfield's *A true reporte of the deathe and martyrdome of M. Campion* of 1582 (cat. 90):

> O God from sacred throne behold our secret sorowes here,
> Regard with grace our helplesse griefe amend our mournfull cheere.
> The bodies of thy Saintes abrode are set for foules to feede,
> And brutish birds devour the flesh of faithful folke in deede.

The same verse was also bluntly proclaimed as an epigraph on the title page of Robert Parsons' *An Epistle of the Persecution of Catholickes* (1582). Father Garnet even asserted that a papal indulgence had been granted "to all those that did devoutlie for the conversion of England say . . . the psalme 78, *Deus, venerunt gentes*."[5]

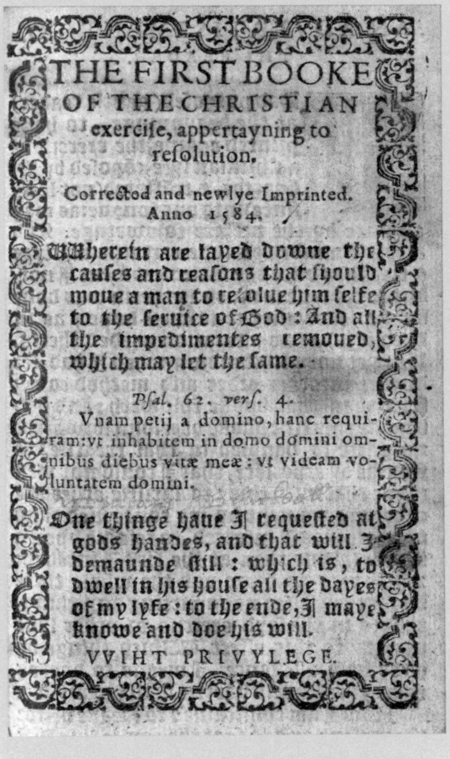

THE FIRST BOOKE
OF THE CHRISTIAN
exercise, appertayning to
resolution.

Corrected and newlye Imprinted.
Anno 1584.

Wherein are layed downe the causes and reasons that should moue a man to resolue him selfe to the seruice of God: And all the impedimentes remoued, which may let the same.

Psal. 62. vers. 4.

Vnam petij a domino, hanc requiram: vt inhabitem in domo domini omnibus diebus vitæ meæ: vt videam voluntatem domini.

One thinge haue I requested at gods handes, and that will I demaunde still: which is, to dwell in his house all the dayes of my lyfe: to the ende, I maye knowe and doe his will.

VVIHT PRIVYLEGE.

Robert Parsons, *The first booke of the Christian exercise, appertayning to resolution.* [Rome], 1584.

• origin/source
• one who: attacks aggressively/refutes principles/opinions of others; practices disputation/controversy

/ *crye oute vpon theese Theues*

But what of Englishmen outside the Catholic community? How would they have interpreted the texts of Byrd's "political" motets? Interestingly enough, non-Catholics may very well have construed the same texts and themes in terms of their own religious and political persuasions. Byrd, once again, best illustrates the point. Effectively in the service of two masters (the pope and the queen), he composed, on the one hand, "Exsurge, quare obdormis, Domine?" for *Cantiones Sacrae II* (1591), presumably in support of the Catholic cause. On the other hand, he also composed "Arise, O Lord, why sleepest thou?," an English translation of the same text and one of his most popular "anthems," which suggests God was on the Protestant side. This anthem survives in many manuscripts, not only Anglican liturgical sources, but also secular manuscripts, including some of obvious Catholic provenance.

English Protestants had had their own equivalents of the martyr Edmund Campion, of course, during the notorious religious persecutions of "Bloody" Mary Tudor's reign in the 1550s. Perhaps it should not be surprising, therefore, that the text of Psalm 78, which appears in Byrd's most strongly worded "protest motet," fits just as well in the mouths of an earlier generation of Protestant martyrs and anti-Catholic polemicists as it did in Jesuit writings. Nicholas Ridley, the reformist Bishop of London martyred with Thomas Cranmer and Hugh Latimer for the Protestant faith in Oxford in 1555, had quoted the very same psalm near the end, as recorded in *A frendly farewel . . . unto all his true lovers and frendes in God, a litle before that he suffred for the testimony of the truthe of Christ his Gospell*, 1559 (cat. 92):

> I may wel complaine on them [the Catholics] and crye oute vpon theese Theues with the Prophet, saying *Deus venerunt gentes in hereditatem tuam. &c. Psal. 79.* O Lord God the gentiles, heathen nations are come into thy heritage, they haue defiled thy holye Temple, and made Ierusalem an heape of stones, . . . these robbers haue rushed oute of their dennes and hath robbed the Churche of Englande of all the foresaide holye Treasoure of God. (sig. B1v)

Ridley's words achieved much broader circulation when John Foxe quoted them in his widely published *Actes and monuments of matters most speciall and memorable, . . . wherein is set forth at large . . . the great persecutions agaynst the true martyrs of Christ, . . . as now lately practised by Romish prelates, especially in this realme of England and Scotland.* Walter Haddon also turned to verse 3 of the psalm, "Effuderunt sanguinem," part 3 of Byrd's motet, in his condemnation of "papistry," *A sight of the Portugall pearle, that is, the aunsvvere of D. Haddon maister of the requests vnto our soueraigne lady Elizabeth . . . against the epistle of Hieronimus Osorius a Portugall, entitled Pearle for a Prince* (1565):

(See p. 84.)

> Auant with thys your barkynge after your bloudye bittes, you monstruous howlyng wolues. . . . You your selues made those Antychristian fyers, you behelde the naked bodyes burning so long as the synewes wold contein them. . . . Play not the hypocrite thus both to byte and whine. As for *cruor* (that is bloude) it is the papistes peculier and lineal badge. Popelinges they are of whom it is written: *Effuderunt sanguinem sanctoru[m] et in eo inebriati sunt*: They shede the bloud of sainctes, and sucked thereof, vntill they were droncken. (sig. C2v–C3v)

Some of Byrd's general themes, which could be read in terms of Catholics' plight, could also be—and apparently were—heard in Protestant terms. Protestant polemicists regularly made *Rome* out to be Babylon, while England or London became Jerusalem, for example. Jesuit rhetoric had regularly portrayed persecuted English Catholics as Israelites in bondage in Egypt, but for early seventeenth-century English patriots and Protestants, the theme of Israel's deliverance became the favorite symbol for the "deliverance" of England and King James I from the "Papist" Gunpowder plotters on 5 November 1605.

Significantly, English composers had shown very little interest in the archetypical "deliverance" text, Psalm 114 of the King James version, during Elizabeth's reign. No musical settings of "When Israel came out of Egypt and the house of Jacob from among the strange people" survive between Byrd's rather plain festal psalm setting for Easter Evensong (from early in Elizabeth's reign) and Michael East's much more animated setting for voices and instrumental accompaniment, published in his *Third Set of Books* of 1610 (p. 78). East very probably composed his consort anthem in quick response to the recent deliverance of "the house of Jacob" with Jacob easily standing for James I. The work achieved extraordinary popularity. Scribes copied it, not only into virtually all the most important Jacobean and Caroline secular manuscript collections, but also into a surprising number of sacred sources, where they might have been expected to eschew its extroverted, madrigalian style (somewhat indecorous for church use). Such widespread acceptance, quite out of proportion to the anthem's musical quality, suggests that East's "When Israel came out of Egypt" became a favorite way to commemorate November 5 in Protestant and loyalist circles, whether in formal church services or in pious music-making at home.

Generations of English Protestant sermonizers confirmed the anthem's appropriateness. Year after year they returned to its theme at annual commemorations of Guy Fawkes Day:

> But the rather must we & truly may we say of it as was said of the night in which the *Isralites* went out of *Egypt. It is a day to be kept holy to the Lord, it is that day of the Lord which all the children of England must keepe throw out their generations*, as an eternall presedent of Gods

> watchfull eye in the preseruation of our Church and state, and an euerliuing testimony of the neuer dying cruelty of Iesuited *Romish* Catholiques.[6]

> Beloved, this dayes deliverance, which Gods right hand hath wrought for this Land, is much like to the delivery of *Israel* out of *Egypt*; for *Rome* is *Egypt* mystically, . . . and we were delivered from the bondage of *Rome* this day, and wee were delivered from the tyranny of the Pope of *Rome*, . . . shall we not then remember this day, wherin we came out of *Egypt*?[7]

Interestingly enough, half a century later, Israel was still England, but the Roundheads who had subjugated England to the servitude of the Commonwealth temporarily stood in for the "Papists" as the Pharoahs:

> Verily, your Majesty [King Charles II] with all your Protestant Subjects, after such a stupendious, glorious deliverance from their la[t]e usurping *Pharoahs*, . . . have just cause to sing aloud to the God of their Salvation . . . *Blessed be the Lord God of* England *from everlasting to everlasting . . . Bl[e]ssed be the Lord thy God, who delighted in thee, to set thee upon his Throne, to be King for the Lord thy God. Because the Lord thy God Lov[e]d* Israel *(England, Scotland and Ireland)* TO ESTABLISH THEM FOREVER, THEREFORE MADE HE THEE KING OVER THEM.[8]

In the immediate aftermath of the Gunpowder Plot, other newly-composed anthems that achieved unusual popularity were also very likely responses to the event. They ring the changes on biblical phrases that regularly reappear later in sermonizers' commemorations of the plot of 1605. The words of Matthew Jeffries' setting of verses from Psalm 124, "If the Lord himself had not been on our side," for example, which appears in several London sources from the 1610s and 1620s, echo in preachings from James I's reign and well beyond, commemorating England's deliverance.

> . . . if the Lord himselfe had not watched ouer his Church, if the Lord himselfe had not written England in the palmes of his hands, if the Lord himselfe had not kept King *Iames* as the apple of his eye, if the Lord himself had not been on our side (now may Gods Israell in England say) if the Lord himselfe had not been on our side, when they rose vp against vs; if the Lord himself had not . . . deliuered our soules out of that horrible gunpowder pit; these bellowing Buls of Basan, and Canon-mouthed-hell-hounds would haue made on this day such a roare, that all Christendome should have felt it. . . .[9]

/ the eccho of our rejoycings might carry terrour and trouble

> *If it had not been the Lord who was on our side, now may Israel say: If it had not been the Lord, who was on our side, when men rose up against us: Then they had swallowed us up quick,* &c. Let *Israel* NOW especially say and glory hereof. . . . Let *Israel* now say, . . . *MANY, MANY a time have they afflicted me, yet they have not prevailed against me*. . . . for thus we sometimes find God himself, as it were, decking his name with new Titles, taken from the Mercies and Deliverances which he hath wrought for his People, *I am the Lord thy God which brought thee out of the Land of Egypt, out of the house of bondage; and the Lord which brought up, and which led the seed of the house of Israel, out of the North-country*. . . . Therefore with all the most signal Praises, let *Israel* now say, and say aloud too, that, if possible, the eccho of our rejoycings might carry terrour and trouble over all their Papal Monarchy. . . .[10]

No fewer than eight other early seventeenth-century composers also set "If the Lord himself had not been on our side," which had been virtually ignored by their Elizabethan counterparts. This evidence reinforces the probability that musical versions of this psalm were Protestant anthems for rejoicing and remembrance in the aftermath of the Gunpowder Plot.

In such writings and anthems, King James I often becomes the biblical King David: "Not onlie is your M[ajesty] . . . in spirituall disposition a faithful *David*, for your burning zeal to Gods glorie, yea and more than *David*, because more continent than hee," proclaimed "I. A." in *The Muses welcome to the high and mightie prince Iames*, commemorating the king's visit to Scotland in 1617. "And that thy Royall *David* long may liue / To try thy cause against that man of *Gath*, / Bring downe the length of dayes vpon his head, / And blesse the partner of his Royall Bed," exclaimed Richard Niccols in *The Three Sisters Teares* (1613), lamenting the death of Henry, prince of Wales. This suggests that musical invocations of King David, such as the popular "Hosannah to the son of David," set by both Orlando Gibbons and Thomas Weelkes; Gibbons' "O all true faithful hearts" ("for he our David from the snares of death hath freed"); and Matthew Jeffries's "Lord, remember David" would all have been heard as references to the English royal family, whether James I or his sons.

Most striking in this regard is the singular outpouring of musical laments by King David, most dating from the second decade of the seventeenth century. These sorts of texts, including "When David heard that Absalom was slain" (set half-a-dozen times by Michael East, Thomas Tomkins, and Thomas Weelkes, among others); "When David heard that Jonathan"; "O Jonathan, woe is me"; "O Jonathan thou wast slain"; "O Jonathan how wert thou slain"; "O my son Absalom, my son"; "And the King was moved"; "Saul and Jonathan"; and "Then David mourned," virtually never set to music in England before 1610, suddenly burgeon. Thurston Dart first suggested that the "When David heard" settings were a response to the untimely death in 1612 of James I's heir, Henry, prince of Wales, who was widely perceived as England's great hope for the future.[11] Henry's death prompted numerous elegies and other poetic effusions, and it makes sense that composers would also have followed suit.

Folger MS V.a.412 (cat. 106) testifies to the popularity of such musical elegies invoking King David, particularly in London musical circles close to court. The copyist of this single surviving partbook, from what must once have been a set of five or six books, can be identified as the early seventeenth-century London organist Benjamin Cosyn,[12] organist of Dulwich College and Charterhouse, whose hand is best known from the "Cosyn Virginal Book" in the British Library and from another large keyboard manuscript in the Paris Conservatoire. His hand also appears in manuscripts that once belonged to the important Jacobean music collector and vicar of St. Stephen's, Walbrook in London, Thomas Myriell, with whose manuscripts the Folger source shares several concordances and some variant readings. Pamela Willetts has suggested that Folger MS V.a.412 reflects Cosyn's musical activities at Dulwich College and Charterhouse, where music figured prominently.[13]

Amidst many madrigals copied directly from printed sources and a few anthems, Cosyn copies no fewer than five David laments into the Folger source. These include Thomas Weelkes's "O my son Absalom," part 2 (only) of the well-known "When David Heard" (one of the most popular David laments even down to our own day), and also Weelkes's comparably popular "O Jonathan, woe is me for thee." Another, more musically pedestrian, "O my son Absalom, my son," which Cosyn attributed to Weelkes in the Cosyn Virginal Book, also turns up in the manuscript, where Cosyn declines to hold Weelkes responsible for it. An "O Jonathan, how wert thou slain" survives in no other source but Folger, while "And the king was moved" reappears in Myriell's large manuscript anthology, *Tristitiae Remedium*, ascribed to Richard Dering. These sorts of musical effusions on 2 Samuel 18, so favored by Cosyn and his London associates, continued to be composed for much of the decade. They found their way into print at least as late as 1622, when Thomas Tomkins included his own "When David heard" (dedicated to Thomas Myriell) in his *Songs of 3. 4. 5. And 6 Parts*. The David laments continued to be copied into other manuscripts through the 1630s and into the 1640s, by which time any associations with Prince Henry's untimely death may well have been forgotten.

These various musical settings of sacred texts, given new meaning when heard in particular historical circumstances by listeners ready to hear, suggest that English musicians, whether Catholic or Protestant, discovered how to make their music speak to their distinct religious and political realities, even though the words they used might be the same. Through these ambiguous, often indirect sorts of expression, Elizabethan and Jacobean composers, most notably William Byrd, maintained potentially effective voices in their time, which we are now beginning to hear afresh.

hesitantly acting/speaking through lack of self-confidence; reserved, unassertive
commonly accepted/supposed; assumed to exist

1 For details of de Ligny's experiences in England, see John Harley, *William Byrd, Gentleman of the Chapel Royal* (Aldershot, 1997), 142–44. This book is the most exhaustive compendium of archival material related to Byrd and his family.

2 Byrd's support of the Catholic cause was treated somewhat diffidently by E. H. Fellowes in *William Byrd*, 2d ed. (London, 1948), 36–46, and has been discussed much more extensively over the years by Joseph Kerman, most recently in "Music and Politics: The Case of William Byrd (1540–1623)," *Proceedings of the American Philosophical Society* 144 (2000): 275–87, but also in *The Masses and Motets of William Byrd* (Berkeley and Los Angeles, 1981). The present discussion of Byrd's "political" motets draws heavily upon Craig Monson, "Byrd, the Catholics, and the Motet: The Hearing Reopened," in *Hearing the Motet*, ed. Dolores Pesce (New York, 1997), 348–74. Apart from Kerman's *The Masses and Motets*, the most insightful and sensitive discussions of Byrd's *Gradualia* appear in the prefaces to Philip Brett's editions of *Gradualia I* and *II* in *The Byrd Edition*, vols. 5–7 (London, 1989–1997).

3 Harley, *William Byrd*, 143 (my translation).

4 Garnet and Southwell are quoted in Monson, "Byrd, the Catholics, and the Motet," 353.

5 Ibid., 362.

6 George Hakewill, *A comparison betvveene thje dayes of purim and that of the powder treason for the better continuance of the memory of it* (London, 1626), sig. E2v.

7 Thomas Vicars, *Edom and Babylon against Jerusalem, . . . Occasioned by the most happy deliverance of our church and state (on November 5. 1605.) From the most bloody designe of the papists-gunpowder-treason* (London, 1633), sig. A4r.

8 William Prynne, *The first and second part of the signal loyalty of gods true saints and pious Christians . . . toward their kings* (London, 1660), sig. A4r–v.

9 John Boys, *An exposition of the last psalme delivered in a sermon at Pauls Crosse the fifth of November 1613* (London, 1613), sig. A5r–v.

10 John Reynolds, *Vituli Labiorum. Or, a thanksgiving sermon, in commemoration of our great deliverance from the horrid powder-plot, 1605. And also of Gods merciful discovery of a bloody conspiracy against his majesties person, and the Protestant religion, 1678. Both intended by the Papists* (London, [1678]), sig. D3v–D4r.

11 Thurston Dart, "Two English Musicians in Heidelberg in 1613," *Musical Times* 111 (1970): 29. For a more detailed examination of the laments and their putative connection with Prince Henry, see Irving Godt, "Prince Henry as Absalom in David's Lamentation," *Music and Letters* 62 (1981): 318–30.

12 Craig Monson, *Voices and Viols in England, 1600–1650: The Sources and the Music* (Ann Arbor, 1982), 39.

13 Pamela J. Willetts, "Benjamin Cosyn: Sources and Circumstances," in *Sundry Sorts of Music Books: Essays on the British Library Collections*, ed. Chris Banks, Arthur Searle, and Malcolm Turner (London, 1993), 142.

"If any of you be mery let hym synge psalmes":
The Culture of Psalms in Church and Home

Nicholas Temperley

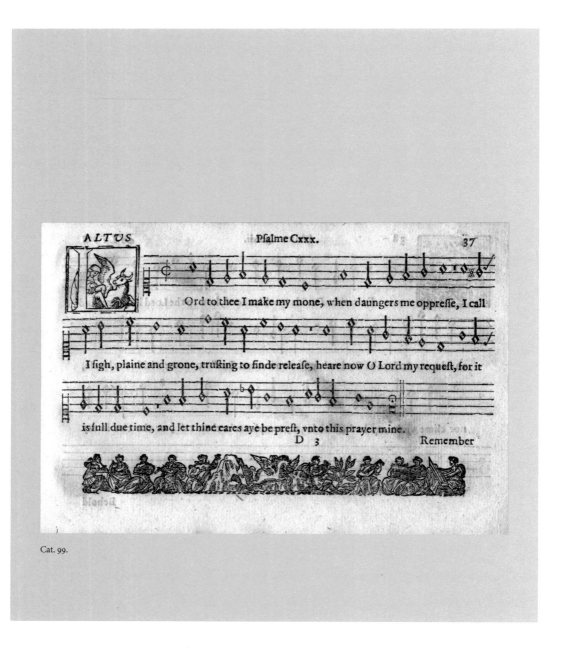

Cat. 99.

/ *when we sing them, we are certain that God puts the words in our mouth*

The psalms of David loomed large in the consciousness of the English for two centuries after the Reformation. That was the time when phrases from the psalms entered everyday speech: "from strength to strength" (84:7), "at their wits' end" (107:27), "the apple of [my] eye" (17:8), "my cup runneth over"(23:5), and many more. This exhibition shows how the psalms were favored by all classes of society as literature, as song, and as liturgy, for public worship and for private contemplation.

The medieval church had required the chanting of certain Latin psalms in the Office by priest and choir. It had also encouraged the use of a group of psalms to assist private meditation; these found their way into many primers and manuals in English prose translation. Especially popular were the "Seven Penitential Psalms" (6, 32, 38, 51, 102, 130, 143) and the "Fifteen Psalms" (120–34), also largely penitential or admonitory.[1] What was new in the reformed churches was the idea that psalms were the ideal vehicle for the people's praise of God. This principle was embraced by Jean Calvin, who did not share Luther's fondness for the Latin liturgical hymns or the *geistliche Gesänge* of German tradition yet saw the value of public expressions of praise: "Look where we may, we will never find songs better, nor more suited to the purpose, than the psalms of David: which the Holy Ghost himself composed. And so, when we sing them, we are certain that God puts the words in our mouth, as if he himself sang in us to magnify his praise."[2] Notice that Calvin did not expressly exclude non-scriptural hymns. But he used his growing influence to encourage the singing of psalms, and his views prevailed in non-Lutheran strands of Protestantism, including those now called Anglican, Puritan, and Presbyterian.

A text that was frequently cited in support of this position was James 5:13. The Coverdale version of 1539 reads, "If any of you be vexed, let him praye. If any of you be mery, let him synge psalmes" (see title page of cat. 103). Though the apostle James may not have had any particular songs in mind, the literalism of the reformers took the verse as a specific reference to the 150 canonical psalms. And the verse encouraged the use of psalms in private as well as in church. Another verse, Colossians 3:16, seemed to allow a wider choice of texts: "psalms, hymns & spiritual songs." Finally Psalm 148:12 established the important point that all should join the singing: "Young men and maidens, old men and children, praise the name of the Lord."

The *Book of Common Prayer*, published in 1549 and prescribed for worship by the Act of Uniformity of the same year, was very largely made up of translations of portions of the Latin Mass and Office. But it contained a unique "Table for The Ordre of the Psalmes, to be sayed at Matins and Evensong." This was justified in the preface by pointing out that "of late tyme a fewe of them have been dailye sayed (and ofte repeated) and the rest utterly omitted."[3]

The 1539 Great Bible translation, principally composed by Miles Coverdale, was adopted as the standard prose version and later (1662) incorporated in the *Book of Common Prayer*. It was not displaced by

• manservant; an officer of the English royal house-hold

/ *our grace taketh pleasure to hear them sung*

the King James version of the Bible; most people from 1611 onwards had two different prose translations of the psalms ready at hand; and undoubtedly, they were widely read in private, both silently and aloud in family prayers, as well as heard in church as part of Morning and Evening Prayer. In ordinary churches they were spoken, verse by verse, in alternation by priest and people, though in course of time the people's part dwindled into silence and was left to the parish clerk. In cathedrals and other well-endowed sanctuaries they were chanted daily by the choir, accompanied on the organ to the Gregorian psalm tones, either in unison or harmony. The practice has continued from 1549 to the present, with brief interruptions in 1553–1558 and 1645–1660. It was not until the late seventeenth century that the composition of new specimens, called "Anglican chants," developed. In addition, psalms were the source of texts for the great majority of anthems sung by cathedral choirs and in the Chapel Royal.

But the reformers' desire for the psalms to become the universal song of the people came up against the awkward fact that they are in prose. The only kind of song that untutored people could be expected to sing was the kind they knew already: the rhymed strophic ballad, repeating the same music for each stanza. For this reason Calvin had adopted *metrical* psalms as the basis of church song, accepting the resulting departures from literal translation in the interest of having all join in the singing. The core of his metrical psalter was the work of Clément Marot, a court poet who had turned to the versification of some of the psalms in about 1532. After Marot's death in 1544, Calvin commissioned Théodore de Bèze to finish the task of translating all 150 psalms. The complete French psalter was published at Geneva in 1562, with a splendid set of tunes.

Similarly, the more ardent of the English reformers took the versified "court" psalms of Thomas Sternhold, groom of the robes to Henry VIII and Edward VI, as the basis for their own metrical psalter. Sternhold, in the preface to his first publication of *Certayne Psalmes Drawen into English Metre* (ca. 1549), dedicated them to Edward VI, "trusting that as your grace taketh pleasure to hear them sung sometimes of me, so ye will also delight not only to see and read them yourself, but also to command them to be sung to you of others." After Sternhold's death in 1549, a complete edition of his twenty-seven psalm versions was published by John Hopkins, a country clergyman, who added a further seven of his own.

Queen Mary I (Mary Tudor) restored the Catholic liturgy in 1554. In anticipation of this, a stream of several thousand Protestants left to find a home on the Continent where they would be free to worship as they pleased. Frankfurt was the main center, until a dispute arose between the "prayer book" party that wished to follow the *Book of Common Prayer* and those who sought a more radical reform. The latter group—the Puritans—moved to Geneva under their leaders John Knox and William Whittingham. There they naturally came under the close influence of Calvin, whose sister Whittingham married. It was in Geneva that the first musical edition of Sternhold and Hopkins' psalms was published as an appendage to the new service book: *One and fiftie Psalmes of David in Englishe metre, whereof .37. were made by Thomas Sterneholde: and the rest by others.* The imprint is 1556 and the preface dated 10 February 1556 (cat. 86). The seven new psalms were the work of Whittingham, who also revised Sternhold's versions: "Conferred with the Hebrewe, and in certeyn places corrected as the text and sens of the Prophete required." The service book specified two psalms for particular uses: 103 at communion and 128 after the marriage service. There were fifty-two tunes, three of them adapted from the French Genevan psalter. A second edition of 1558 added more versions and tunes.

The new tunes in these books are mostly bland, unshapely, and unmemorable by comparison with those of the French psalter. Whittingham, unlike Calvin, could not call on some of the best musicians of his country but had to make do with whatever talent was available in the small band of exiles. There is much to suggest that the tunes, though original, derived from a tradition of courtly songs, deprived of their accompaniment (since the Geneva exiles would not allow organs or choirs in the service) and thus tending to lose their rhythmic vitality. A very similar type of tune is found in Hall's *Court of Vertue* (cat. 87), which is known to be a moralistic parody of *The Court of Venus*: the tunes may be those to which the original verses had been sung. Considering that an important part of the designed function of metrical psalms was to replace "amorous and obscene songs" in the affections of the people, the Puritans may have welcomed the adaptation to moral texts of tunes or types of tune associated with erotic secular ballads. The title page of John Day's harmonized psalm book of 1563 says that the psalms might be "song to al Musical instruments" and were now "set forth for the encrease of vertue: and aboleshyng of other vayne and triflyng ballades." (See also cat. 99, dedication.)

When Elizabeth I decided to pursue a moderately Protestant church polity, she sought a compromise between the two parties in the reformed church, "some declaring for Geneva, and some for Frankfurt."[4] In her *Injunctions* of 1559, following the reintroduction of the prayer book, she showed characteristic subtlety. She did not explicitly countenance metrical psalms, but she allowed that "in the beginning, or in the end of common prayers, either at morning or evening, there may be sung an hymn, or such like song, to the praise of Almighty God, in the best sort of melody and music that may be conveniently devised, having respect that the sentence of the hymn may be understood and perceived."[5] This was taken to authorize both anthems in choral service and metrical psalms in congregational worship, yet it did not quite make either of them a part of the official liturgy.

The queen also granted a joint monopoly for the publishing of metrical psalms to two leading printers, William Seres and John Day. Seres made little use of his privilege, but Day, the printer of *Certaine*

The side of a leaf (as of a manuscript) that is to be read second; a left-hand page; opposite of recto, a right hand page, read first

Notes (cat. 88), began the series of psalm books that would soon become universal. They are now generally known as the "Old Version" (or "Sternhold and Hopkins") to distinguish them from Tate and Brady's *New Version of the Psalms* (1696). He took the Geneva books as the starting point, adding more psalm versifications by Hopkins and several other authors. He also used material from a psalm book without tunes published at Wesel in about 1557, which represented the Frankfurt or "prayer book" party. In particular, he included metrical canticles, creeds, and hymns to which Puritans might have objected and placed them before and after the 150 canonical psalms.

When all the psalms had been versified, Day published the result in 1562 as *The whole booke of Psalmes, collected into Englysh metre by T. Starnhold I. Hopkins & others: conferred with the Ebrue, with apt notes to synge them withal, faithfully perused and alowed according to thordre appointed in the quenes maiesties Injunctions.* Cat. 101 and 103 are later editions of this work. It was surpassed in the number of its editions only by the Bible and prayer book (with which it was often bound). The opening shown in cat. 103 illustrates once again the political compromise inherent in the Elizabethan settlement of religion. The verso explains a pedagogical device intended to ensure that all the people sang the psalms, rather than leaving them to trained choirs—a Puritan goal. But the recto shows that the first two songs in the book were a translated Latin Office hymn and an original hymn, neither of which could claim biblical authority.

The combination of Day's printing privilege, the citation of the queen's *Injunctions* on the title page, and the binding of it with the prayer book soon created a widespread impression that the psalm versions and hymns of the Old Version were the only ones authorized for use in church. (This fiction was not legally challenged until 1820.) It is certain that it soon became the only book in normal use and that weekly singing in church soon made many of its texts and tunes as familiar a part of the culture as the Bible itself. Congregations relished the chance to sing. The Puritan associations of the psalms were forgotten as they became a national possession—indeed the only form of organized singing in most people's lives. Church psalmody was nominally led by the parish clerk, solitary survivor of the small musical staff of chantry priests and clerks that had existed in many parish churches in Henry VIII's time. But in the absence of effective professional direction or accompaniment, it soon became a self-regulating crowd performance not unlike that of a stadium of football fans. Over the generations it tended to slow down, while complexities in the tunes were gradually lost.[6]

The tunes printed in the psalm book, with a few exceptions such as PSALM 100 (now called OLD 100TH), soon fell out of use, especially those of irregular meter derived from the French Genevan psalter. They were replaced by a set of sturdy four-line tunes, of unknown origin but certainly beginning to come in before 1580. By 1592 Thomas East, in publishing a harmonized edition of the Old Version, set the great

/ *to be sung or plaide upon the lute, orpharyon, citterne or base violle*

majority of the psalms to these new tunes, and in 1594 he stated that a mere four of them were used for the psalms "in most churches of this Realme" (cat. 97).

It is unlikely that four-part harmony such as East provided was within the reach of parish churches, where choirs were unknown in his time. Cathedrals and endowed choral foundations could have used them but hardly in sufficient quantity to justify publication. East's book belongs, instead, to a series of books intended for domestic use in affluent homes. Day's 1563 collection has already been mentioned. John Cosyn (cat. 99) and William Damon also preceded East, while Richard Allison and Thomas Ravenscroft (cat. 96) followed him. These compilers presented the psalm settings as substitutes for secular songs, which they characterized with varying degrees of disapproval. Allison's arrangements (1599) were "to be sung or plaide upon the lute, orpharyon, citterne or base violle."

But East and Ravenscroft differed from the others in important respects. As well as providing harmonized tunes underlaid with the first verse of a psalm, they printed all the other verses of the psalm below and repeated some tunes for many psalms so that their books can be regarded as harmonized editions of the Old Version. Perhaps East hoped his book might be used in church as well, though he was too prudent to mention this in the title or preface, as it might have been seen as pushing the pace of reform. Ravenscroft followed suit, but he also dedicated his book to the archbishop of Canterbury and named most of the tunes after cathedrals and choral foundations.

Whereas Cosyn and Allison printed their own harmonizations, East and Ravenscroft commissioned leading musicians of the time, though not those who held leading church positions. East's roster consisted of Allison, Blancks, Cavendish, Cobbold, Dowland, Farmer, Farnaby, Hooper, and Kirby; Ravenscroft added another eleven names, including his own. Unlike the others, these two books entered the permanent repertory. East's was three times revised and reprinted, and Ravenscroft's was a revision of East's. On 27 November 1664, Samuel Pepys took part in a sing-through of "Ravenscroft's four-part psalms, most admirable music," with two other men and a boy. The New England "Bay Psalm Book" of 1640 also referred to Ravenscroft's tunes. In the 1670s, John Playford "was much importuned by some persons in the West Country to set out a new edition of Mr Ravenscroft's Psalms."[7]

If formal harmonization of the psalm tunes was rarely heard in church, there is evidence of a practice of improvised harmonization, perhaps a survival of faburden—the fifteenth-century practice of improvising largely parallel counterpoints to chant. When a well-known tune was sung, one or two skilled singers might add a descant above it, generally moving to the nearest available consonance, with an occasional cadence suspension. In course of time the descant was perceived as the main melody and became separated from its mother tune. One tune, usually known as OXFORD, was especially prone to this practice.

/ a most Excellent-large-plump-lusty-full-speaking-Organ

It may be itself a derivative of one of the ancient psalm tones, which had regularly been chanted in faburden. No fewer than three four-line tunes that were popular in the seventeenth century fit perfectly as descants to OXFORD; one of them, LITCHFIELD, is shown alongside OXFORD itself in cat. 98. The other two cases were pointed out by Charles Butler, who said that the mean and tenor of OXFORD had been "made two several tunes, (under the names of Glassenburie and Kentish tunes) with other parts set unto them," though his example confused the tunes concerned (cat. 33).[8]

By the time of the Civil War, metrical psalms could be recruited by both sides, as eye-witnesses reported. In November 1640, the House of Commons attended church at St. Margaret's, Westminster, according to custom, but during the communion service, which was no doubt conducted in Laudian style by that time, some members "began to sing some of Hopkins's metre, and disturbed the office. . . . The Commons, it seems, had a mind to acquaint the people with part of their design."[9] But during the siege of York in 1644, when those loyal to the king took refuge in the Minster, the whole congregation sang a psalm according to custom, led by the choir and "a most Excellent-large-plump-lusty-full-speaking-Organ."[10]

Psalms continued to be favored in educated circles, where there was growing discontent with the perceived crudity of the Old Version. George Sandys, a poet who dedicated each of his published works to Charles I, brought out a new set of paraphrases of the psalms and other biblical lyrics in 1636, and selections were set to music by the Lawes brothers, leading musicians of the court. Henry Lawes's *Choice Psalmes Put Into Musick, for Three Voices* (cat. 102) was also dedicated to the king. Rather than arrange the common tunes, Lawes composed entirely original settings and added some by his deceased brother William. Perhaps for this reason they had little impact on general practice.

In 1645 Parliament abolished the *Book of Common Prayer* and substituted a Presbyterian order of service that called for metrical psalms. But neither of the new versions of psalms adopted by Parliament (those of William Barton and Francis Rous) made much headway in the churches, even when the practice of lining out was adopted.[11] The people, by and large, went on singing the psalms and tunes they knew, in a slower and slower tempo and in a manner that approached heterophony. The practice continued with little change after the Restoration. But it was a case of survival rather than progress. Only two new psalm tunes were printed in England between 1644 and 1671.[12]

The leading reformer of the period was John Playford, stationer, musician, royalist, and clerk to the Temple Church. Sensing a steady decline in standards, he embarked on a campaign to preserve and improve the singing of the old psalms, with their tunes correctly sung and, if possible, with harmony. During the Commonwealth he had to offer the tunes ostensibly for domestic recreation, since the authorities did not approve of rehearsed or accompanied singing in worship. He first included nine Old Version psalms with monophonic tunes in *A Booke of New Lessons for the Cithern and Gittern* (1652). Six years later he placed some of the common psalm tunes, with basses, in a new edition of his *Introduction to Music*, with some guidance to parish clerks as to how to choose the appropriate tune for a given psalm and how to set the pitch (cat. 98).

When the king came into his own again in 1660, the Company of Stationers, which had held the monopoly in psalm printing since 1603, allowed Playford to thoroughly revise the Old Version in a conservative direction, and he prepared a grand folio edition for parish clerks (1661) in the now archaic black-letter type. It paid special attention to the appropriate matching of tunes and words. He also issued a single leaf of organ settings of psalm tunes for the benefit of cathedrals and the few parish churches that had acquired instruments.[13]

Playford's most ambitious project was *Psalms & Hymns in Solemn Musick* (cat. 100), published in 1671. Here again he prudently combined church and home use. He recommended accompaniment by organ, lute, or viol. But the settings are for four-part male choir, and it is clear from the preface that he yearned for the choral solemnity that he believed had once infused the singing of the psalms in church. Indeed he presented a number of copies of the book to the Company of Parish Clerks of London, and supervised their weekly practices; the Company had his settings copied out in manuscript partbooks (no longer extant).[14] There was little hope that such singing could be introduced in parish churches, even in London; choirs were as yet unknown, and there was only one clerk in each parish. The enterprise was doomed to failure, and the book was never reprinted.

Playford learned his lesson, and his next effort was a complete edition of the Old Version published in 1677, *The Whole Book of Psalms . . . Compos'd in Three Parts* (cat. 43). Even this was a little ahead of its time, and it was not widely used before Playford's death in 1686/7. But when voluntary choirs began to form in the 1690s, Playford's son Henry obtained the Company of Stationers' leave to print a second edition, and others followed in close succession, extending eventually to the twentieth in 1757. The straightforward three-voice settings, set out so that they could also be used with keyboard accompaniment, turned out to be just the right thing for the new reform movement based on a choir leading the congregation. They were also an early example of a uniquely English invention: the ambiguous G clef, designed for trebles and tenors alike.

Of the two domains of psalm singing in the early modern period, the private one was beginning to decline, though devotional settings were still found occasionally throughout the eighteenth century. Psalm singing in public worship, on the other hand, was about to enter a vigorous revival, after a long sleep lasting much of the seventeenth century. Poets, musicians, and clergy joined forces to raise psalmody once more to an acceptable level.

Detail, cat. 52.

1 See Francis Procter, *A History of the Book of Common Prayer* (London and Cambridge, 1864), 12–15.

2 Jean Calvin, "La forme des prieres et chants ecclesiastiques," in *Pseaumes octantetrois de David, mis en rime Francoise . . . par Clement Marot . . . et trentequatre par Theodore de Besze* (Geneva: Jean Crespin, 1551), A7r–v; translation mine.

3 *The First and Second Prayer Books of King Edward the Sixth* (London and Toronto, 1910), 4.

4 H. Robinson, ed., *Zurich Letters*, Parker Society Publications vol. 52 (Cambridge, 1846), 17.

5 Walter H. Frere, ed., *Visitation Articles and Injunctions of the Period of the Reformation*, Alcuin Club Collections nos. 14–16 (London and New York, 1910), 16:8.

6 For a full account of church psalmody in this period, see Nicholas Temperley, *The Music of the English Parish Church* (Cambridge, 1979), especially chapters 2–5.

7 John Playford, *The Whole Book of Psalms . . . Compos'd in Three Parts* (London: W. Godbid for the Company of Stationers, 1677), preface.

8 Charles Butler, *The Principles of Musik* (London: John Haviland for the author, 1636), 44; see also Temperley, *Music of the English Parish Church*, 2 vols. (Cambridge and New York, 1979), 1:74.

9 J. Collier, *An Ecclesiastical History of Great Britain*, ed. F. Barnham, 9 vols. (London, 1841), 8:194.

10 Thomas Mace, *Musick's Monument* (London: T. Ratcliffe and N. Thompson for the author, 1676), 19.

11 The reading aloud of each line of text by a precentor or parish clerk, before the line was sung by the congregation.

12 See Temperley, *Hymn Tune Index*, 4 vols. (Oxford and New York, 1998), 3:192–93, tunes 536, 537. The tunes in the census are arranged in chronological order of first printing.

13 Inserted in some copies of Playford's *Musick's Hand-Maid* (London: for J. Playford, 1678): see Temperley, "John Playford and the Metrical Psalms," *Journal of the American Musicological Society* 25 (1972): 353–55.

14 Ibid., 357.

Catalogue of the Exhibition

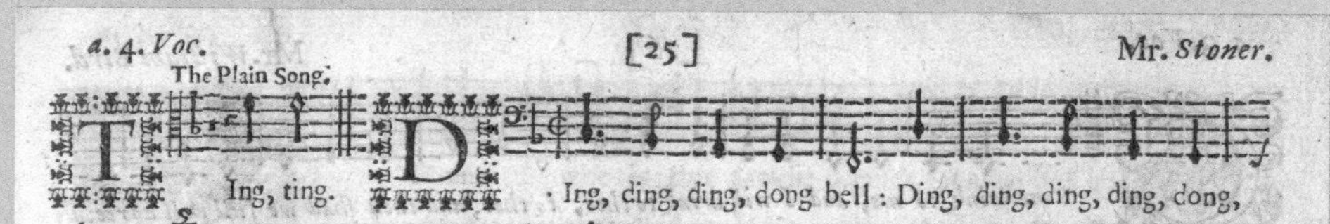

Catch that catch can: or the musical companion. Containing catches and rounds for three and four voyces. London, 1667.
Previous page: Detail, cat.13.

"The perpetuitie of ringing": The Sounds of Bells

For Ben Jonson's character Morose, "a gent that loues no noise," the bells were the worst of all, driving him to a padded room.[1]

> *Cle.* O, i' the Queenes time, he was woont to goe out of Towne euery Satterday at ten a clock, or on Holy-day-eues. But now, by reason of the sicknesse, the perpetuitie of ringing has made him deuise a roome, with double walles, and treble seelings; the windores close shut, and calk'd: and there he liues by Candle-light.[2]

Not everyone had Morose's reaction: legend has it that Princess Elizabeth (later Queen Elizabeth I) found the bells of All Hallows Staining a comfort during her imprisonment in the Tower of London and donated new bell ropes to the church.

Bells marked the passage of time, day and night. Diarist Samuel Pepys writes (16 January 1660), ". . . I sat up till the bell-man came by with his bell, just under my window as I was writing of this very line, and cried, 'Past one of the clock, and a cold, frosty, windy morning.' I then went to bed and left my wife and the maid a-washing still." Bells signaled the beginning of services. John Donne's famous devotion reminds us, "As therefore the *Bell* that rings to a *Sermon*, calls not upon the *Preacher* onely, but vpon the *Congregation* to come; so this *Bell* calls vs all."[3] They recorded moments of civic celebration or alarm, the arrival of personages, or the birth of an heir to the throne. As Donne explains, "Who bends not his *eare* to any *bell*, which vpon any occasion rings?" And, of course, they tolled the death knell.

Church bells had characteristic sounds that helped demarcate the geography of a parish. One definition of a cockney is someone born within the range of the Bow bell, the bells of St. Mary-le-Bow. Donne would leave a legacy in his will for the upkeep of these bells.

England developed a distinctive form of bell-ringing known as change ringing, in which all of the bells in a peal or tuned set would be rung to an ever-changing pattern ("ringing changes").[4] The sounds of change ringing became so pervasive that they found their way into many compositions, including William Stonard's four-voice catch, "Ding dong ding dong bell." The narrator of this mock lament (death has "stopt the breath of him I lov'd so well") asks for order so that "we may ring his Knell." He also seems to describe the practice of ringing a handbell, known as the lich-bell, before the corpse in a funeral procession: "Hark, hark, I hear the Belman near, I hear the bell come ringing; go Belman on before, and stand at the dore, for now the Corse is bringing; make ready all anon, that we may be gone, for all the Bells are ringing, Ding, dong."[5]

• criticize/rebuke/punish somebody severely

1. Thomas Ravenscroft (ca. 1590–ca. 1635)
Deuteromelia: or the seconde part of musicks melodie, or melodius musicke. Of pleasant roundelaies; K. H. mirth, or freemens songs. And such delightful catches
London: [T. Snodham] for Thomas Adams, 1609
Folger STC 20757 c. 2
Sig. D1: "The great bels of Oesney"

Composer and theorist Thomas Ravenscroft captured the sounds of everyday life in his three collections of songs and catches, *Pammelia*, *Deuteromelia*, and *Melismata*.[6] Ross Duffin argues that the "K. H." of the title page is the King's Head Tavern near Guildhall and that the "freemens songs" were sung by London's free men, members of guilds and companies. Ravenscroft had been deeply involved with the London theater as one of the boy actors of St. Paul's. His three-voice round reflects the sounds of bells, in this case from the Augustinian abbey in Oseney, west of Oxford. The abbey was dissolved in 1539, and in 1546 its large bell went to Christ Church where it is preserved in Tom Tower. Great Tom was recast in 1626, an event which Richard Corbett (1582–1635), dean and later bishop, memorialized in a poem that celebrates the bell's new life as well as its past:

> Rejoyce with Christ Church, looke higher, Oseny,
> Of Gyante belles the famous treasury.
> . . .
> Nere greive, old Oseny, at thy heavy fall.
> Thy reliques build thee up againe. They all
> Florish to thy glory; Their sole fame
> When thou are not will keepe great Osenys name.
> This Tom was infant of thy mightie steeple:
> Yet hee is Lord controuler of a people.[7]

Ravenscroft's round keeps the Oseney name alive as well, recording a sound that hadn't been heard for half a century.

2. Samuel Chidley (1616–in or after 1672)
Bells founder confounded, or Sabinianus confuted: with his damnable sect. Written by a lover of musick, especially in churches
[London, 1659?]
Folger C3834b
Sig. A3

Samuel Chidley was a Leveller and radical protestant separatist who believed in iconoclasm, the destruction of everything that could be considered "papist," including "the Popish bells." His capsule history of religion in England (p. 2) castigates monarchs from Henry VIII to the late king (Charles I) for leaving "monuments of idolatry" undestroyed.[8]

3. David Melvill (fl. 1600–1612)
Ane buik off roundells whairin thair is conteined songs and roundells that may be sung with thrie four fyue or mo uoices haifing prettie and plesante letters sum in latin and sum in Inglish quhilks ar an hundreth in number collected and notted by david melvill, 1612
M1490 .M535 A5 Case
Music Division, Library of Congress, Washington, D.C.
P. 100: "Jak boy ho boy newis"

In *The Taming of the Shrew* (4.1), Grumio asks, "Why, 'Jack boy, ho boy!' and as much news as wilt thou." This four-voice round, found in Melvill's book of rounds and two earlier sources, refers to

person/store that sells stationery

the jack, the mechanical figure that strikes the bell in a clock. The bell in this four-voice round ("roundell") sounds both the news and the death knell for the unfortunate cat: "Jak boy ho boy newis/ The cat is in ye vall [well]/ Let ws ring now for hir knell/ Ding dong, ding dong bell." The little-known collector of these pieces and scribe of the manuscript may be the elder brother of Church of Scotland minister James Melville (1556–1614).[9]

4. Angelo Rocca (1545–1620)
De campanis commentarius a Fr. Angelo. Roccha Episcopo. Tagastensi, et Apostolici Sacrarij Praefecto elucubratus, ad. sanctam. ecclesiam catholicam directvs
Rome: Guglielmo Facciotti, 1612
Folger Acc. 158588
Plate after sig. A4

Large tower bells such as the one illustrated by Angelo Rocca ("campana a XXIIII hominibus pulsata") are traditionally associated with timekeeping and the calling of people to services. Within monastic communities, like the one that Rocca entered at the age of seven, bells sounded the canonical hours, the prescribed times throughout the day and night when the monks assembled for prayer. It was largely in response to the needs of monasteries that mechanical timekeepers came into being in the late thirteenth century. The word "clock" was derived from the French *cloche* or German *glock*, meaning bell, and the earliest tower clocks sounded the hours but had no faces or hands.

The bell Rocca illustrates is one of those in the Cathedral Church of Saint Lambert in Liège, where there are twelve small bells to strike the hours and eight larger ones. Maximum striking of the large bells requires twenty-four men, twelve pulling the ropes of half the bells from one side while twelve pull the ropes of the remaining bells from the opposite side.
(Rachel Doggett)

5. Fabian Stedman (1640–1713)
Campanalogia: or, the art of ringing improved. With plain and easie rules to guide the practitioner in the ringing all kinds of changes. To which is added, great variety of new peals
London: W. Godbid for W. S., 1677
Folger S5374
Sig. D7: "Peals upon five Bells," Grandsire 1 and 5

Fabian Stedman was a stationer and member, and later steward and master, of the Society of College Youths, a bell-ringing society. He seems to have collaborated with Richard Duckworth in the publication of *Tintinnalogia* (1668), the first treatise devoted to change ringing. His *Campanalogia* (the preface is signed "F. S.") shows the considerable advances in the art (and mathematics) of change ringing taking place during the seventeenth century.

Change ringing is a method of ringing bells in rows, in which the order of bells changes from row to row; there are rules governing the changes (for example, each bell can sound only once in each row and can move only one position at a time). Grandsire is one of the earliest methods devised for ringing an odd number of bells; "double" refers to a peal or tuned set of five bells. The numbers are a system of notation to show the changes; they refer to the bells (1 is the treble or smallest bell).[10]

• a parish officer dealing with petty offenders

6. Thomas Dekker (ca. 1572–1632)
The belman of London. Bringing to light the most notorious villanies that are now practised in the kingdome. Profitable for gentlemen, lawyers, merchants, cittizens, farmers, masters of housholdes, and all sorts of seruants to mark, and delightfull for all men to reade
London: [E. Allde] for Nathaniell Butter, 1608
Folger STC 6482
Title page

Equipped with bell, lantern, long staff, and dog, the bellman illustrated on the title page of Thomas Dekker's popular pamphlet would be a familiar character in most English towns. He was the town crier, a beadle, and the "*Centinell* of the Cittie, the watchman for everie ward. . . ." As he made his rounds, the bellman would ring at intervals, announcing the hour and confirming all was at peace. When Dekker asks "why with such a jangling and balling, and beating at Mens doores, he went about to waken either poore men that were over-wearied with labour, or sick men that had most need of rest," the bellman explains that his late-night ringing doesn't disturb citizens. Instead, it is "musiqu[e] to charme them faster with sleepe," blending into the other night sounds of a city at rest.
(Leigh Anne Palmer)

7. Claes Jansz Visscher (1586/7–1652)
Londinum florentissima Britanniae urbs, emporiumque toto orbe celeberrimus
[ca. 1625]
Folger GA795.L6 V5 1625 Cage

This view of London by Dutch engraver Claes Visscher was originally printed in 1616. Taken from the south bank of the Thames, where the Globe and other theaters are situated, it looks northward, showing many of the dozens of church steeples inside the city walls. Each had its own distinctive bell sounds: Bow Church, St. Lawrence Pultney, St. Dunstan in the East, and St. Paul's Cathedral, destroyed by the Great Fire of London in 1666. The heads of those who were executed are displayed at the entrance to the London Bridge.
(Georgianna Ziegler)

Detail, cat. 7.

Lawne as white as driven Snow, Cypresse black as ere was Crow, Gloves as
Sweet as damaske Roses, Maskes for faces & for Noses, Bugle Bracelets
Necklace Amber, perfumes for a Ladye's Chamber, Gold Coyfes & Stoma=
=chers for my Ladds, for: //: to give their Deere's Pins & Potinge sticks
pins: //: & potinge sticks of steele what maydes lack what: //:

Cat. 9.

a very typical example

"Songs for man, or woman, of all sizes": Street Music

Imagine a world where life's necessities were to be found hawked on the streets by vendors. We have just a taste of that today with people selling newspapers to drivers stopped at a red light or scalpers trying to sell tickets before a big game. But imagine if that were the distinctive sound of city life? Autolycus from *The Winter's Tale* is the archetypal vendor. He sings:

Lawn as white as driven snow,
Cypress black as e're was crow,
Gloves as sweet as damask roses,
Masks for faces and for noses,
Bugle bracelet, necklace amber,
Perfume for a lady's chamber,
Golden quoifs and stomachers
For my lads to give their dears,
Pins and poking-stickes of steel,
What maids lack from head to heel,
Come buy of me, come. Come buy, come buy.
Buy, lads, or else your lasses cry.
Come buy.
(*Winter's Tale* 4.4.254–66)

While no known setting of this song dates back to Shakespeare's day, a setting by John Wilson (1595–1674) survives, published in his *Cheerfull Ayres or Ballads* (Oxford, 1660 [1659]; see cat. 9 for a manuscript copy).

The sounds of the cries are captured in musical compositions by Ravenscroft, Gibbons, Dering, and others.[11] And the images of the criers became a genre in their own right. Typically the vendor is represented by the object being sold—as in John Savage's engraving of a ballad seller, "A Merry New Song," first published in 1668 in Marcellus Laroon's *The Cryes of the City of London.*[12]

8. Thomas Ravenscroft (ca. 1590–ca. 1635)
Melismata. Musicall phansies fitting the covrt, citie, and covntrey hvmovrs. To 3, 4, and 5. voyces
London: William Stansby for Thomas Adams, 1611
M1690 .R25 c. 1
Music Division, Library of Congress, Washington, D.C.
Sig. D: "Broomes for old shooes"

What songs would have been heard in London's streets around the year 1600? This composition, "Broomes for old shooes," hints at that lost soundscape by assembling some of the "cries" that were sung daily in urban England. There are vendors calling out the items they have for sale—footwear, seafood, fresh fruit, straw. A tinker and a woodcutter volunteer their services. The night watchman urges citizens to secure their homes from theft and fire. Meter and rhyme are absent here, so we may be sure that this composition quotes real street cries, not poeticized ones. As for its music, it may hint at authentic melodies, but its real aim is different and more subtle. Notated as a single melody, it is in fact meant to be superimposed upon itself and sung as a "round" or canon for four voices. Thus Voice 2 starts singing the tune only at the point when Voice 1 reaches the words "New Oysters"; and so on, until all four voices are in play, creating a layered polyphony—or is it a cacophony?—of popular song. In real life, these street cries would have had to vie not only with one another, but also with songs emerging from the surrounding cityscape. The Elizabethan commentator John Case neatly depicts the scene for us: "manual labourers, and Mechanicall artificers of all sorts, keepe such a chaunting and singing in their shoppes, the Tailor on his bulk, the Shomaker at his last, the Mason at his wal, the shipboy at his oare, the Tinker at his pan, and the Tylor on the house top."[13] Clearly there was no shortage of song in the streets of early modern England.
(John Milsom)

9. J[ohn] W[ilson] (1595–1674)
A scrapbook of seventeenth-century Shakespearean songs, ca. 1675
Folger MS V.a.437
Fols. 1–5 (reconstructed as a single sheet): "Lawne as white as driven snow"

In *The Winter's Tale* 4.4, Autolycus sings this peddler's song. He is selling lawn (a kind of fine linen), cypress black (crepe), gloves, masks, a bugle-bracelet, an amber necklace, perfume, golden coifs, stomachers, pins, poking-sticks—"what maids lack from head to heel." This manuscript copy is a later setting of the text, first published in 1659/60; once a large sheet, it was cut up and pasted into the scrapbook. Wilson was associated with the King's Men between 1614 and 1629 and may be the Iacke Wilson mentioned in the First Folio.[14]

10. John Hilton (1599–1657), compiler
Catch that catch can: or a choice collection of catches, rounds, and canons: being three or foure parts in one. Collected and published by John Hilton Batchelor of Musick. The second edition corrected and enlarged by J. Playford
London: W. G. for John Benson and John Playford, 1658
Folger H2037

(See p. 10.) • (1512) a vigorous English dance traditionally performed by men wearing costumes/bells

Sig E2: Mr. Thomas Holmes, "Will you buy a new merry Book, or a doleful Ditty"

Thomas Holmes (1606–1638) was organist at Winchester Cathedral and then, from 1633, Gentleman of the Chapel Royal. A dozen of his catches have survived in mid-century prints. In this four-voice catch, a ballad seller hints at the contents of one of his ballads: "[H]e took her 'bout the middle so small, he threw her down, but that was not all . . . ," stops the story abruptly and urges, "therefore quickly come and buy, and read for your penny, come my hearts, 'tis as good a bargain as e're you had any. . . ."[15]

11. Marcellus Laroon (1653–1702)
The cryes of the City of London drawne after the life. In 74 copper plates
London: Henry Overton, 1711
Folger DA688.L2 Cage
No. 13: "A Merry new Song"

Representations of street criers evolved from individual broadsides filled with tiny figures in rows to publication of large individual portraits in book form. The brainchild of printseller Pierce Tempest, *The Cryes of the City of London* first appeared in 1687. This bestseller was expanded and reprinted many times until 1821. The 1711 edition was the first of the editions published by Henry Overton. The engraver was John Savage (fl. 1680), who was responsible also for cat. 80. Samuel Pepys owned a copy of this engraving; he cut off the title and added an identification: "Rog.r Teasdell & M.rs Parker–Ballad-Singer."[16]

12. Thomas Morley (1557–1602)
Madrigalls to fovre voyces newly pvblished by Thomas Morley. The first booke
London: Thomas Est, 1594
Folger STC 18127 c. 2
Tenor, no. XVIII: "Hoe who comes heere"

This madrigal by Thomas Morley vividly evokes one of the most celebrated entertainments of early modern England: the antics of a team of morris dancers. The scene takes place out of doors and begins typically with the dramatic entry of the all-male dancing team. Then, to the evident delight of the women in the audience, the main dance takes place to the noise of jingling bells on the dancers' legs, supported by the music of bagpipes and drums. Testosterone, energy, and the display of lithe dancing bodies (fueled by plenty of ale) made the morris dance a boisterous ritual, and it was enjoyed in pre-Puritan England by all ranks of society, from royalty and gentry down to commoner and beggar. Latterly condemned by churchmen as "ungodly," it was never wholly outlawed. Today there are still thriving teams of morris dancers in many of England's rural communities. Thomas Morley's madrigal, scored for four voices of roughly equal range, is notated in high clefs, as if meant for an ensemble of women singers. It can also be sung an octave lower by four men.
(John Milsom)

Io ſon quel Geminian caldaroſtaro
Che voglio 'l nome mio ſar noto al mondo.
E perche nel gridar, non trouo paro,
Con mia voce conquaſſo à Pluto il fondo.
Superioꝝ licentia.
Meſſer Gioanni Orlando mio galante,
Ornato di uertù degna e pregiata,
A uoi ſol dono queſto bel ſembiante.
F. Villamena F.
O fuſto ben compito, a me ſi caro
Ritratto ſol per farmi piu giocondo.
Ch' eſſendo hoggi da molti riguardato,
Mi glorio ſol del mio felice ſtato.
Cum Priuilegio.

Cat. 13.

13. Francesco Villamena (ca. 1566–1624)
Engraving: "Io son quel Geminian caldarostaro"
[Italy, ca. 1600]
Folger ART 259532

It would be hard to imagine a picture that more clearly evokes the sound of a street crier bawling out his message than Francesco Villamena's roast chestnut seller. Flinging one arm back, he contorts his face, throws his body forward, and bellows at the top of his lungs. In the poem below, the chestnut seller claims his cry is unmatched, since his voice can shake Pluto in the depths of the underworld. The roiling clouds above show that he can also disturb the heavens.

Villamena engraved five other images for his series of street criers, but this one more than the others portrays the cry itself. If it were not for the fact that the poem below identifies the figure as Geminiano the roast chestnut seller ("Geminian caldar[r]ostaro") the man's trade would be unknown. We do not see a brazier. The contents of the bucket are hidden from us. His cavernous mouth, however, is unavoidable.

Although the street vendor is a lowly subject and Geminiano's facial expression can only be called grotesque, there is nothing clumsy about Villamena's bold, sweeping engraved lines. It is a tour de force of the Mannerist style. He gives a humorous subject the graphic weight of a god or hero. Like the engraving of the ballad singers (cat. 11), a copy of this engraving was in Samuel Pepys's collection.
(Erin Blake)

AN
ANTIDOTE
AGAINST
MELANCHOLY:
Made up in PILLS.
Compounded of *Witty Ballads*, *Jovial Songs*, and *Merry Catches*.

These witty Poems though sometime may seem to halt on crutches,
Yet they'l all merrily please you for your charge, which not much is.

Printed by *Mer. Melancholicus*, to be sold in *London* and *Westminster* 1661.

Cat. 14.

"*Fidlers*, who are properly call'd a *Noise*": Tavern Sounds

"A Tavern is an Academy of Debauchery, where the Devil teaches the seven deadly sins instead of Sciences, a Tipling-School a degree above an Ale-house," writes John Earle in *The Character of a Tavern* (London, 1675). And in this place "'Tis a Bedlam of Wits, where men are rather *mad* than *merry* . . . there another repeating scraps of old Plays, or some Bawdy Song, this speaking *Latine*, and a fourth *Nonsence*, whilst all with loud hooting and laughing confound the noise of *Fidlers*, who are properly call'd a *Noise*, for no Musick can be heard for them."[17] Earle is scathing in his sketch of a fiddler: "A new song is better to him then a new Jacket; especially if bawdy, which he calls merry: & he hates naturally the *Puritan*, as an enemy to his mirth."[18] Fiddlers are universally reviled—street musicians considered vagabonds or beggars.[19] Stephen Gosson, defending his *Schoole of Abuse* (cat. 76), complained, "London is so full of unprofitable Pipers and Fidlers, that a man can no soner enter a taverne, but two or three caste of them hang at his heeles, to giue him a daunce before he departe; therefore let men of grauities examine the case, & iudge uprightly, whether the sufferance of such idle beggars be not a greeuous abuse in a common wealth."[20]

Pepys names over one hundred taverns in his diaries, and his visits not infrequently included music. On 27 March 1661 he went to his favorite tavern, the Dolphin, with friends, "And in our mirth, I sang and sometimes fiddled (there being a noise of fiddlers there) and at last we fell to dancing."

• any of several white wines imported to England/Canary Islands during the 16th/17th centuries
• one who draws/paints on a surface; who outlines in sharp detail \lim\ lim-(n)er

14. N. D.
An antidote against melancholy: made up in pills. Compounded of witty ballads, jovial songs, and merry catches
[London]: Mer. Melancholicus, 1661
Folger D66a
Title page

This collection, with words only and no music, contains ballads, songs, and catches—typical pub fare. The engraving on the title page is a later state of the title page by William Marshall (fl. 1617–1650) for Richard Braithwaite's 1617 *A Solemne Joviall Disputation . . . Briefly Shadowing the Law of Drinking*. The two scenes juxtapose upper and lower classes. In the upper, Apollo dispenses "nectar ut Ingenium" to five gentlemen; they are drinking and smoking at an inn whose sign reads "Poets Impalled w^{t} Laurell Coranets." In the lower scene, in a tavern signed with a "Rose" and identified in the earlier state as "Puddlewharf," a bagpiper is providing music for dancing. The two fiddlers placed between the scenes have been added to this version of the engraving.[21]

15. John Hilton (1599–1657), compiler
Catch that catch can: or the musical companion. Containing catches and rounds for three and four voyces. To which is now added a second book containing dialogues, glees, ayres, & ballads, &c. Some for two three foure voyces
London: W. Godbid for J. Playford, 1667
Folger H2039 c. 1
Sig E2: Dr. William Child, "If any so wise is that Sack he despises"

This catch, a drinking song that extols the virtue of sack, was composed by Dr. William Child (1606/7–1697), organist at St. George's Chapel, Windsor, before and after the Interregnum, and after the Restoration a member of the Chapel Royal. Known as a composer of anthems and services, Child appears frequently in Pepys's diaries as a dinner companion, an occasional partner in informal music sessions, and someone who could harmonize an unfigured bass, something apparently beyond Pepys's ability. The gist of this song is that only sack will cure a hangover: "But be sure overnight if this Dog do you bite, you take it henceforth for a warning, soon as out of your bed, to settle your head, take a hair of his tail in the morning." On 3 April 1661, Pepys actually took this advice, which we, to this day, call hair of the dog.

16. Stephen Batman (ca. 1542–1584)
A christall glasse of christian reformation, wherein the godly maye beholde the coloured abuses vsed in this our present tyme. Collected by Stephen Bateman Minister
London: Iohn Day, 1569
Folger STC 1581 bd. w. STC 1585 c. 2
Sig. E3

Batman, a clergyman and chaplain to Archbishop Matthew Parker for whom he collected nearly seven thousand books, is best known as the translator of Bartholomaeus Anglicus's thirteenth-century encyclopedia, *Batman uppon Bartholome*. Trained as a limner, he makes good use of images in his writing, as shown in this exposition of vice and virtue. It is not surprising that this account of gluttony would be situated in a tavern.

· énflame with love
· tears (archaic)
· paper cut four from a sheet

17. Thomas Ravenscroft (ca. 1590–ca. 1635)
A briefe discovrse of the true (but neglected) vse of charact'ring the degrees by their perfection, imperfection, and diminution in measurable musicke, against the common practise and custome of these times. Examples whereof are exprest in the harmony of 4. voyces, concerning the pleasure of 5. vsuall recreations. 1 Hunting, 2 hawking, 3 dauncing, 4 drinking, 5 enamouring. By Thomas Rauenscroft, Bachelor of Musicke
London: Edw: Allde for Tho. Adams, 1614
Folger STC 20756
Sig. E, no. 12: "Tobacco fumes away all nastie rheumes"

Ravenscroft, described in a dedicatory poem as twenty-two years old, dedicated this volume to the Senators of Gresham College, London, where he had attended lectures on music. The first half, "The Discourse," consists of a short treatise (just twenty-two pages —four sheets in quarto format) concerning the proper notation of rhythm, based on older Continental practices. The second, "The Harmonies," consists of compositions by Ravenscroft and others organized into common "Recreations." This tribute to the virtues of tobacco comes in the section on drinking.

18. Humphrey Mill (fl. 1639–1646)
A nights search· discovering the nature and condition of all sorts of night-walkers; with their associates. As also, the life and death of many of them. Together with divers fearfull and strange accidents, occasioned by such ill livers. Digested into a poeme by Humphry Mill
London: Richard Bishop for Laurence Blaicklock, 1640
Folger STC 17921 c. 1
Sig. Q5, sect. 43

Poet and godly reformer Humphrey Mill, functioning as a "rhyming constable" cataloguing London's underworld, produced a text that could later be recommended by fictional whores as a sort of guidebook.[22] James Turner describes it as "part pornographic jest and part vigilante patrol-work." In this sketch of a tavern, a fiddler who has earned nothing on the day ("For want of custome he alone did play/ The lamentable tune of *Welladay!*") turns up at a tavern at night to give a music lesson "having tun'd his Viall." Mill, in characterizing the fiddler, represents the common view that fiddlers were low lifes:

> Thou art no Begger, but thou do'st invade,
> And trench most grosly on the beggers trade.
> Crowd, crowd away, let us thy absence borrow:
> Then thou maist play to night, and beg to morrow.

19. Thomas Wharton (1648–1715)
A new song
[London, 1688–89]
Folger W1577A
"Ho Brother Teague dost hear de Decree"

Politician Thomas Wharton claimed authorship of this ballad text, written in the dialect of an Irish Catholic peasant who is thrilled with James II's appointment of the Catholic Richard Talbot (1630–1691), the first earl of Tyrconnell, as Lord

Deputy of Ireland in 1688. The virulently anti-Catholic text, quoted here, reflects the fears of Anglo-Irishmen:

Ho! Brother *Teague* dost hear de Decree,
Lil – li Burlero Bellen a – la,
Dat we shall have a new Debittie,
Lil - li Bur-le – re Bullen a – la,
Le-ro, Le-ro, Le-ro Le-ro,
Lil-li Bur-le-ro, Bullen a la,
Le – ro, Le – ro, Le – ro, Le – ro,
Lil – li Burlero Bellen a la.

Ho by my Shoul it is a T—t [Talbot], . . .
And he will Cut all de *English* Troat, ...

Though by my shoul de *Inglish* do Prat, . . .
De Law's on Dare side, and *Chreist* knows what, ...

But if Dispence do Come from de Pope, . . .
Weel hang *Magno Carto* & demselves in a Rope, ...

And the good T—t is made a Lord, . . .
And he with brave Lads is coming aboard, ...

Who'! all in *France* have taken a swear, . . .
Dat day will have no Protestant h—r [heir] . . . .

O but why does he stay behind, . . .
Ho by my shoul 'tis a Protestant wind, . . .

Now T—l [Tyrconnell] is come a-shore, . . .
And we shall have Commissons gillore, ...

And he dat will not go to M—ss [Mass], . . .
Shall turn out and look like an Ass, ...

Now now de Hereticks all go down, . . .
By *Chreist* and *St. Patrick* the Nation's our own, ...[23]

Printed anonymously and with no date or publisher, this ballad is clearly seditious. Wharton would later claim that it helped drive James II from the throne.

This is a rare example of a ballad with the actual music rather than the customary reference to a particular tune. The tune, known by the pseudo-Irish refrain "Lilli burlero," became exceedingly popular, and is still used as a signature tune by the BBC.[24]

20. *The country lawyers maid Joan, containing her languishing lamentation for want of a man, which at length she met with, being her masters man Mark. Tune of Turn Coat of the Times. Licensed according to Order*
[London]: for P[hilip]. Brooksby, J[onah]. Deacon, J[osiah]. Blare, and J[ohn]. Back, [ca. 1688–1692]
Folger Acc. 249840

This ballad is about a country lawyer's maid who succeeds in putting an end to her complaint—"The Grief I sustain, for want of a Man,/ There's no body knows but I"—thanks to lusty Mark, a country lawyer's clerk. He "tickl'd her in the dark;/ he litt on the very Vein,/ The place of her grief and pain,/ And caus'd her to laugh amain." The tune appears as early as 1658.

21. *The cloath-worker caught in a trap: or, a fool and his mony soon parted. Being a true relation of a cloath-worker, dwelling in Thames-street, who was wished by an old woman to a maid near Pauls*

Church-yard, perswading him she had money at use, being a meer plot of the maiden and she to cheat him of his money, knowing him to be none of the wisest, cheated him of forty pound. . . . The tune is, How now Jocky whither away. Or The tyrant
London: for W. Thackeray, T. Passenger, and W. Whitwood, [between 1666 and 1679]
Folger Acc. 249839

This ballad, preserved in only a handful of copies, tells the story of a not very bright but venal "cloath-worker" tricked into giving forty pounds to his would-be young wife, who he thought had money of her own. The final stanza, "My couetous humour did meet with a cross;/ And I was rewarded with forty pound loss,/ A Prouerb to all men, lo here I will be,/ A Fool and his Money's soon parted we see," is an early instance of this proverb. Of the two tunes listed, "The tyrant" or "Now the tyrant hath stolen" is mentioned on over twenty ballads printed between 1650 and 1695.[25]

22. *The lamentable and tragicall history of Titus Andronicus, with the fall of his five and twenty sons in the wars of [t]he Goaths, with the ravishment of his daughter Lavinia by the empresse [t]wo sons, through the means of a bloody Moor, taken by the swor[d] of Titus in the war, with his revenge upon them for their cruell an in humane act. To the tune of Fortune my foe*
[London]: for F. Coles, T. Vere, and VV. Gilbertson, [1661]
Folger L252a

It is not certain which came first—the ballad known as "Titus Andronicus' Complaint" or Shakespeare's tragedy, first published in 1594. Ross Duffin argues that Shakespeare's double reference to "noble minds" in the first scene may indicate that he knew the ballad, which begins, "You noble minds."[26] The tune, "Fortune my foe," can be traced to ballads dating as early as the 1580s; it had a notable career in instrumental arrangements by such composers as William Byrd, John Dowland, and Thomas Tomkins. An early owner of Yonge's *Musica Transalpina* (cat. 73), Conyers D'Arcy, has scribbled the tune into the Folger copy.

23. *An excellent ballad, iutituled* [sic], *the constancy of Susanna, to an excellent new tune*
[London]: for F. Coles, J. Wright, T. Vere, W. Gilbertson, [1655?]
Folger E3782a bd. w. E3804h

Ross Duffin has found references to "There dwelt a man in Babylon," the first line of a *Constancy of Susanna* ballad, in *The Merry Wives of Windsor* (3.1), *The Merchant of Venice* (4.1) and *Twelfth Night* (2.3), sung by Sir Toby.[27] A ballad entitled "of the godly constant wife Susanna" was registered in 1562–1563, possibly surviving as a text in Folger MS V.a.438. This version, "There dwelt a man in Babylon," was first printed in ca. 1620. The "lady, lady" refrain suggests that it is to be sung to the tune for "King Solomon," found in two sixteenth-century English manuscripts.

· a brief comic show/entertainment

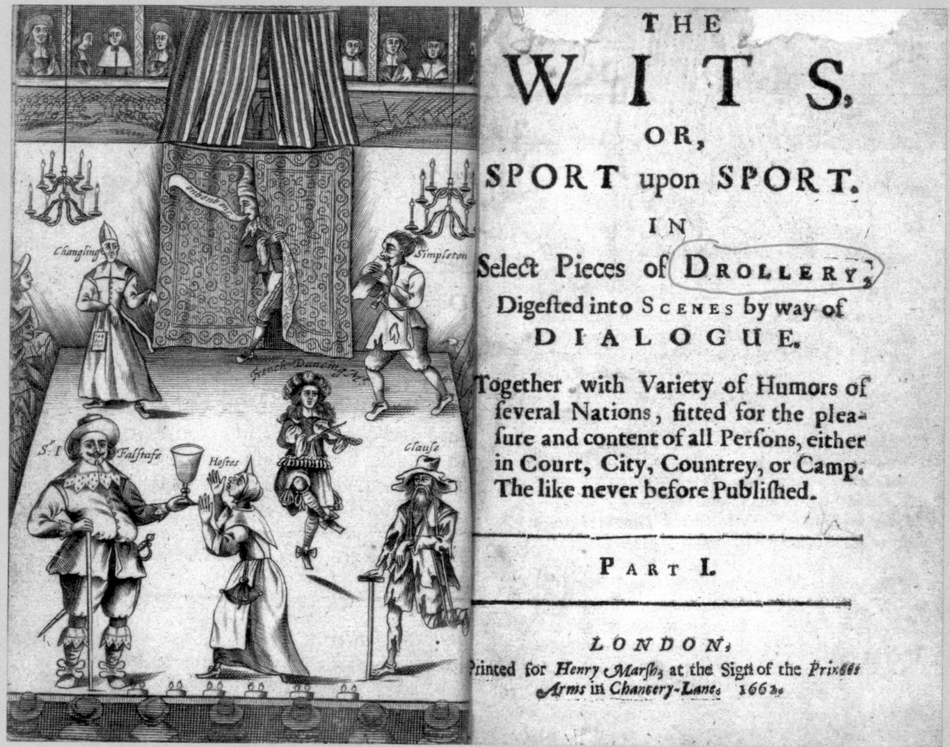

THE
WITS,
OR,
SPORT upon SPORT.
IN
Select Pieces of DROLLERY,
Digested into SCENES by way of
DIALOGUE.
Together with Variety of Humors of
several Nations, fitted for the plea-
sure and content of all Persons, either
in Court, City, Countrey, or Camp.
The like never before Published.

PART I.

LONDON,
Printed for *Henry Marsh*, at the Sign of the *Princes*
Arms in *Chancery-Lane*. 1662.

Cat. 27.

“Would you have a love song?”: Music on Stage

In *Twelfth Night* (2.3), Sir Toby and Sir Andrew join Feste, portrayed by Robert Armin, in a comic concert. Feste sings a love song, “O mistress mine, where are you roaming?” Then the three engage in a kind of drunken musical repartee, with catches and ballads galore—titles unfamiliar to us, but well-known to Shakespeare’s audience. The scene evoked is a tavern, as Malvolio complains:

> “My masters, are you mad? Or what are you? Have you no wit, manners, nor honesty but to gabble like tinkers at this time of night? Do you make an ale-house of my lady’s house, that you squeak out your coziers’ catches without any mitigation or remorse of voice?”

This scene captures some of the functions of music in English theater: interpolated songs, set pieces to evoke the role of music in the real world, instrumental interludes to help set or reflect the mood.[28] While much of the music for the Elizabethan stage has been lost, its existence is made clear through songs found in the texts or cues indicating performance. The survival of a rare musical sketch in the Folger copy of Fulwell’s *Like Wil to Like* (cat. 26) is thus a fortunate happenstance.

24. Robert Armin (1563–1615)
The history of the two maids of More-clacke, vvith the life and simple maner of Iohn in the hospitall. Played by the Children of the Kings Maiesties Reuels. VVritten by Robert Armin, seruant to the Kings most excellent Maiestie
London: N[icholas] O[kes] for Thomas Archer, 1609
Folger STC 773 c. 1
Title page

Robert Armin replaced Will Kemp as the clown in Shakespeare's company, the Lord Chamberlain's Men, in 1599 and played such roles as Feste in *Twelfth Night*, the Fool in *King Lear*, and possibly Autolycus in *The Winter's Tale.*[29] In *Twelfth Night* (2.3), he sings free-standing songs but also ballads and rounds, cued through first-line tags such as "There dwelt a man in Babylon" (cat. 23), the ballad about the constancy of Susanna.

25. Commonplace book, ca. 1600–ca. 1650
Folger MS V.a.399
Fol. 16v: "As you came fro[m] Walsingham"

This commonplace book preserves the text for an early version of the ballad "Walsingham": "As you came from Walsingham/ from that holy land,/ Met you not with my true love/ by the way as you came?" The second stanza, which begins "How should I your true love know," makes clear that Ophelia is alluding to this ballad in her song, "How should I your true love know" (*Hamlet* 4.5).[30]

26. Ulpian Fulwell (1545/6–by July 1586)
An enterlude intituled/ Like wil to like quod the Deuil to the colier, very godly & ful of pleasant mirth. Wherin is declared not onely what punishment foloweth those that wil rather folowe licentious liuing, then to esteem & folowe good councel: and what great benefits and commodities they receiue that apply them vnto vertuous liuing and good exercises. Made by Vlpian Fulwel. Fiue may easely play this enterlude
Lo[n]don: Iohn Allde, [after 1568?]
Folger STC 11473.2
Sig. F2v: Anonymous, textless three-voice composition (two phrases)

Andrew Sabol suggested that this manuscript addition to Fulwell's morality play could be the music for the song that concludes the drama, "Where like to like is matched so," sung by the characters Vertuous Life, Honour, and Good Fame.[31] The music is preserved only in this source, which is itself the only surviving exemplar of this edition. The music is something of a puzzle. It seems to be two versions of enough music to set two eight-syllable lines (four measures). The bass (staves 3 and 6) is the same in both, and staff 6 seems to be a clean version of the music at the beginning of staff 3. The upper voices in the first version are in the treble and contratenor range. In the second version, they are notated for contratenor and tenor. The crudeness of the writing and the existence of two versions may suggest that this is a composer's draft.

Cat. 26.

27. Henry Marsh (fl. 1663–1664), compiler
The wits, or, sport upon sport. In select pieces of drollery, digested into scenes by way of dialogue. Together with variety of humors of several nations, fitted for the pleasure and content of all persons, either in court, city, countrey, or camp. The like never before published. Part I
London: for Henry Marsh, 1662
Folger W3218
Frontispiece and title page

Drolls are short comic scenes, frequently excerpted from plays, that were performed in makeshift settings during the Commonwealth when theater was prohibited. The bookseller Henry Marsh compiled this collection of drollery and published it after the Restoration. The frontispiece offers a valuable glimpse of a mid-seventeenth-century indoor stage, though it may not represent one specific theater.[32] The stage is populated with characters from several drolls, including the French dancing master with a violin, and Sir John Falstaff. Above the stage, the striped curtains cover a place that could be used as the musicians' gallery. This is the first illustration to show an English stage lit by chandeliers and candles in front.

28. Thomas Morley (1557–1602)
The first booke of ayres. Or little short songs, to sing and play to the lute, with the base viole. Newly published by Thomas Morley Bachiler of Musicke, and one of the gent. of her Maiesties Royall Chappel
London: [H. Ballard for] VVilliam Barley, the assigne of Thomas Morley, 1600
Folger STC 18115.5
Sig. C, no. VI: "It was a louer and his lasse"

This is the only copy of Morley's *First Booke of Ayres* that has survived, and it is incomplete, lacking the final signatures. The music is printed in folio using "tablebook" layout that enables several musicians to sit around a table and sing from a single book. A singer reading the texted cantus part can be accompanied by a lutenist reading from tablature. A third musician, playing the bass viol and sitting opposite them, can read the untexted bass line. It is unknown whether Morley composed this song for the play *As You Like It* (5.3) or whether Shakespeare included a song already in circulation.[33]

29. Miscellany of catches, glees, and rounds, ca. 1625
Folger MS V.a.409
Fol. 17: Anonymous, "What shall he haue that kill the deere"

Ross Duffin identified this manuscript as the earliest source for the four-voice round that closes *As You Like It* (4.2). A later version was published by John Hilton (1599–1657) in his 1652 *Catch that Catch Can* (cat. 47). The text of the song,

> What shall he haue that kill the deere
> his leather skin and hornes to weare
> [omitted: Then sing him home the rest shall beare this burthen]
> take thou noe scorne to weare the horne
> it was a crest 'fore thou wast borne
> thy fathers father wore it
> and thy father bore it
> the horne the horne, the lusty horne
> is not a thing to laugh to scorne.

omits line 3 from the First Folio, "Then sing him home the rest shall beare this burthen," that is in effect a performance direction, "an invitation by Jaques to join in the round."[34]

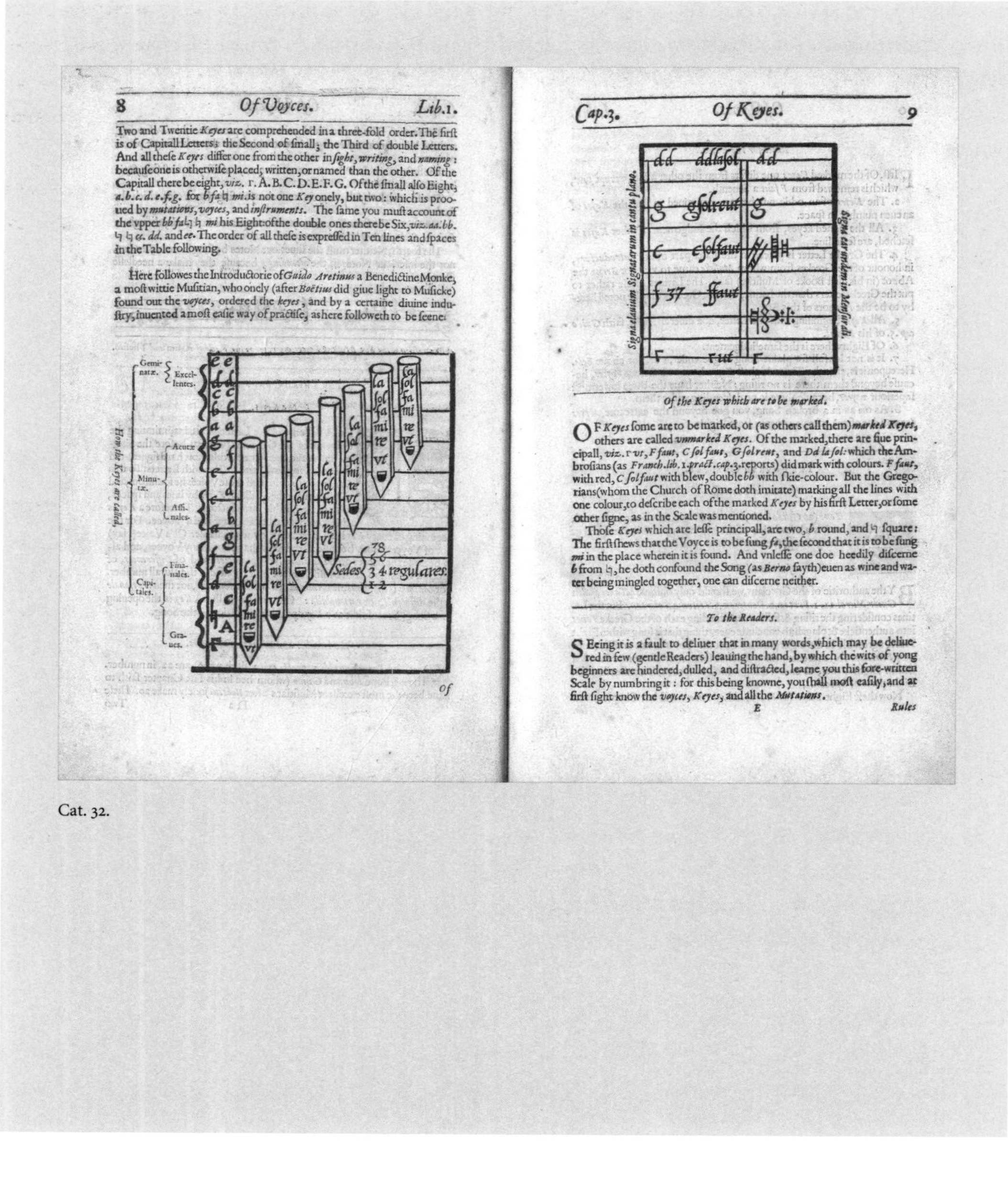

8 *Of Voyces.* *Lib.*1.

Two and Twentie *Keyes* are comprehended in a three-fold order. The first is of Capitall Letters; the Second of small; the Third of double Letters. And all these *Keyes* differ one from the other in *sight*, *writing*, and *naming*: because one is otherwise placed, written, or named than the other. Of the Capitall there be eight, *viz.* Γ. A. B. C. D. E. F. G. Of the small also Eight, *a. b. c. d. e. f. g.* for *b fa* ♮ *mi*. is not one *Key* onely, but two: which is prooued by *mutations*, *voyces*, and *instruments*. The same you must account of the vpper *bb fa* ♮ ♮ *mi* his Eight: of the double ones there be Six, *viz. aa. bb.* ♮ ♮ *cc. dd.* and *ee*. The order of all these is expressed in Ten lines and spaces in the Table following.

Here followes the Introductorie of *Guido Aretinus* a Benedictine Monke, a most wittie Musitian, who onely (after *Boëtius* did giue light to Musicke) found out the *voyces*, ordered the *keyes*, and by a certaine diuine industry, inuented a most easie way of practise, as here followeth to be seene.

Of

*Cap.*3. *Of Keyes.* 9

Of the Keyes which are to be marked.

OF *Keyes* some are to be marked, or (as others call them) *marked Keyes*, others are called *vnmarked Keyes*. Of the marked, there are fiue principall, *viz.* Γ *vt*, *F faut*, *C sol faut*, *G sol reut*, and *Dd la sol*: which the Ambrosians (as *Franch. lib.* 1. *pract. cap.* 3. reports) did mark with colours. *F faut*, with red, *C sol faut* with blew, double *bb* with skie-colour. But the Gregorians (whom the Church of Rome doth imitate) marking all the lines with one colour, to describe each of the marked *Keyes* by his first Letter, or some other signe, as in the Scale was mentioned.

Those *Keyes* which are lesse principall, are two, *b* round, and ♮ square: The first shews that the Voyce is to be sung *fa*, the second that it is to be sung *mi* in the place wherein it is found. And vnlesse one doe heedily discerne *b* from ♮, he doth confound the Song (as *Berno* sayth) euen as wine and water being mingled together, one can discerne neither.

To the Readers.

SEeing it is a fault to deliuer that in many words, which may be deliuered in few (gentle Readers) leauing the hand, by which the wits of yong beginners are hindered, dulled, and distracted, learne you this fore-written Scale by numbring it: for this being knowne, you shall most easily, and at first sight know the *voyces*, *Keyes*, and all the *Mutations*.

E *Rules*

Cat. 32.

“To sing your part sure”: Music Education

Being able to read music at sight, to sing a part securely, and to play an instrument such as the lute, viol, or virginal were regarded as important goals of upper-class education.[35] Amateurs could learn music from manuals or textbooks that taught the rudiments of music, or they could study with musicians employed as tutors. One of the treasures of the Folger Shakespeare Library is a lutebook that records lessons given by John Dowland, England’s premier composer of lute songs and other music for the lute.

Instruction usually began with the gamut, the musical scale comprised of letters and solmization or solfa syllables; the name derives from the Greek letter gamma combined with the solmization syllable *ut*. Students were advised

> *To attaine the skill of Musicks Art,*
> *Learne* Gam-ut *up and down by heart,*
> *Thereby to learn your Rules and Spaces,*
> *Notes names are known knowing their places.*[36]

Several forms of the gamut exist: Thomas Morley and Ornithoparchus (as translated by Dowland) present Continental versions, while Charles Butler uses a version of the fixed four-note scheme common in England. The music lesson in *The Taming of the Shrew* (3.1) offers a humorous take on the gamut (“gamouth”).

> *Hortensio,* as *Litio:* Madam, before you touch the instrument,
> To learn the order of my fingering
> I must begin with rudiments of art,
> To teach you gamut in a briefer sort,
> More pleasant, pithy, and effectual
> Then hath been taught by any of my trade.
> And there it is in writing fairly drawn.
> *Bianca:* Why, I am past my gamut long ago.
> *Hortensio:* Yet read the gamut of Hortentio.
> *[Giving her a paper.]*

• (14c) loosel styled/irregular in measure esp. for burlesque/comic effect; also: marked by triviality/inferiority

Bianca reads

"*Gamut* I am, the ground of all accord:
A re, to plead Hortensio's passion;
B mi, Bianca take him for thy lord,
C fa ut, that loves with all affection;
D sol re, one clef, two notes have I;
E la mi, show pity or I die."
Call you this "gamut"? Tut, I like it not,
Old fashions please me best. I am not so nice
To change true rules for odd inventions.

30. John Playford (1623–1686/7)
An introduction to the skill of musick, in three books. The first contains the grounds and rules of musick, according to the gam-ut, and other principles thereof. The second, instructions and lessons both for the bass-viol and treble-violin. The third, the art of descant, or composing of musick in parts, in a more plain and easie method than any heretofore published. By John Playford. The eleventh edition, corrected and enlarged
London: Charles Peregrine for Henry Playford, 1687
Private collection
Sig. E8: metrical psalm tunes with manuscript solfa syllables

Many of the surviving copies of the numerous editions of Playford's popular *Introduction to the Skill of Musick* show signs of heavy use. In this one, a reader has written in solfa syllables using the prevailing English four-note system, familiar to Americans through shape-note hymnody. *Ut* and *re* are dispensed with, leaving *mi fa sol la*. The signature determined where the *mi* would be placed. In Psalm 113 the *mi* is on B, while in the other three psalms (with a flat in the signature) it is on E. Playford and many other writers use doggerel verse to teach the placement of *mi*.

31. Thomas Morley (1557–1602)
A plaine and easie introdvction to practicall mvsicke, set downe in forme of a dialogue: deuided into three partes, the first teacheth to sing with all things necessary for the knowledge of pricktsong. The second treateth of descante and to sing two parts in one vpon a plainsong or ground, with other things necessary for a descanter. The third and last part entreateth of

* Why and how did he come to know German well enough to translate?
• one of encyclopedic learning \päl-i-math\ poly + manthanein to learn

composition of three, foure, fiue or more parts with many profitable rules to that effect. With new songs of, 2. 3. 4. and .5 parts. By Thomas Morley, Batcheler of musick, & one of the gent. of hir Maiesties Royall Chappell
London: Peter Short, 1597
Stationer's Register: Entered to P. Short and W. Hoskins 9 October 1596
Folger STC 18133 c. 2
Sig. B3

Thomas Morley was organist at St. Paul's, Gentleman of the Chapel Royal from 1592 until his death, and from 1598 holder of the patent for publishing music. He dedicated his music textbook to his teacher William Byrd. *A Plaine and Easie Introduction* has long been regarded as the most important English treatise on music, no doubt because of its imposing appearance. In this opening, Morley shows the "Scale of Musicke" or "Gam" (gamut), a combination of letter-names for the pitches (for example, F), with solmization syllables (for example, *fa ut*), keyed to the musical staff (the lines and spaces) through clefs (for example, the bass clef). His use of italics in this passage may indicate that he is quoting another text.

32. Andreas Ornithoparchus (ca. 1490–after 1518)
John Dowland (1562–1626), translator
Andreas Ornithoparcvs his micrologvs, or introduction: containing the art of singing. Digested into foure bookes. Not onely profitable, bvt also necessary for all that are studious of musicke. Also the dimension and perfect vse of the monochord, according to Guido Aretinus. By Iohn Dovland lvtenist, lute-player, and Bachelor of Musicke in both the uniuersities
London: [Thomas Snodham] for Thomas Adams, 1609
Stationer's Register: Entered 20 January [1609]
Folger STC 18853
Sig. E

Why lutenist and composer John Dowland should have chosen to translate a German music textbook * first published nearly a century earlier (1517) is not known. Dedicated to Robert Cecil, first earl of Salisbury, it contains material that had little practical use in early seventeenth-century England. Ornithoparchus's version of the gamut, faithfully reproduced by Dowland, probably from one of the editions published in Cologne between 1524 and 1540, represents the seven hexachords (each one consisting of six syllables: *ut re mi fa sol la*) as organ pipes. The ten-line staff, showing the clefs used in chant (*cantu plano*) and polyphony (*mensurabili*), was the standard way for students to learn to compose.

33. Charles Butler (1560–1647)
The principles of musik, in singing and setting: vvith the two-fold use therof, [ecclesiasticall and civil.] By Charles Butler Magd. Master of Arts
London: Iohn Haviland for the author, 1636
Folger STC 4196 c. 1
Sig. C1v-C2r

Charles Butler was a schoolteacher and then, from 1600 until his death, vicar at Wootton St. Lawrence (near Basingstoke). A polymath, he discovered the matriarchal organization of bee colonies, published treatises on rhetoric and grammar, and

• the art of writing words with the proper letters according to standard usage; the representation of the sounds of a language by symbols

130 created an original system of orthography. His music treatise, often dismissed today because of its unorthodox spelling, was highly praised by Roger North; it offers an important explanation of the concept of "key." Butler devised a seven-note solmization system, introducing a newly invented seventh syllable, *pha*, and using *mi* to explain the placement of flats in the key signature.

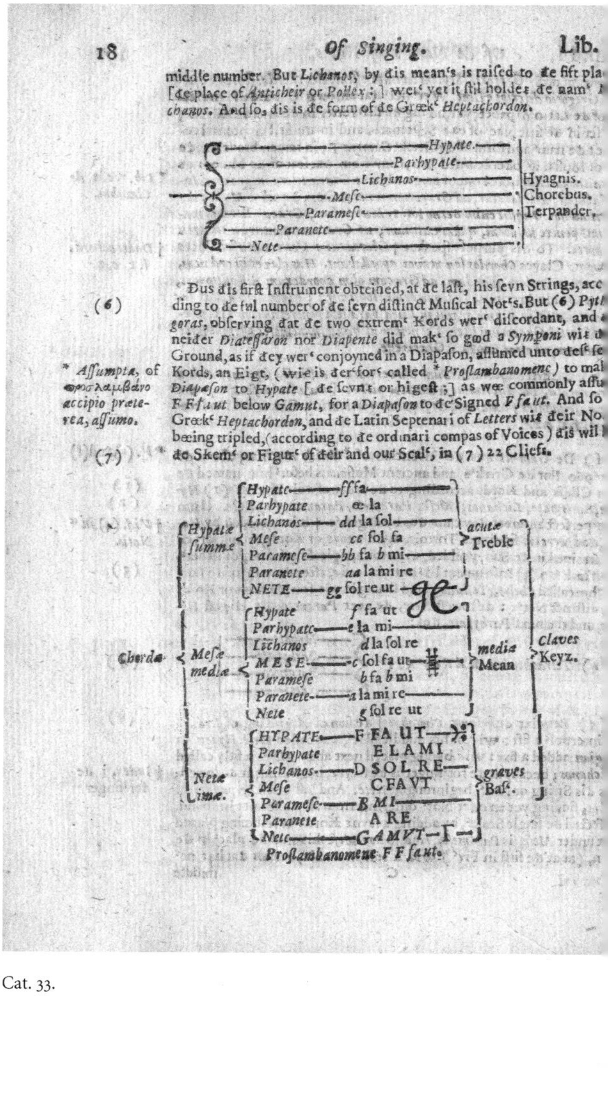
18 Of Singing. Lib.

middle number. But *Lichanos*, by đis mean's is raised to đe fift pla [đe place of *Anticheir* or *Pollex*;] wer' yet it stil holdeđ đe nam' *Lichanos*. And so, đis is đe form of đe Greek' *Heptachordon*.

(6) Đus đis first Instrument obteined, at đe last, his sevn Strings, acc ding to đe ful number of đe sevn distinct Musical Not's. But (6) *Pyth goras*, observing đat đe two extrem' Kords wer' discordant, and neiđer *Diatessaron* nor *Diapente* did mak' so good a *Symphoni* wiđ đ Ground, as if đey wer' conjoyned in a Diapason, assumed unto đes' se Kords, an Eigt, (wiċ is đer'for' called * *Proslambanomene*) to mak *Diapason* to *Hypate* [đe sevnt or higest;] as wee commonly assu F F fa ut below *Gamut*, for a *Diapason* to đe Signed *F fa ut*. And so Greek' *Heptachordon*, and đe Latin Septenari of *Letters* wiđ đeir No being tripled, (according to đe ordinari compas of Voices) đis wil đe Skem' or Figur' of đeir and our Scal', in (7) 22 Cliefs.

* *Assumpta*, of προσλαμβάνω accipio præterea, assumo.

Cat. 33.

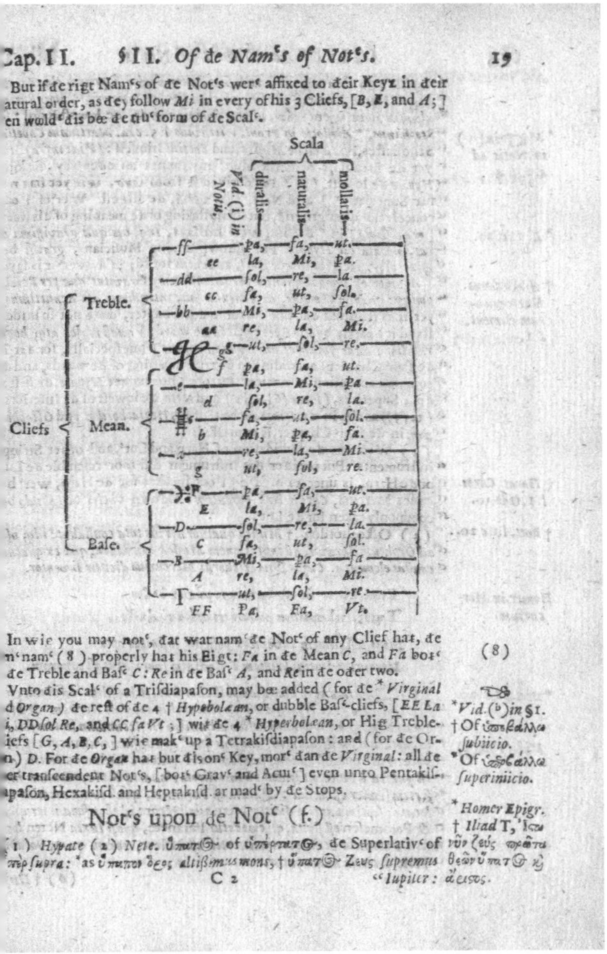
Cap. II. §II. *Of de Nam's of Not's.* 19

But if de rigt Nam's of de Not's wer' affixed to deir Keyz in deir atural order, as dey follow *Mi* in every of his 3 Cliefs, [*B*, *E*, and *A*;] en would' dis bee de tru' form of de Scal'.

In wic you may not', dat wat nam' de Not' of any Clief hat, de n' nam' (8) properly hat his Eigt: *Fa* in de Mean *C*, and *Fa* bot' de Treble and Bas' *C*: *Re* in de Bas' *A*, and *Re* in de oder two. (8)

Vnto dis Scal' of a Trisdiapason, may bee added (for de * *Virginal* d *Organ*) de rest of de 4 † *Hypobolean*, or dubble Bas'-cliefs, [*EE La i*, *DD sol Re*, and *CC fa Vt*;] wit de 4 * *Hyperbolean*, or Hig Treble-iefs [*G*, *A*, *B*, *C*,] wic mak' up a Tetrakisdiapason: and (for de Or-n.) *D*. For de *Organ* hat but dis on' Key, mor' dan de *Virginal*: all de er transcendent Not's, [bot' Grav' and Acut'] even unto Pentakis-apason, Hexakisd. and Heptakisd. ar mad' by de Stops.

*Vid. (b) in §1.

*Homer Epigr.

† Iliad T,

Not's upon de Not' (f.)

(1) *Hypate* (2) *Nete*. ... of ..., de Superlativ' of ... *supra*: * as ... *altissimus mons*, † ... Zeus *supremus* ... "*Iupiter*: ...

C 2

34. The "Dowland" lutebook (catalogued as "A commonplace book of songs and dances for the lute"), ca. 1600
Folger MS V.b.280
Fols. 22v–23r: John Dowland, "My Lady Hunsdons Allemande"; Dowland (arr.), "What if a day"

John Dowland (1562–1626) was the greatest English composer of his time for the lute, writing solos, songs, and music for five viols and lute. Folger MS V.b.280 is called "The 'Dowland' lutebook" because it contains signatures and other examples of Dowland's handwriting and just might have been in his family until sold to Henry Clay Folger in 1926. The manuscript contains many easy pieces, still used by lute teachers today, as well as some of the finest music for very skilled players. Dowland, the last of three main copyists in the book, entered only three pieces; the final one is incomplete. "My Lady Hunsdons Allemande," rather untidily written on the left-hand page, was one of Dowland's best-known pieces, which he signed and to which he added his Oxford degree. He was probably writing at speed during a lesson with an experienced player, pointing out some of the finer points of performance. On the right, hardly any neater, is his simple arrangement of the popular tune "What if a day" for a less advanced pupil. Seemingly only the first four lines were studied in one lesson; the end was probably added at the next. Not only does Dowland use a much broader pen, but the note-values are halved, either by mistake or to show that there was more than one way to notate a straightforward piece like this. Dowland's other entries show how the note values and pitches of lute tablature relate to those of ordinary music.[37]
(Ian Harwood)

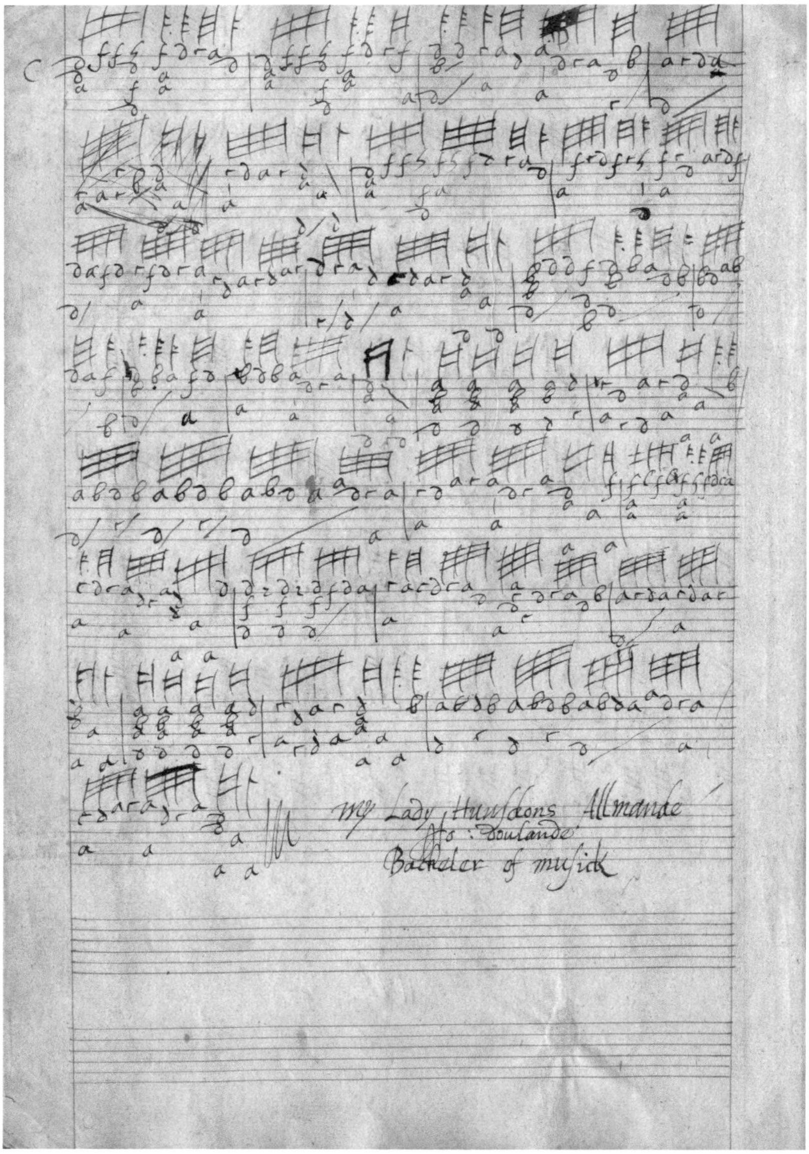

Cat. 34.

35. Thomas Greeting (d. 1682)
The pleasant companion: or new lessons and instructions for the flagelet
London: for J. Playford, 1680
Folger G1875a
Title page

A violinist and wind player, Greeting became a member of the Chapel Royal in 1674; he also served as a musician for the daughters of James, duke of York. A proponent of the flageolet, a kind of pipe similar to a recorder, he published this collection of music, which includes an instruction manual, in 1667; it went into several editions. The music is notated in a form of tablature that enables the amateur player to perform without knowing conventional staff notation. This sort of instruction manual, in the characteristic small (octavo) oblong format, enabled amateurs to learn their instruments, with or without a tutor.

The flageolet was Samuel Pepys's favorite instrument and references to it are found throughout his diaries. He hired Greeting to teach him and his wife ("Up, and there comes to me Drumbleby [a pipe maker] with a flagelette made to suit with my former, and brings me one Greeting, a master to teach my wife. I agree by the whole with him, to teach her to take out any lesson of herself for 4*l*," 28 February 1667) and bought a copy of *The Pleasant Companion.* Pepys carried his flageolet in his pocket and often played in taverns or while traveling; it was his "pleasant companion."

Of 3. voc.
I.
ALTVS.
FLy Loue aloſt, to heauen & looke out Fortune,& &c. Fly
loue aloſt, to heauen & looke out Fortune, Then ſweetly,ſweetly, ſweetly hir im-
portune, That I from my Ca-liſto beſt beloued, As you & ſhe ſet downe, be neuer mo-
ued, As you & ſhe ſet downe,:||: be ne-uer moued, And loue, to Ca-ri-
mel ſee you cõmend me,cõmend me,:||: cõmend me, Fortune for his ſweet
ſake,:||: may chaũce befriend me. Fortune for his ſweet ſake,:||: may
chaũce bee-friend me. And loue, to Carimel ſee you cõmend me,cõmend me,:||:
cõmend me, Fortune for his ſweet ſake,:||: may chaũce be-
friend me. Fortune for his ſweet ſake, Fortune for his ſweet ſake may chãce bee-friend mee.
B.

Cat. 37.

"A perfect and true Copie": Music Printing in England

The development of a technology for printing polyphonic music from movable type began about 1500 in Italy. An English printer, John Rastell, began to use the single-impression method in the early 1520s, before it was adopted on the Continent.[38] This technique, which uses type fonts with both notes and staves, allowed each page to be printed once and made commercial music printing possible.

England, however, did not become a major center for music printing on the scale of Venice or Antwerp; the 100+ titles published between 1575 and 1625 were about ten percent of the output of just one of the printers active in Venice.[39] One reason may have been the distinctive system of royal patents (monopolies) that put musicians themselves in charge of the music publishing process. In 1575, as Monson writes, "Queen Elizabeth granted Byrd and Tallis the exclusive right to print any 'songe or songes in partes, either in English, Latine, Frenche, Italian, or other tongues that may serve for musicke either in Churche or chamber, or otherwise to be either plaid or soonge' for a period of twenty-one years. The monopoly extended to the printing of music-staff paper, while other booksellers were even forbidden to import or market music from abroad."[40] The first-fruits of this monopoly, the 1575 *Cantiones . . . Sacrae* ("Songs which because of their Subject Matter are called Sacred"), dedicated to Elizabeth (cat. 36, 60), turned out to be a financial disaster. Monson writes, "In 1577 Tallis and Byrd lamented to the queen that the 'lycense for the printinge of musicke . . . hath fallen oute to oure greate losse and hinderaunce to the value of two hundred markes at the least'. They had apparently overestimated England's incipient music market."[41]

From 1588 on, Byrd's printer was Thomas East (ca. 1540–1608), the most important English music printer of the time (represented by no fewer than fifteen volumes in this exhibition).[42] East shrewdly navigated the restrictions of a royal monopoly and the system of registration imposed by the Company of Stationers. He registered titles during the brief period when the monopoly was not assigned and printed hidden editions when the supply of legal copies ran out. Of the four copies of John Wilbye's first book of madrigals in the Folger Library, only one belongs to the true first edition of 1598 (cat. 37); the other three (cat. 38, 39, 40) were printed in 1605 or 1606, to judge from the paper; it takes an attentive eye to notice the differences. The case of Dowland's second book (cat. 42) wound up in court, thus furnishing valuable information about the practices of the trade; two of East's apprentices were caught printing and selling extra copies.

Although the scale of English music publishing was small, this means of transmitting music helped develop new audiences. Musicians—amateur or professional—typically performed from individual parts. Vocal music was generally printed in partbooks (one for each voice—known variously as superius or cantus, medius or contratenor or quintus, altus, tenor, bassus, sextus), at first in oblong quarto (like cat. 36) and later in upright quarto format. Lute songs were published in folio, sometimes in table layout so that performers sitting around a table could read from the same opening.

without attracting observations done secretly, often with skillful avoidance of detection and in violation of custom, law, or authority

36. Orlando di Lasso (1532–1594)
Recveil dv mellange d'Orlande de Lassvs, contenant plvsievrs chansons tant en uers Latins qu'en ryme francoyse, a quatre, & cinq parties
London: Thomas Vautrollier, 1570
Folger STC 15266 bd. w. STC 23666 c. 2
Superius, title page

This is an example of a "binder's copy," in a contemporary parchment binding, assembled by an unknown owner. It contains two music books published by the Huguenot printer and exile Vautrollier (d. 1587), both using the same woodcut border and design for the title pages; the other title is the 1575 *Cantiones, qvae ab argvmento sacrae vocantvr* by Thomas Tallis and William Byrd. (For another copy, see cat. 60.) Vautrollier brought out this selection of chansons (*Recueil du Mellange*) by the great Flemish composer Orlando di Lasso (1530 or 1532–1594), drawn from Le Roy and Ballard's *Mellange d'Orlande de Lassus* published in Paris in 1570. About half of these secular chansons were turned into sacred *contra-facta* for Protestant readers. Richard Freedman argues that Vautrollier ordered the collection as a kind of spiritual journey: "And in closing with an almost narrative sequence that prepares the reader to wait with 'solid hope' and 'living faith,' the book emerges as a site where spiritual meanings are discovered in familiar musical objects."[43] The volume is dedicated to the earl of Arundel, a prominent Catholic and patron of music. The note, "Thomas Hamond of Hawkdon in the Countie of Suff: oweth thiese bookes. Aprill. 5th. Ao. 1635," identifies one of the seventeenth-century owners of this volume as the music collector Thomas Hamond (d. 1662), whose manuscripts are important records of amateur musical taste during the reign of Charles I.[44] This exemplar is the only copy of Lasso's *superius* to have survived.

37. John Wilbye (1574–1638)
The first set of English madrigals to 3.4.5. and 6. voices: newly composed by Iohn Wilbye
London: Thomas Este, 1598
Stationer's Register: entered 7 August [1598]
Folger STC 25619.3
Altus, sig. B: "Fly Loue aloft"

Thomas East published the first edition of John Wilbye's very popular first book of madrigals in 1598 at a time when the monopoly for printing polyphonic music was vacant. He protected his investment by registering the title with the Company of Stationers, and he reprinted the book surreptitiously in ca. 1605–1606. (A second hidden edition dates from after East's death.) This edition includes a dedication to Sir Charles Cavendish.

38. John Wilbye (1574–1638)
The first set of English madrigals to 3.4.5. and 6. voices: newly composed by Iohn Wilbye
London: Thomas Este, 1598 [i.e., 1605 or 1606]
Folger STC 25619 c. 3
Altus, sig. A2: "Fly Loue aloft"

Despite the date on the title page, this copy of Wilbye's first book is actually a hidden edition—reset to resemble the first edition, which had been completely sold out—printed in 1605 or 1606.[45] East would have had to pay to print this title in 1605 and so he pretended that it was the 1598 edition for which he owned the rights. Note the absence of the letter of dedication, and minor differences in the music and in the signature found in the lower right-hand corner, used to identify the gathering. This hidden

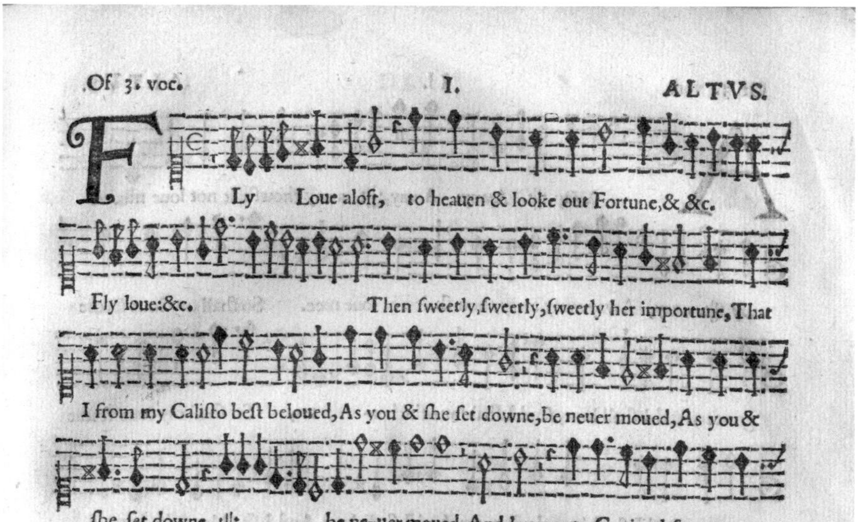
Of 3. voc.
I.
ALTVS.
FLy Loue aloft, to heauen & looke out Fortune,& &c.
Fly loue:&c. Then sweetly,sweetly,sweetly her importune,That
I from my Calisto best beloued,As you & she set downe,be neuer moued,As you &
she set downe, :||: be ne-uer moued,And loue, to Ca-rimel see you com-
mend me,commend mee,to Ca:&c. commend mee,Fortune for his sweet sake,
:||: may chaũce befriend mee.Fortune for his sweet sake,:||: may
chance be-friend me,& loue, to Carimel see you cõmend me,cõmend me,:||:
commend mee,Fortune for his sweet sake,:||: may chance be-
friend me.Fortune for his sweet sake,Fortune for his sweet sake,may chãce befriẽd me.
A.ij.

Cat. 38.

edition was printed on paper left over from a 1604 publication. Given the actual date of printing, it comes as no surprise that this copy is bound with two books of about the same time: Wilbye's *Second Set of Madrigales* (London, 1609, STC 25619a c. 3) and Michael East's *Third Set of Bookes* (London, 1610, STC 7462 c. 3).

Cat. 39.

39. Binder's copy, owned by "C. S." [Sir Charles Somerset (ca. 1588–1665)]
Folger STC 25205 c. 2 v. 1; STC 25204 c. 2; STC 25206 c. 2; STC 25619 c. 2; STC 25619a c. 2; STC 25119 c. 2
Altus parts, bound in one volume
Binding: contemporary blind-stamped calf binding, with a central ornament of a Tudor rose surrounded by garter and foliage, and surmounted by a crown, with the initials "C" and "S" on either side; evidence of ties; "Altus" stamped in gilt on the front cover

This altus volume, together with the quintus (Folger STC 25205 c. 2 v. 2), is all that remains from a set of five owned by Sir Charles Somerset and listed in an inventory of 1622 (items 19–25).[46] Somerset, who also owned cat. 74, gathered Weelkes's *Madrigals to 3.4.5. & 6. Voyces* (London, 1597), Weelkes's *Ballets and Madrigals* (London, 1608), Weelkes's *Madrigals of 5. and 6. Parts* (London, 1600), Wilbye's *First Set of English Madrigals* (London, "1598," i.e. 1605 or 1606), *Wilbye's Second Set* (London, 1609), and Watson's *First Sett of Italian Madrigals Englished* (London, 1590) and bound them as a set. Binder's copies reveal the tastes of a particular owner.

40. John Wilbye (1574–1638)
The first set of English madrigals to 3.4.5. and 6. voices: newly composed by Iohn Wilbye
London: Thomas Este, 1598 [i.e., 1605 or 1606]
Folger STC 25619 c. 1
Quintus, sig. C2v, facing altus, title page

In the early seventeenth century, this set of partbooks was bound with a dozen other titles into a large binder's copy, like the ones in cat. 36, 39, and 74; each volume contained the music for a single voice or part. The nineteenth-century book collector Henry Huth (1815–1878) had the books disassembled and rebound by F. Bedford so that all the volumes or parts of an individual title were bound together. (The end of the quintus part faces the beginning of the altus.) In this configuration the music could no longer be used for performance. This copy, dated 1598 on the title page, was printed in 1605 or 1606, part of the same hidden edition as cat. 38 and 39.

41. Orlando Gibbons (1583–1625)
The first set of madrigals and mottets of 5. parts: apt for viols and voyces. Newly composed by Orlando Gibbons, Batcheler of Musicke, and organist of his Maiesties honourable chappell in ordinarie
London: Thomas Snodham, assigne of W. Barley, 1612
Folger STC 11826 c. 2
Altus, sig. A3: "The siluer Swanne"

This set of partbooks of Gibbons' 1612 book of madrigals and motets consists of the cantus and altus parts only. They were assembled from unrelated copies, presumably at the time of their binding by Rivière and Son. The altus is in the state buyers would have expected to find it in bookshops, with untrimmed rough edges. "The siluer Swanne" is one of Gibbons' best-known madrigals.

42. John Dowland (1562–1626)
The second booke of songs or ayres, of 2. 4. and 5. parts: vvith tableture for the lute or orpherian, with the violl de gamba. Composed by Iohn Dovvland Batcheler of Musick, and lutenist to the king of Denmark: also an excelent lesson for the lute and base viol, called Dowlands adew. Published by George Eastland, and are to be sould at his house neere the greene Dragon and Sword, in Fleetstreete
London: Thomas Este, assigne of Thomas Morley, 1600
Stationer's Register: Entered to T. East 15 July [1600]
Folger STC 7095 bd. w. STC 7092
Title page

We gain valuable information about the book trade from a lawsuit brought by the publisher George Eastland against the printer Thomas East, two of whose apprentices sold unauthorized copies.[47] East, anticipating that this volume would be commercially successful, bought the rights for future editions from Eastland once the first edition of 1,025 copies was sold out. Unbeknownst to the novice publisher Eastland, East also cleverly registered a copy with the Stationers' Company to make a further claim on the property. The connection of this book with an early phase of the Essex revolt—it contains in effect musical apologies to the queen—may have made it too topical after Essex's execution; in contrast with the very popular first book (cat. 58), it was never reprinted.

[1]
A
PASTORAL ELEGY
On the DEATH of
Mr. John Playford.
[Note, The Notes with this Mark * over them, are to be ſung Demiquavers.]
The Words by Mr. Tate.
Set by Mr. Henry Purcell.
Entle Shepherds, you that know the Charms of Tune—ful Breath, that
Harmony in Grie——f can ſhow, Lament, Lament, for Pi——ous The—ron's Death!
Theron, the good, the friend-ly Theron's gone! Theron, Theron, the good, the friend-ly Theron's
Soft.
Loud.
gone! Ren ———ding Mountains, weeping Fountains, groaning Dales, and ecchoing Vales, if
A

Cat. 49.

“A much larger Banquet than you had before”: Playford and New Markets

The abolition of the *Book of Common Prayer* services in 1645 and the dissolution of royal and cathedral musical organizations during the Commonwealth forced professional musicians into private employment as music tutors and helped to develop a broad-based audience of enthusiastic musical amateurs. Stationer John Playford shrewdly provided music for this new market—instruction manuals, country dances, catches, songs, and psalms. A committed royalist, he used music to help sustain royalist aspirations during the Interregnum.[48]

43. John Playford (1623–1686/7)
The whole book of psalms: with the usual hymns and spiritual songs; together with all the ancient and proper tunes sung in churches, with some of later use. Compos'd in three parts, cantus, medius, & bassus: in a more plain and useful method than hath been formerly published
London: W. Godbid for the Company of Stationers, 1677
Folger Acc. 167– 105q
Title page

This three-part harmonization of the psalms was Playford's studied effort to create a useful guide to remedy the state of psalm singing. In it Playford considered both the practical restrictions of church performance and the need to revive and beautify the music of the service. These qualities eventually led to the adoption of this psalmbook and the revival of English psalmody.
(Stacey Houck)

44. John Playford (1623–1686/7)
An introduction to the skill of musick, in two books. The first contains the grounds and rules of musick, according to the gam-ut, and other principles thereof. The second, instructions and lessons both for the basse-viol and treble-violin. By John Playford. To which is added, the art of descant, or composing of musick in parts, by Dr. Tho. Campion; with annotations thereon by Mr. Chr. Simpson. Also the order of singing divine service in cathedrals
London: A[nne]. G[odbid]. and J[ohn]. P[layford]. for John Playford, 1679
Folger P2481
Title page and frontispiece (portrait of Playford signed "F.H. van. Houe sculp." [Frederick Hendrick van Hove, 1628?–1698, engraver])

This treatise is part of a series of editions that began in 1654. Here, in its eighth edition ("carefully corrected"), is one of the first appearances of a section detailing the order of the divine service in cathedrals, which underscores Playford's concern for correct musical practices in the church. Editions of the *Introduction* continued to appear regularly until 1730. (For other editions, see cat. 30, 98.)
(Stacey Houck)

45. John Playford (1623–1686/7), copyist
Autograph fragments (catalogued as "Music by John Wilson for two songs from *The Tempest*"), ca. 1650–1667
Folger MS V.a.411
Fol. 11r: [Robert Johnson], "Full fathom five" (*Tempest* 1.2)

This manuscript fragment, originally part of a set of Playford partbooks now in the Euing Music Collection at the University of Glasgow Library, R.d.58–61, was copied by Playford and records a version of Robert Johnson's piece, "Full fathom five." This work was most likely written for a Jacobean restaging of Shakespeare's *The Tempest.* Although Playford and Johnson never met, Playford probably received the piece from Johnson's fellow theater musician John Wilson.[49]
(Stacey Houck)

1. Cantus Primus.
A. 3. Voc.
3
Dr Wilson
11
Full fathom fiue thy father lyes of his bones are Corrall made those are
pearles that were his eyes nothing of him that doth fade but doth suffer a
sea change into some thing rich & strange Sea nimphs howerly ring his
knell hark now I heare them hark :||: ding dong Bell Ding ding
ding dong bell Ding ding ding dong Bell Ding ding ding dong Bell

Cat. 45.

· a song in homophic style for three or more unaccompanied male voices · chordal · obscene; lewd; boisterously / humorously indecent

46. John Playford (1623–1686/7)
The musical companion, in two books. The first book containing catches and rounds for three voyces. The second book containing dialogues, glees, ayres and songs for two, three and four voyces. Collected and published by John Playford practitioner in musick
London: W. Godbid for John Playford, 1673
Folger P2490
Title page

This collection is an expansion upon the successful series started by John Hilton in 1652 with his *Catch that Catch Can* (cat. 47). As he acknowledged in an earlier edition of 1667, Playford performed many of these pieces with his own music society. The widespread appeal of these pieces gave rise to the development of the catch and glee clubs of the eighteenth century. (Stacey Houck)

47. John Hilton (1599–1657)
Catch that catch can, or a choice collection of catches, rovnds, & canons for 3 or 4 voyces collected & published by John Hilton Batch: in Musick
London: for John Benson & John Playford, 1652
Folger H2036
Title page

Catches and rounds had long been popular vocal genres in England. However catches, more so than rounds, were intended to be humorous and often bawdy. Though they were entertaining convivial pieces by design, Hilton's pieces often echoed social concerns of the day. This collection was enlarged in 1658 and continued to grow under the title *The Musical Companion* (cat. 46). (Stacey Houck)

48. *Select ayres and dialogues for one, two, and three voyces; to the theorbo-lute or basse-viol. Composed by John Wilson Charles Colman doctors in musick. Henry Lawes William Lawes Nicholas Laneare William Webb gentlemen and servants to his late Majesty in his publick and private musick. And other excellent masters of musick*
London: W. Godbid for John Playford, 1659
Folger W2909 c. 1
Title page

The series *Select Ayres and Dialogues*, of which this is the last and largest edition, was Playford's attempt to offer a sampling of serious, court-influenced songs to the general public. That the series continued and grew suggests that it was well received; for the upper classes it was nostalgic, and for the lower classes the series likely belonged to a category of improvement books that taught fine speech and manners. This binder's copy also contains two books of ayres by John Gamble and three by Henry Lawes, all published between 1653 and 1659. (Stacey Houck)

49. Nahum Tate (1652–1715), author
Henry Purcell (1659–1695), composer
A pastoral elegy on the death of Mr. John Playford
[London: printed for Henry Playford, 1687]
Folger T203
Sig. A

This pastoral elegy for the music publisher John Playford was written by Nahum Tate and set to music by Henry Purcell. Here, the shepherds are entreated to lament Playford in the guise of

Theron. The symbolism associated with this name is probably derived from King Theron of Acragus (488–472 BCE), an ancient Greek ruler who promoted the arts. Such a tribute embodies the high esteem with which Playford was regarded by Restoration artists.
(Stacey Houck)

148
Euterpe.
4
Euterpe, She is the Muse that with swett Sounds and
Mellodye deliteth men, and hath her name of Euterpe,
which signifyeth to delyte:

Cat. 51.

The Trevelyon Miscellany

Thomas Trevelyon (Trevilian) was probably employed in the London textile trade. He compiled two massive visual miscellanies, the earlier in the Folger collection, the later (1616) in the Wormsley Library in England.[50] Trevelyon's manuscript reflects the values and mind-set of a committed Protestant, providing stories that he describes as historical, prophetical, and evangelical—an extraordinary array of topics. He draws on images and texts found in books, as well as single-page engravings, many of them by Flemish engravers.

50. Thomas Trevelyon (b. ca. 1548)
Trevelyon Miscellany, 1608
Folger MS V.b.232
Fol. 158v: "The seaven liberal sciences"

This page presents "The seaven liberall sciences"; *musica, geometry, astronomia,* and, on the reverse side (fol. 158r), *grammatica, dialectica, rhetorica, arithmetica.* Trevelyon used a set of engravings by Hans Sebald Beham (1500–1550) as his model. An angel plays a portative organ, against which is leaning a viol. This image could be construed to contradict the text, a commonplace extolling learning over mere practice: "Musicke teacheth men to sing and to make difference of tymes as well by voice as instrument, therefore he that doth not make musick by art, according to art, is not a musition but a crowder." A "crowder" is a fiddler, playing a "crowd," a kind of fiddle.

51. Thomas Trevelyon (b. ca. 1548)
Trevelyon Miscellany, 1608
Folger MS V.b.232
Fol. 148r: "Evterpe"

This page comes from a series of the nine muses, a very popular theme in early modern England. Euterpe is the muse of music: "She is the Muse that with swett sounds and Mellodye deliteth men, and hath her name of Euterpo, which signifyeth to delyte:" For this series Trevelyon copied engravings from the workshop of Philips Galle, after Maarten de Vos (1532–1603). Euterpe sits playing a straight trumpet held in her right hand. In her left hand she holds a strange wind instrument with characteristics of both shawm and recorder. At her feet and beside her are a bagpipe, crumhorn, case of flutes, flute, cornett, and trumpet.[51]

52. Thomas Trevelyon (b. ca. 1548)
Trevelyon Miscellany, 1608
Folger MS V.b.232
Fol. 189r: "Synging men"

The image of "Synging men" illustrates a collection of biblical verses about music, for example, "Speakieng vnto your selues in spsalmes, and spirituall songs, singing and making melodie to the Lorde in your hearts: Ephe 5:19." The figure on the left is a stock character whom Trevelyon used a number of times. The two men hold one music book while the figure on the left points to another; two other books float nearby. The four books each supply the music for one part: M(edius), CT (contratenor), T(enor) and B(assus). The music is, appropriately enough for the Protestant Trevelyon, a setting of a psalm tune, apparently found only in this source.[52]

189
Syngīg men
M
B
C T
T
And David ſpake the words of this ſong vnto the Lord. what time the
Lord had deliuered him out of the handes of all his enimies, and out of the
hande of Saul: 2: Samuel: 22: i: Speakieng vnto your ſelues in ſpſalmes. and ſpi-
rituall ſongs, ſinging and making melodie to the Lorde in your hearts: Ephe
5: 19: Sing yee vnto the Lorde anew ſong: let his prayſe be heard in the
Congregation of Saints: Let Iſrael reioyce in him that made him. and let
the children of Zion reioyce in their Kyng: Let them prayſe his Name
with the flute: let them ſing prayſes vnto him with the tembrell and harpe;
For the Lorde hath pleaſure in his people: hee wyll make the meeke glorious
by deliuerance: Let the Saints bee ioyfull with glory: let them ſing loude vpon
theire beds: Pſalmes: 149: 1: to 8: Prayſe yee God in the ſounde of the trumpet
prayſe yee him vpon the Viole and the harpe: Prayſe yee him with soun
cimbals: prayſe yee him with high ſounding ſimbals: Prayſe yee hi
and flute: prayſe yee him with Virginalles and organs: Pſalmes:
Then ſang Deborah, and Barak, the ſonne of Abinoam. the ſame
Prayſe yee the Lorde for the auenging of Iſrael, and for the pe
them ſelues willingly: Judges: 5: 1: 2: Then ſang Moſes and
Iſrael this ſong vnto the Lorde. and ſayd. I will ſing vnto
hee hath triumphed glorioſly: the horſe and him that rode
ouer throwen in the Sea: Exodus: 15: 1: Lord. now lettest thou
peace. according to thy worde: For mine eyes haue ſene thy ſaluati

Cat. 52.

Cat. 53.

"Strike vp a noise of Viols"

Introduced into England early in the sixteenth century, the viola da gamba—a fretted instrument of six strings played with a bow—became extremely popular among both professional and amateur musicians. A chest or set of viols typically consists of two each of treble, tenor, and bass. While composers wrote fantasias and other kinds of instrumental music specifically for viol consorts, performers also played vocal music, often advertised as "apt both for viols and voyces."

53. John Strong
Treble Viol
16th century?
Folger ART Inv. 1047

Back: two-piece, burr elm (?), "book-matched" so that pattern repeats each side of the central join
Ribs: burr wood similar to back
Soundboard: spruce
Neck, fingerboard, pegbox, scroll, and pegs: not original
Bridge: not original
Label (not original): "Made in Som [piece of label missing] set/ by John Strong/ Given to D. Re d by Be Co."
An internal pencil note on the soundpost back-plate reads: "Restored by/ Chickering and Sons./ under the direction of/ Arnold Dolmetsch/ November 1906/ Boston, U.S.A."

The three instruments (cat. 53, 54, 62) were among those acquired by the Folger Shakespeare Library in 1930 from Arnold Dolmetsch (1858–1940), an important pioneer of the concept of playing early music on the instruments for which it was conceived. He provided a handwritten description, signed and dated 19 December 1930, which is in the Folger archives. At this date, Dolmetsch was settled in England, but he had spent the period 1905–1909 working with Chickering and Sons of Boston, MA, in charge of the construction of harpsichords and clavichords and the restoration of old instruments in general. When earlier plucked and bowed instruments dropped out of use during the nineteenth century, lutes tended to be preserved (if at all) simply as beautiful decorative objects. Viols, on the other hand, were sometimes given a new lease of life by conversion into violins, violas, or violoncellos, involving the substitution of a new neck, fingerboard, pegbox, and scroll of entirely different style, suitable for four strings instead of the original six or seven. In addition, the smaller viols often had the depth of their bodies reduced so that they could be held under the chin as members of the violin family.

This is an outstanding example of an English viol with "festooned" outline, using the ornate figure of "burr wood" for the back and ribs. This may well be elm (walnut and ash have also been suggested) "book-matched" on the back so that the pattern is identical each side of the central join. The restoration at Chickering's probably involved the removal of a nineteenth-century viola-style neck, pegbox, and scroll, and their replacement by something more appropriate to a six-stringed viol. The present rather shallow ribs may have been reduced in the viola phase or may be original; some smaller viols were apparently held against the breastbone or on the arm, in the early playing position of the violin family, for which deeper ribs are cumbersome.
A sale catalogue of 1892 includes an "antique viol by John Stroud," which may be a misreading for "John Strong" and refer to this instrument. It is not known whether Dolmetsch acquired it then, bringing it with him when he joined Chickering, nor how it remained in his possession for sale to the Folger nearly a quarter of a century later.
(Ian Harwood)

• ? (a specialized word)

54. Anonymous
Bass Viol
17th century?
Folger ART Inv. 1048

Back: three piece, sycamore or maple
Ribs: sycamore or maple; upper and central bouts original, bottom bout replaced
Soundboard: spruce
Neck, fingerboard, pegbox, scroll, and pegs: not original
Bridge: not original
Label: none present

Arnold Dolmetsch suggested no maker for this bass viol but considered it English of "about 1615." It has since been ascribed to George Miller (ca. 1665) because of its soundboard decoration, but although the later date seems more likely the attribution is doubtful; such patterns were part of the general English tradition. So was the shape, with twin outlines of inlaid "purfling" (three thin strips of wood, dark-light-dark, glued together and inserted edgewise, to show the contrasting colours), the spruce soundboard, and the figured sycamore or maple for the back and ribs. The three-piece back has a central strip with a classic lozenge-shaped purfling pattern in the center, and two "wings" completing the outline. With an original string length of some 28½ inches (72.4 cm), this was considered "typical of the larger consort bass" by twentieth-century observers. However, in the seventeenth century even a 30-inch (76.2 cm) instrument was a "division" viol, suitable for rapid solo passage-work, whereas a full-size "consort bass" required a string-length of 32 inches (81.3 cm). Many modern players find this size unacceptably large and suggest that the English inch has changed (it has not), but it was confirmed by the 1995 discovery in France of just such an instrument made by Henry Jaye of Southwark in 1621, which, appropriately restored, has almost exactly this string-length.
(Ian Harwood)

55. Tobias Hume (ca. 1579–1645)
Captaine Hvmes poeticall musicke. Principally made for two basse-viols, yet so contriued, that it may be plaied 8. seuerall waies vpon sundry instruments with much facilitie. 1 The first way or musicke is for one bass-viole to play alone in pares, which standeth alwaies on the right side of this booke. 2 The second musicke is for two basse-viols to play toghether. 3 The third musicke, for three basse-viols to play together. 4 The fourth musicke, for two tenor viols and a basse-viole. 5 The fift musicke, for two lutes and a basse-viole. 6 The sixt musicke, for two orpherions and a basse-viole. 7 The seuenth musicke, to vse the voyce to some of these musicks, but especially to the three basse-viols, or to the two orpherions with one basse-viole to play the ground. 8 The eight and last musicke, in consorting all these instruments together with the virginals, or rather with a winde instrument and the voice
London: Iohn VVindet, 1607
Folger STC 13957.2
Title page

Soldier, amateur composer, and passionate advocate for the viola da gamba ("Gambo Violl"), Hume left two published collections of instrumental music and songs. The 1607 collection, which survives in four exemplars, was dedicated to three different

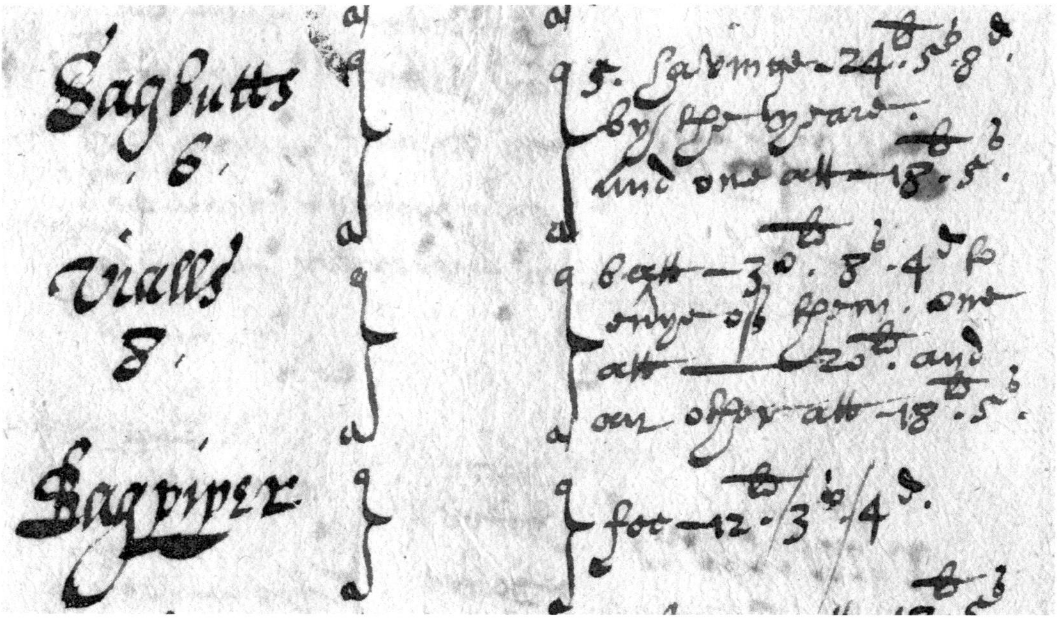

Detail, cat. 59.

patrons: Queen Anne (who rewarded him with one hundred shillings), "Philip [Howard,] earle of Arundel" (Thomas Howard was actually the earl of Arundel in 1607), and Christopher Hatton (ca. 1570–1619). The Folger exemplar, which omits sigs. A–F and has the title page printed on sig. G, bears a dedication to "Philip, earle of Arundel." Many of the pieces are associated with members of the Jacobean court, for example, "Sweet Ayre. The Earle of Arundels favoret." The title page gives a range of possibilities or "orchestrations" for the music.[53] Hume specifies in his letter to the reader that "Your Viols must be tuned as the Lute" but indicates other possible tunings in the music.

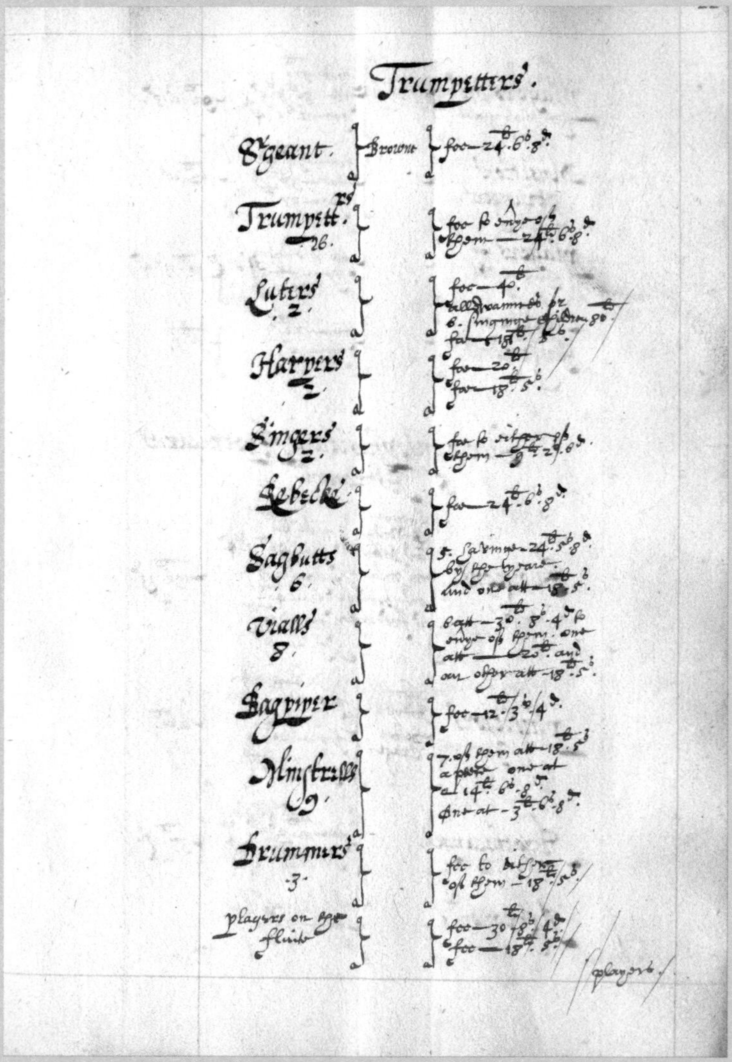

Trumpetters.

Sergeant — Browne — fee — 24li. 6s. 8d.

Trumpetters 26 — fee to every of them — 24li. 6s. 8d.

Luters 2 — fee — 40li. / [illegible] / 6. singinge children — 80li. / fee — 18li. 5s.

Harpers 2 — fee — 20li. / fee — 18li. 5s.

Singers 2 — fee to either of them — 24li. 6s. 8d.

Rebecke — fee — 24li. 6s. 8d.

Sagbutts 6 — 5. [illegible] — 24li. 5s. 8d. by the yeare and one att — 18li. 5s.

Vialls 8 — 6 att — 30li. 8s. 4d. to every of them, one att — 20li. and one other att — 18li. 5s.

Bagpiper — fee — 12li. 3s. 4d.

Minstrells 9 — 7 of them att — 18li. 5s. apeece, one at 14li. 6s. 8d. One at — 3li. 6s. 8d.

Drummers 3 — fee to either of them — 18li. 5s.

players on the flute — fee — 30li. 8s. 4d. / fee — 18li. 5s.

players

Cat. 59.

“Greet Elyza with a ryme”: Music at Court

Queen Elizabeth, indeed every monarch, had a special role in the national musical culture. The court maintained the Chapel Royal as well as a large number of instrumentalists. Elizabeth was known as an accomplished amateur musician; she was even portrayed holding a lute, the most popular aristocratic instrument of the day. Her influence on music can be seen through her patronage of Tallis, Byrd, Ferrabosco, and Morley.[54]

• symbolic truth about humans expressed in fiction

56. Crispijn van de Passe (1564–1637)
After Maarten de Vos (1532–1603)
Engraving: *Terra* (Earth)
Crispin de Passe, [ca. 1590]
Folger ART 259051

This engraving, from about 1590, comes from a set illustrating the Four Elements, all of which are in the Folger collection. They belong to a series of allegorical subjects (the five senses, the four seasons, etc.). In this instance de Passe is using exemplary figures rather than personifications. "Terra" is a complex allegory, still not completely deciphered, in which music represents love, in both positive and negative senses. In the background are several scenes, including the harvesting of fruit, dancing to the music of a bass viol, flute, and lute, and an amorous tryst. In the central image, a man playing the lute looks at a woman seated next to him, who is holding open a music book. Another music book lies open on the table in front of them; the text, "Susanna," a reference to one of the many musical elaborations of the biblical story of Susanna and the Elders, faces the viewer rather than the musicians. The other objects on the table are also richly symbolic—the series of instruments (cittern, flute, recorder, cornett, and violin), a lizard, a bowl of fruit, and a plate of carnations in sand.[55] The Latin hexameters begin with a somewhat altered version of Lucretius, *De Rerum Natura*, II.992ff, and end with a newly composed moralizing couplet.

Humorum guttas mater cum Terra recepit;
Foeta parit nitidas fruges, arbustaque laeta,
Et genus humanum, parit omnia secla ferarum:
Pabula cum praebet, quibus omnes corpora pascunt,
Et dulcem ducunt vitam sobolemque propagant:
Unde etiam merito maternum nomen adepta est.
Luxuriem ergo cave partis quae parcere nescit,
Donorumque Dei, quae Terra haec gignit, abusum.

When mother Earth has received the drops of moisture [from the sky], she teems and gives birth to gleaming crops and flourishing trees, and human kind, she gives birth to all the races of beasts; when she provides the fodder from which all feed their bodies, and draw sweet life and beget offspring; whence indeed she has deservedly acquired the name of mother. Therefore avoid self-indulgence, which knows not how to save what it has gained, and the abuse of God's gifts, which this Earth produces.
(Translation: Leofranc Holford-Strevens)

57. Thomas Morley (1557–1602)
Madrigales the triumphes of Oriana, to 5. and 6. voices: composed by diuers seuerall aucthors. Newly published by Thomas Morley, Batcheler of Musick, and one of the gentlemen of hir Maiesties honorable chappell
London: Thomas Este, the assigne of Thomas Morley, 1601
Folger STC 18130
Altus, title page

The eighteenth-century historian of music, John Hawkins, was the first to identify the madrigals in this collection as a tribute to Queen Elizabeth. They all end with some version of "then sang the shepherds and nymphs of Diana, long live Oriana." Jeremy Smith has recently challenged this view of Oriana's identity, suggesting instead that OriANA may be Anna of Denmark and the collection a musical statement of the case made by the ill-fated Robert Devereux, second earl of Essex, that Elizabeth be succeeded by James VI and his wife, Anna.[56]

Cat. 57, sig. D3.

58. John Dowland (1562–1626)
The first booke of songes or ayres of fowre partes with tableture for the lute: so made that all the partes together, or either of them seuerally may be song to the lute, orpherian or viol de gambo. Composed by Iohn Dowland lutenist and Batcheler of musicke in both the vniversities. Also an inuention by the sayd author for two to playe vpon one lute
[London]: Peter Short, 1597
Stationer's Register: Entered 31 October [1597]
Folger STC 7091
Sig. K: "His golden locks time hath to siluer turnde" (for Sir Henry Lee)

This is the first in the great series of lute books in folio format that would be published between 1597 and 1632. The song, "His golden locks," honors Sir Henry Lee, who retired from his position as Queen's Champion during the Accession Day (November 17) festivities in 1590: his "lover's songs shall turn to holy psalms." It can be performed by voice and lute or by four voices; the layout makes possible a performance by musicians seated around a table.

59. [A general collection of all the offices of England with their fee], 1608
Folger MS V.b.119
Fol. 22: "Trumpetters"

This unpublished Jacobean document shows an organization of the musical establishment typical since the time of Henry VIII.[57] The categories of musicians include those involved with ceremonies of state ("trumpeters") as well as instrumental ensembles and other musicians: "Luters," "Harpers," "Singers," "Rebecke," "Sagbutts," "Vialls," "Bagpiper," "Minstrells," "Drummers," "Players on the fluite," "players on the virginalls," "Musitions strangers," "players of Enterludes," and "Maker of instrumentes." Only one name is listed: "Browne." This refers to Benedict Browne, Serjeant Trumpetter.

The court establishment consisted of the Chapel Royal, with thirty-two gentlemen (chaplains and singing men) and twelve boy choristers, and the King's Musick (instrumentalists and a few singers). During the reign of James I, there were some sixty-five to seventy professional musicians, including members of the household of Queen Anne and the prince of Wales.[58]

60. Thomas Tallis (ca. 1505–1585)
William Byrd (between 1540 and 1543–1623)
Cantiones, qvae ab argvmento sacrae vocantvr, qvinqve et sex partivm, avtoribvs Thoma Tallisio & Guilielmo Birdo Anglis, serenissimæ Regineæ Maiestati à priuato sacello generosis, & organistis
[London]: Thomas Vautrollier, 1575
Folger STC 23666 c. 1
Contratenor, letter patent; bassus, title page

In the seventeenth year of her reign, Queen Elizabeth granted Thomas Tallis and his former pupil William Byrd a joint monopoly on the publication of music in England. Their gift in return was an elegantly produced book of motets, seventeen by each composer, dedicated to Elizabeth and featuring a short version of the royal license in each of the partbooks. The full title of the 1575 *Cantiones* translates, somewhat coyly, as "songs which on account of their subject matter are called sacred." Latin motets were not entirely free of political suspicion in Elizabethan England—but, as the preface makes clear, the composers (and their patron) wanted to meet the international musical community on its own terms, with a book for sophisticated collectors and singers. Despite its sacred subject matter and refined style, it appears to have been intended primarily as domestic chamber music; there is no evidence of its use in actual church services.[59] The contents are eclectic, ranging from elaborate canons to large-scale settings of devotional monologues by the church fathers Augustine and Isidore.
(Kerry McCarthy)

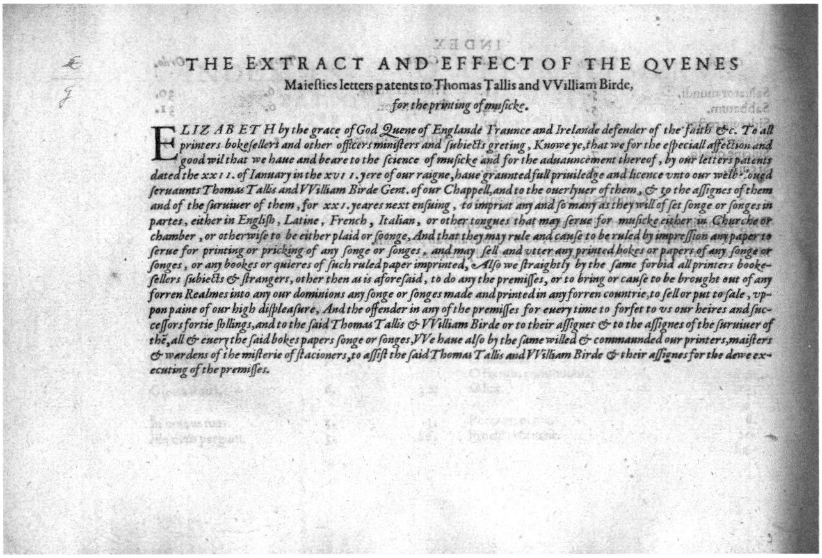

THE EXTRACT AND EFFECT OF THE QVENES
Maiesties letters patents to Thomas Tallis and VVilliam Birde,
for the printing of musicke.

ELIZABETH by the grace of God Quene of Englande Fraunce and Irelande defender of the faith &c. To all printers bokesellers and other officers ministers and subiects greting, Knowe ye, that we for the especiall affection and good wil that we haue and beare to the science of musicke and for the aduauncement thereof, by our letters patents dated the xxii. of Ianuary in the xvii. yere of our raigne, haue graunted full priuiledge and licence vnto our welbeloued seruaunts Thomas Tallis and VVilliam Birde Gent. of our Chappell, and to the ouerlyuer of them, & to the assignes of them and of the suruiuer of them, for xxi. yeares next ensuing, to imprint any and so many as they will of set songe or songes in partes, either in English, Latine, French, Italian, or other tongues that may serue for musicke either in Churche or chamber, or otherwise to be either plaid or soonge, And that they may rule and cause to be ruled by impression any paper to serue for printing or pricking of any songe or songes, and may sell and vtter any printed bokes or papers of any songe or songes, or any bookes or quieres of such ruled paper imprinted, Also we straightly by the same forbid all printers bookesellers subiects & strangers, other then as is aforesaid, to do any the premisses, or to bring or cause to be brought out of any forren Realmes into any our dominions any songe or songes made and printed in any forren countrie, to sell or put to sale, vppon paine of our high displeasure, And the offender in any of the premisses for euery time to forfet to vs our heires and successors fortie shillings, and to the said Thomas Tallis & VVilliam Birde or to their assignes & to the assignes of the suruiuer of thē, all & euery the said bokes papers songe or songes, VVe haue also by the same willed & commaunded our printers, maisters & wardens of the misterie of stacioners, to assist the said Thomas Tallis and VVilliam Birde & their assignes for the dewe executing of the premisses.

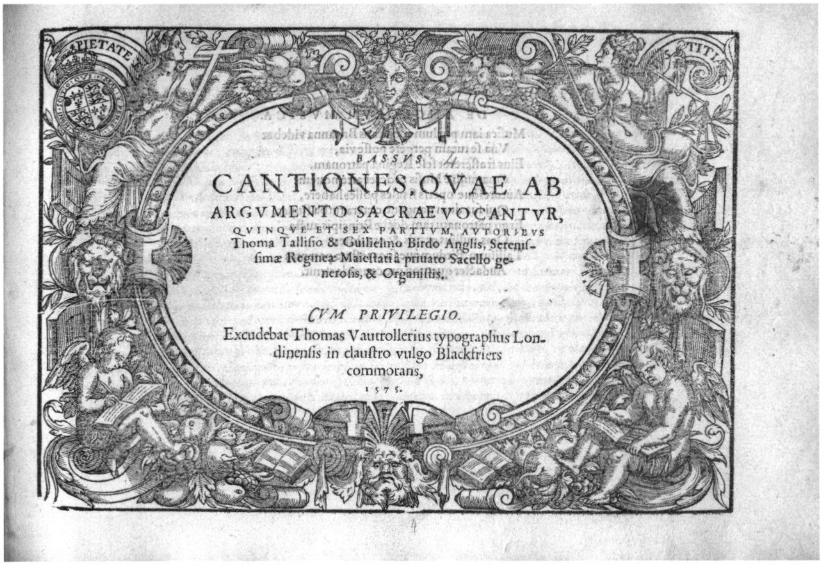
BASSVS
CANTIONES, QVAE AB
ARGVMENTO SACRAE VOCANTVR,
QVINQVE ET SEX PARTIVM, AVTORIBVS
Thoma Tallisio & Guilielmo Birdo Anglis, Serenissimæ Reginea Maiestati à priuato Sacello generosis, & Organistis.
CVM PRIVILEGIO.
Excudebat Thomas Vautrollerius typographus Londinensis in claustro vulgo Blackfriers commorans,
1575.

Cat. 60.

162

61. Commonplace book, ca. 1571–ca. 1600
Folger MS V.a.159
Fol. 4v: "Blame not my lute"

According to John Ward, the music at the beginning of this manuscript miscellany (fols. 3–21) is the work of two or possibly three unidentified scribes, with scribes A and B working in 1559 and soon thereafter, and scribe C in the 1570s.[60] Scribe A was probably "the anonymous author of the play 'July and Julian', which begins on fol. 94, someone who was likely a schoolmaster and amateur lutenist-composer." He notates the music in a very sketchy, abbreviated fashion, as though he were writing a kind of shorthand for himself. The setting, which bears the first line of Wyatt's poem "Blame not my lute" (barely visible in the left-hand margin), consists of a well-known harmonic pattern of Italian or Spanish origin, known by the name "Cara cosa," notated as a series of chords without rhythmic values.

62. Michielle Harton
Lute
Padua, 1598
Folger ART Inv. 1002

Body: 35 ribs of shaded yew, each with half-and-half brown heartwood and white sapwood
Soundboard: close-grained spruce, with original intricate carved rose-pattern soundhole
Bridge: original, but see below
Neck and Fingerboard: original poplar with ebony and ivory veneer; see below
Pegbox: original beech, veneered with ebony and ivory; see below
Strings: originally 17 (single treble and eight paired, i.e. nine "courses"); now 18 (single treble, eight paired and single bass, i.e. ten "courses")
Maker's label: visible through the rose:
In Padova, Michielle Harton [printed]
1 5 9 8 M L [handwritten]

In a 1904 article about this instrument in *The Connoisseur* magazine, Arnold Dolmetsch wrote that the soundboard had sunk in just above the bridge and, "wanting to make it playable, I had to take off its belly in order to repair it." Two photographs show the lute minus its soundboard but otherwise in original condition. The caption gives the overall length as "2 ft 10 in." or 34 inches (86.4 cm). Dolmetsch later shortened the neck after removing the pegbox, which was then reassembled with an additional small bracket or "treble rider" for the highest string. Finally, some of the string holes in the original bridge were plugged and redrilled. The overall length in its present cut-down state is 30¼ inches (77 cm), so Dolmetsch evidently removed 3¾ inches (9.5 cm) from the neck. The current open string length is 27 inches (68.6 cm), but would have been 30¾ inches (78.1 cm) when it left Harton's workshop in 1598. This accords with the earlier comments that viol sizes in the sixteenth and seventeenth centuries were larger than modern players find comfortable. With plain-gut stringing throughout, this implies a pitch level about a tone lower than today's.
(Ian Harwood)

Cat. 62.

Cat. 65.

• a short allegorical entertainment of the 16th/17th centuries performed by masqued actors

"But strike a musique of like harts": Court Masques

In keeping with the elite, courtly culture from which it arose, the court masque brought together an eclectic combination of artistic and intellectual elements, incorporating high and low drama, music, dance, architecture, ornate costumes, elaborate scenes and machines, high-flown philosophical rhetoric, structural and generic intricacy, and complex allegorical and political meaning. Masques were designed to praise the king in exaggerated terms, likening him and his courtiers to mythical gods and heroes. Moreover, by spending lavishly on productions while constructing the masque as a "disposable" entertainment, the monarch and other sponsors of masques showcased their affluence. Because of the form's ephemeral nature, only bits and pieces survive from what must have been a vast corpus of vocal and instrumental music composed for the dozens of masques performed between 1604 and 1641.[61]
(Andrew Walkling)

63. James Shirley (1596–1666)
The trivmph of peace. A masque, presented by the foure honourable houses, or Innes of Court. Before the King and Queenes Majesties, in the banquetting-house at White Hall, February the third, 1633. Invented and written, by James Shirley, of Grayes Inne, gent.
London: Iohn Norton for William Cooke, 1633 [i.e. 1634]
Folger STC 22459
Title page

London's Inns of Court, the hub of the English legal profession, emerged as an important site for the production of masques, revels, and similar entertainments. Occasionally, the Gentlemen of the Inns brought their talents to the royal court to honor some special event. In February 1634, members of all four Inns combined forces to present a lavish masque celebrating the birth of James, duke of York (later James II) and atoning for intemperate remarks made by one of their number, William Prynne, who had insulted the queen and infuriated King Charles I. James Shirley, a playwright and a member of Gray's Inn, provided the text, which extolled the monarch while subtly criticizing some of his more controversial policies. The year 1633 given on the title page reflects "old style" dating, in which the new year did not begin until 25 March. (Andrew Walkling)

64. John Smyth (1567–1640)
Collection of Cholmondeley manuscripts from Condover Hall, ca. 1603–1636
Folger MS Z.e.1 (25)
Pp. 2–3: Anonymous (after James Shirley), "The Manner of the progression of the Masque," 1634

This eight-page manuscript, from a nineteenth-century miscellany of early seventeenth-century documents, was identified in 1988 as a description of the magnificent procession before the performance of *The Triumph of Peace* (cat. 63). The costumed masquers rode on floats and were accompanied by crowds of richly dressed attendants. The portion of the document shown here includes the names of twenty-eight musicians who sat in the floats or rode on horseback, including two trumpeters, two viol players, five lutenists, a harpist, and eighteen singers. Other pages list performers on a variety of instruments, including bagpipes, shawm, jews harp, tongs, "birds," drums, trumpets, lutes, and bass viol, as well as the two composers of the music for this masque, Simon Ives and William Lawes.[62] (Andrew Walkling)

65. Thomas Campion (1567–1620)
The discription of a maske, presented before the Kinges Maiestie at White-Hall, on Twelfth Night last, in honour of the Lord Hayes, and his bride, daughter and heire to the honourable the Lord Dennye, their marriage hauing been the same day at court solemnized
London: Iohn Windet for Iohn Brovvn, 1607
Folger STC 4538
Sig. A2: Anonymous, "Knight of Apollo"

The earliest of four masques Campion wrote for the court of James I, *Lord Hay's Masque* celebrates the marriage of James Hay, Lord Hay (later viscount Doncaster and earl of Carlisle) to Honora

Denny on 6 January 1607. Hay, a Scotsman known for his extravagant lifestyle, was a favorite of James I and a leading patron of masques. Campion's published text includes a rare example of an illustration showing a masquer—usually a member of the nobility or gentry—in costume. The anonymous image is thought to be based on a design by Inigo Jones, who created the outfits and stage sets for many of the court masques. The masquer shown in this engraving is a "Knight of Apollo," one of nine who danced in the performance after being released from an enchantment of the goddess Diana through which they had been metamorphosed into golden trees.
(Andrew Walkling)

66. Thomas Campion (1567–1620)
The description of a maske: presented in the banqueting roome at Whitehall, on Saint Stephens night last, at the mariage of the right honourable the Earle of Somerset: and the right noble the Lady Frances Howard. Written by Thomas Campion. Whereunto are annexed diuers choyse ayres composed for this maske that may be sung with a single voyce to the lute or base-viall
London: E. A[llde and Thomas Snodham] for Laurence Li'sle, 1614
Folger STC 4539
Sig. D2: "Wooe her and win her"

Campion is unusual in having achieved prominence both as a poet and as a composer, and he drew upon his dual talents to create court masques in which music played an especially important role, often providing his own compositions for some of the sung texts. The song "Wooe her and win her hee that can" was written and composed for *The Lords' Masque*, performed on 14 February 1613 to celebrate the marriage of James I's daughter Elizabeth to Frederick, the Elector Palatine. However, it was only printed at the end of Campion's text for *The Somerset Masque* of December 1613, "to fill vp these emptie Pages" that followed several settings by other composers for the later masque. Campion's song is here set for a solo tenor, accompanied by lute (scored in tablature) and a melodic bass instrument. At this moment in the masque, eight male masquers representing stars have been joined by four lady masquers, reanimated at the command of Jove, who had transformed them into statues. After the song, four more ladies are released, allowing the men and women to pair off evenly. The song's second verse nicely articulates Campion's belief in the equal importance of words and music.
(Andrew Walkling)

67. Alfonso Ferrabosco (ca. 1575–1628)
Ayres
London: T. Snodham for Iohn Brovvne, 1609
Folger STC 10827
Sig. G2: "Yes were the loues or false or straying" and "So beautie on the waters stood"

The younger Ferrabosco was the illegitimate son of the Italian madrigal composer Alfonso Ferrabosco (1543–1588), who had served Elizabeth I. He gained prominence as the leading musician at the court of Henry, prince of Wales, where he tutored the prince, composed, and played the viol, helping to introduce the new Italian Baroque style to England.

His 1609 collection of "ayres" contains a number of songs written for masques, including "Yes were the loues or false or straying" and "So beautie on the waters stood" from Jonson's *Masque of Beauty*, performed the same year. Ferrabosco's publication does not identify the masques and plays from which many of the songs are drawn and is clearly intended for use by amateurs in a private setting. The printed page is set up so that, with the book laid flat on a table, the singer can accompany himself on the lute while a viol player sits opposite, reading the upside-down bass line at the top.
(Andrew Walkling)

68. Ben Jonson (1573?–1637)
The workes of Beniamin Ionson
London: Will Stansby, 1616
Folger STC 14751 c. 5
Sig. 4G5 (pages 908–909): *The Masque of Beauty*

Ben Jonson emerged early on as the leading author of masque texts and his progressive innovations over three decades continued to shape the form's development. Jonson signaled his assessment of the importance of masque texts when he included them alongside his plays in his massive folio *Works* of 1616, a volume that strongly influenced the creation of the Shakespeare First Folio of 1623. This opening shows part of *The Masque of Beauty*, performed in 1608 (following a two-year delay necessitated by the production of special wedding masques, including that for Lord Hay, cat. 65). This portion of the text lists the sixteen lady masquers and shows the masque's central sequence of alternating "new" (*i.e.*, specially choreographed) dances and songs—note that two of the songs given here can be seen with Alfonso Ferrabosco's music (cat. 67). At the bottom of page 909, the sequence ends and is followed by the "measures and revels," in which the masquers descend from the stage and take out partners from the audience for an extended interlude of fashionable courtly dances.
(Andrew Walkling)

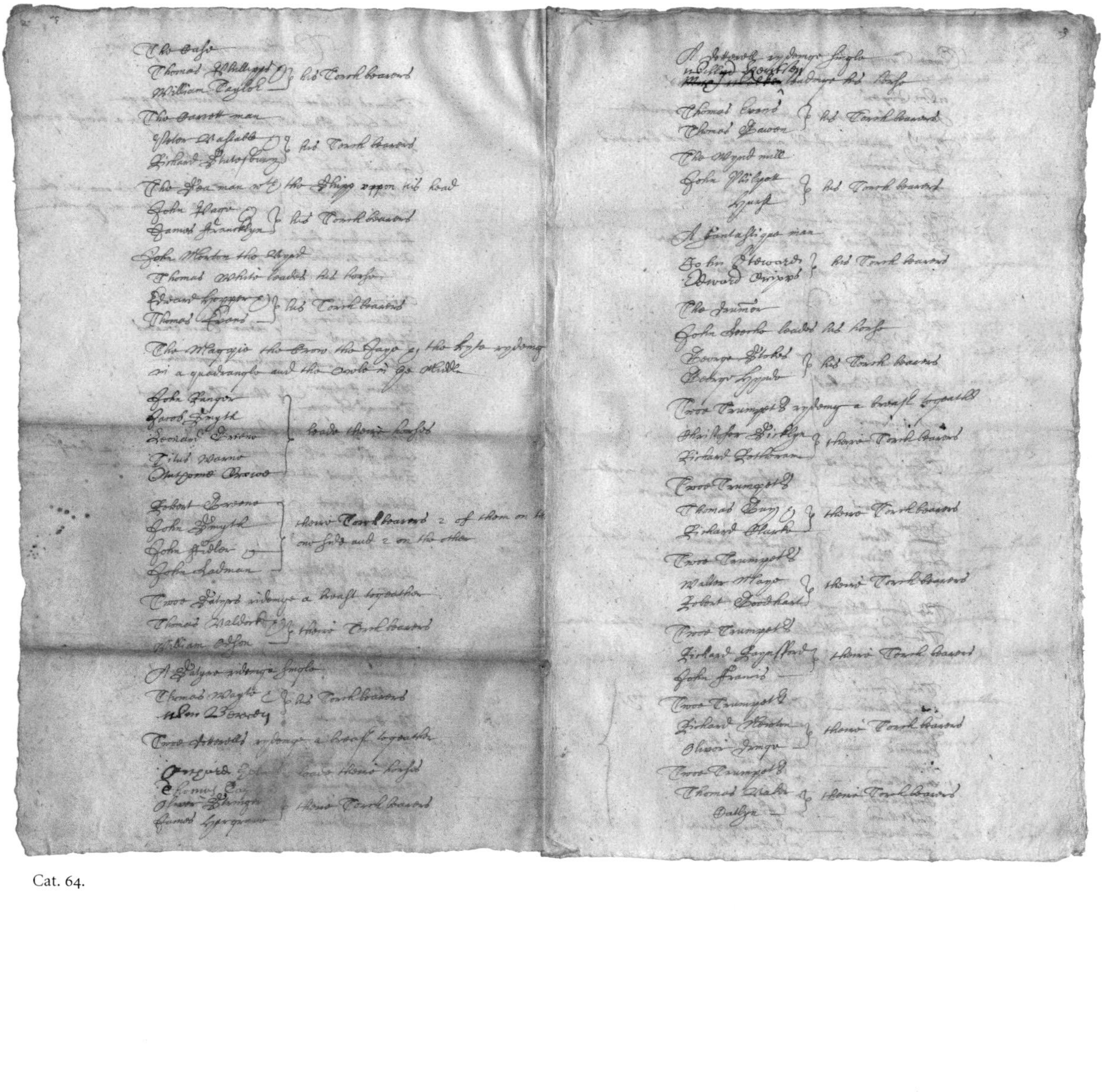

The Hart
Thomas Phillipps } his Torch bearer
William Taylor
The Parrott man
Peter Masfield } his Torch bearer
Richard Shrewsbury
The Sea man wth the Shipp uppon his head
John Ware } his Torch bearer
James Franklyn
John Morton the Ape
Thomas White leaded his horse
Edward Hopper } his Torch bearer
Thomas [illegible]
The Magpie the Crow the Jaye & the kyte rydeing
in a quadrangle and the Owle in the Middle
John Ranger
Jacob Smyth
Leonard Brown } leade their horses
Titus Warne
Anthony Brewe
Robert Browne
John Smyth } their Torchbearers 2 of them on the
John Fidler } one side and 2 on the other
John Hadman
Twoo Satyres rideing a horse together
Thomas Waldork } their Torch bearer
William Odson
A Satyre rideing single
Thomas Wayte } his Torch bearer
[illegible] Browdy
Twoo Ostreches rydeing a horse together
[illegible] leade their horse
Thomas Cay
Oliver Stronge } their Torch bearers
James [illegible]

A Ostrech rydeing single
William Lowther
[illegible] leadinge his horse
Thomas Ewart } his Torch bearer
Thomas Bawen
The Wynd mill
John Philpott } his Torch bearer
[illegible]
A fantasticque man
John Edwards } his Torch bearer
Edward Cripps
The Drumer
John Brooke leaded his horse
George Stokes } his Torch bearer
George Hynde
Twoo Trumpetts rydeing a horse together
Christofer Birkbye } their Torch bearer
Richard Cotheram
Twoo Trumpetts
Thomas Guy } their Torch bearer
Richard Clarke
Twoo Trumpetts
Walter Maye } their Torch bearer
Robert Goodhart
Twoo Trumpetts
Richard Raynsford } their Torch bearer
John Francis
Twoo Trumpetts
Richard Newton } their Torch bearer
Oliver Dinge
Twoo Trumpetts
Thomas Wake } their Torch bearer
Dallyn

Cat. 64.

The Compleat Gentleman, whose *Titles are contained in these* Chapters following.

A 2 TO

Cat. 69.

"After the Italian vein": Amateur Music-Making

Among the upper classes, the ability to "sing your part sure" was essential. Music lovers played and sang, sometimes from printed books, sometimes from their own manuscript notebooks. In many of these sources, especially from the end of the sixteenth and beginning of the seventeenth centuries, there is evidence of a striking predilection for Italian music.

69. Henry Peacham (1578–in or after 1644)
The compleat gentleman fashioning him absolute in the most necessary & commendable qualities concerning minde or bodie that may be required in a noble gentlema[n]. By Henry Peacham. Mr. of Arts some-time of Trinity Coll: in Cambridge
[London]: [John Legat] for Francis Constable, 1622
Stationer's Register: entered 3 July [1622]
Folger STC 19502 c. 1
Sig. P

This scholar, artist, composer, Continental traveler, and prolific writer produced one of the most popular and oft-reprinted conduct books in the seventeenth century. The table of contents of *The Compleat Gentleman* reveals the breadth of Peacham's interests and expertise, offered in aid of the educational formation of young gentlemen. (To these, later editions would add chapters on Travel and Fishing.) Music historians have been particularly interested in Peacham's substantial chapter on music. In addition to the standard encomia to the heaven-sent powers and gifts of music found in many conduct books of the period, Peacham offers this exceptionally concise practical advice: "I desire no more in you then to sing your part sure, and at the first sight, withall, to play the same vpon your Violl, or the exercise of the Lute, priuately to your selfe" (p. 100). Most interesting is his enumeration and description of the best composers to be emulated. *Primus inter pares* for Peacham was William Byrd, who was a professional acquaintance and also a neighbor. Among the Italians singled out for special praise was Peacham's own instructor, Orazio Vecchi. It is worth noting that even by 1622 most of the Italian and English composers mentioned by Peacham were representative of an old-fashioned musical style. (Pamela Starr)

70. Treble partbook, untexted instrumental ensemble and vocal music, and English anthems, (first part) ca. 1590, (second part, possibly autograph of Matthew Jeffries) ca. 1600 (catalogued as "Common-place book containing motets, in nominees, and anthems")
Folger MS V.a.408
Fols. 8v–9r: Claudius Coregens [Merulo], "Another songe" ["Qual maggior segri Aurora"]

Warwick Edwards has associated this manuscript, the sole survivor of a set of five, with Matthew Jeffries (ca. 1558–ca. 1615), a composer and vicar choral at Wells Cathedral from 1579 to at least 1613.[63] This partbook is the only surviving source for four of Jeffries's instrumental pieces as well as five anthems that could well be by him. It also contains two versions of his anthem, "Praise the Lord ye servants."

Musicians—professional and amateur alike—assembled repertories of compositions they liked to sing, or in this case, play, since the texts were omitted from the Continental vocal music. Even after the establishment of commercial music printing in England in the 1570s, music continued to circulate and to be copied into manuscripts. We see in the choice of a madrigal published in 1566 by the Italian composer, Claudio Merulo (1533–1604), called only "Another songe," further evidence of the taste for Italian music.

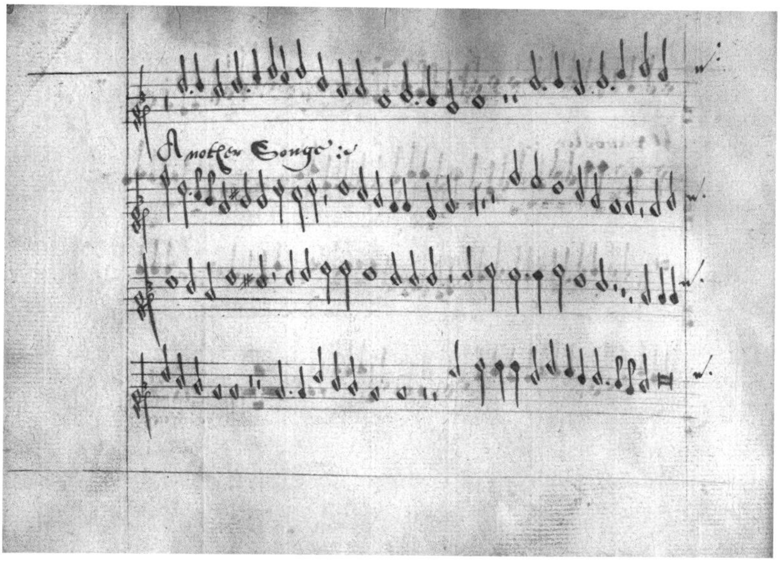

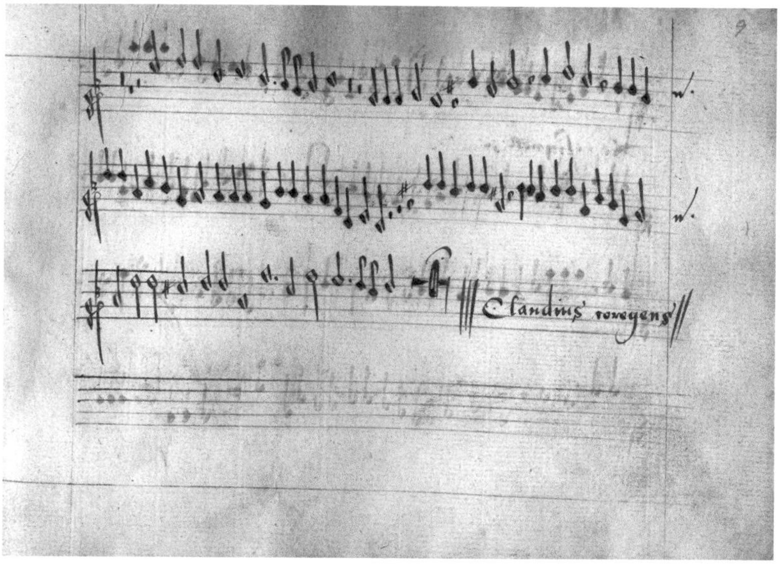

Cat. 70.

71. Randolph Helsby
Autograph letter signed, to Mary Hatton
The Strand, July 2, 1654
Folger MS X.d.493 (10)

In this love letter to Mary Hatton, Randolph Helsby describes a festive outing on the Thames in which the passengers were entertained with "good voyces & singinge of maddrigalls" as they boated from Charing Cross to Hampton and back again. Helsby enjoyed "the sweetlie loud notes" of Mrs. Cicely Wynne and her cousin, Doll, and admired Lady Powell's bravery as she continued to sing despite her voice breaking "awaie from all curbe and time." He recounts the flirtatious antics between Doll and one Mr. Brearton (Doll "worked her eyes, now full of drollerie when he came round aboute her, & then . . . she drops them prettily & here & there cast them aside till he was smill all ouer fantastickly & went nigh stumbling into her lapp"), and the dining and dancing that followed at Mrs. Wynne's house.[64] From this account it is clear that amateurs did not always attain the desired level of competence. (Heather Wolfe)

72. Hannah Woolley (1622 or 1623–ca. 1675)
The gentlewomans companion; or, a guide to the female sex: containing directions of behaviour, in all places, companies, relations, and conditions, from their childhood down to old age: viz. as, children to parents. Scholars to governours. Single to servants. Virgins to suitors. Married to husbands. Huswifes to the house. Mistresses to servants. Mothers to children. Widows to the world. Prudent to all. With letters and discourses upon all occasions. Whereunto is added, a guide for cook-maids, dairy-maids, chamber-maids, and all others that go to service. The whole being an exact rule for the female sex in general
London: A. Maxwell for Dorman Newman, 1673
Folger W3276.8
Sig. F6

Hannah Woolley (or Wooley, as she more frequently styled herself) was one of several women authors who addressed the educational formation of young women in seventeenth-century England. A professional cook and former schoolmistress, Woolley was the author of several popular cookbooks, including *The Ladies Directory* (1661), *The Cooks Guide* (1664), and *The Queen-like Closet* (1670). Although it, too, contains a substantial section devoted to recipes, *The Gentlewomans Companion* was Woolley's most significant offering in the literary genre of the courtesy book. Modeled on the numerous manuals directed at young men, it attempted to define the standards of formation for women of all stations. Woolley's exclusive authorship of this work has been called into question, but scholars attribute much of the text to her.

Of the four recreations "most fitting and proper for young gentlewoman," including music, dancing, drawing, and reading, the performance of music occupies two pages. Woolley does not attempt to offer practical instructions; she is more concerned with the etiquette of public performance: the "do's" and—especially—the "don'ts" of amateur musicianship. Echoes of Woolley's prescriptions linger on in the drawing rooms of Jane Austen's novels.

Woolley completes her discussion of music with the chapter "Of wanton Songs, and idle Ballads." Here she inveighs against the texts that might com-

promise a young woman's innocence in the performance of such songs: "You may easily believe this to be truth, if you consider the multiplicity of vanity and trumpery which stuff these Ballads; how an amorous or rather foolishly fond Virgin forsook Kindred and Country, to run after a stranger and her Lover" (p. 76). As always with such injunctions, they serve to document the enduring popularity of the "idle ballads."
(Pamela Starr)

73. Nicholas Yonge (d. 1619), compiler
Mvsica transalpina. Madrigales translated of foure, fiue and sixe partes, chosen out of diuers excellent authors, vvith the first and second part of La verginella, made by Maister Byrd, vpon tvvo stanza's of Ariosto, and brought to speake English vvith the rest. Published by N. Yonge, in fauour of such as take pleasure in musicke of voices
London: Thomas East, the assigne of William Byrd, 1588
Folger STC 26094
Sextus, sig. B4: Marenzio, "Because my loue" ("Che la mia donna"), second part of "I soung sometime" ("Cantai gia"); table of contents

Nicholas Yonge, known to have served as a singer at St. Paul's Cathedral in London, fed the English mania for Italian music by publishing this anthology of madrigals in English translation; a second volume appeared in 1597. The composers include internationally known figures such as Palestrina, Marenzio, Wert, Lasso, Monte, and Ferrabosco as well as lesser-known Italians and *oltramontani* writing in Italian. The six partbooks were bound together into a single volume, a format which prevents them from being used in performance. Five of the partbooks contain important manuscript additions. The sextus part comes from a different set, a dismembered binder's copy whose volumes contained at least 258 pages, to judge from the manuscript pagination added to coordinate the parts for performance ("256" and "257" are visible on the opening displayed). As in Watson's *Italian Madrigalls Englished* (cat. 75), William Byrd's name appears prominently on the title page. It can also be found in the surely deliberate spelling of "byrd" in the final composition of the volume.[65]

74. Thomas Morley (1557–1602)
Di Tomaso Morlei il primo libro delle ballette a cinqve voci
London: Thomas East, 1595
Folger STC 18118 bd. w. STC 18119
Canto, title page

Thomas Morley, seen here in Italian guise as Tomaso Morlei (printer Thomas East became Tomaso Este!), not only modeled his ballets on the *balletti* of Giovanni Gastoldi but also issued them in two editions, one in English, one in Italian, perhaps in the hopes of increasing sales. The book is dedicated to Robert Cecil, first earl of Salisbury and a member of the Privy Council, who would help Morley obtain the patent for publishing music.[66] Morley described "Balletts, commonlie called *fa las* . . . a slight kind of musick it is & as I take it deuised to be daunced to voices."[67] Morley's *Ballette* was bound with seven other titles, in a handsome contemporary calf-leather binding, with gilt blocked

Cat. 74.

and tooled decorations and the initials C. S., that belonged to Sir Charles Somerset. Somerset bound the books, all of them printed by Thomas East between 1595 and 1608—six by Thomas Morley, one by the Netherlandish composer Orlando di Lasso, and one by Henry Youll—as a set consisting of five volumes, one for each voice part; only the cantus has survived.[68]

75. Thomas Watson (1555/6–1592)
The first sett, of Italian madrigalls Englished, not to the sense of the originall dittie, but after the affection of the noate. By Thomas Watson Gentleman. There are also heere inserted two excellent madrigalls of Master VVilliam Byrds, composed after the Italian vaine, at the request of the sayd Thomas Watson
London: Thomas Este, the assigne of William Byrd, 1590
Folger STC 25119 c. 1
Title page

Thomas Watson, a poet and translator, compiled this volume of Italian madrigals to build on the success of Yonge's *Musica Transalpina* (cat. 73). This important anthology, consisting of twenty-eight madrigals, twenty-three of which were composed by Luca Marenzio, played a significant role in making Italian madrigals accessible to English audiences and musicians. Watson's goal was not a literal translation of the words but rather a text that reflected (or "read") the gestures in the music, or as Watson wrote in the title, "not to the sense of the originall dittie, but after the affection of the Noate." Dedicated to the earl of Essex, the anthology has strong connections to the Sidney circle, including

• (assignee) a person to whom a right/property is ~~assigned~~ legally transferred

five Sidney-related texts. The title page places William Byrd in a prominent position, both as composer (the only English composer in the volume) and a monopolist (he was the sole holder of the patent for printing music, granted by Queen Elizabeth in 1575); the volume was printed under his assigne. Byrd's settings pay tribute to his powerful patron, Queen Elizabeth, asking her to "take well in worth a simply toy."

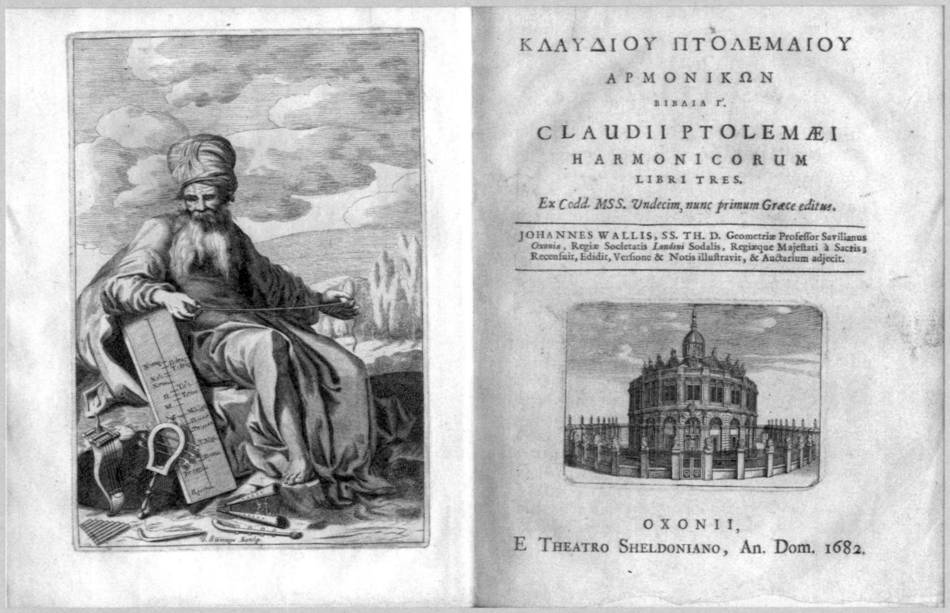
ΚΛΑΥΔΙΟΥ ΠΤΟΛΕΜΑΙΟΥ
ΑΡΜΟΝΙΚΩΝ
ΒΙΒΛΙΑ Γ'.
CLAUDII PTOLEMÆI
HARMONICORUM
LIBRI TRES.
Ex Codd. MSS. Undecim, nunc primum Græce editus.
JOHANNES WALLIS, SS. TH. D. Geometriæ Professor Savilianus Oxoniæ, Regiæ Societatis Londini Sodalis, Regiæque Majestati à Sacris; Recensuit, Edidit, Versione & Notis illustravit, & Auctarium adjecit.
OXONII,
E Theatro Sheldoniano, An. Dom. 1682.

Cat. 80.

• a group of studies (arithmetic, music, geometry, and astronomy) forming the upper division of the seven liberal arts (in medeival* universities [The trivium was the lower division — grammar, rhetoric, and logic.)

"Sciences, and Artes Mathematicall": Speculative Music

* Middle Ages, c. 500 to 1500

While music today is generally thought of as one of the arts, from late antiquity it belonged to the quadrivium with the other mathematical sciences—arithemetic, geometry, and astronomy. Reflecting an age-old divide between *cantor* and *musicus*, the realm of practical music theory—the rudiments of notation and counterpoint—was the purview of professional musicians, while that of the science of music was cultivated by university-trained intellectuals. We see diverse strands of musical thought in seventeenth-century England—from Fludd's occult philosophy, with its interest in cosmology, to Bacon's new experimental philosophy, with its interest in recording the properties of the physical world. Other writers, associated with the Royal Society, explored the mathematical bases of tuning and the emerging field of acoustics.[69]

76. Stephen Gosson (1554–1625)
The schoole of abuse, conteining a plesaunt inuectiue against poets, pipers, plaiers, iesters, and such like caterpillers of a co[m]monwelth; setting vp the flagge of defiance to their mischieuous exercise, [and] ouerthrowing their bulwarkes, by prophane writers, naturall reason, and common experience: a discourse as pleasaunt for gentlemen that fauour learning, as profitable for all that wyll follow virtue. By Stephan Gosson. Stud. Oxon.
London: [T. Dawson] for Thomas VVoodcocke, 1579
Folger STC 12097
Sig. A8

Gosson's little rant about music and the other arts of his day reveals his education in the classics. He describes the power of Chiron, Terpandrus, and Homer and then asks witheringly, "Thinke you that those miracles coulde bee wrought with playing of Daunces, Dumpes, Pauins, Galiardes, Measures Fancyes, or new streynes"—a veritable catalogue of contemporary instrumental music. He cites Pythagoras as condemning those "that judge Musicke by sounde and eare. If you will bee good Scholers, and profite well in the Arte of Musicke, shutte your Fidels in their cases and looke up to heauen: the order of the Spheres, the unfallible motion of the Planets . . ." He rehearses the standard stories, for example, of Terpander, who "never pyped Rogero nor Turkelony [two ballads] . . . but taught them too treade a better measure."

77. Francis Bacon (1561–1626)
Sylva sylvarvm: or a naturall historie. In ten centvries. VVritten by the Right Honourable Francis Lo. Verulam Viscount St. Alban. Published after the authors death, by VVilliam Rawley Doctor of Diuinitie, late his Lordships chaplaine
London: I[ohn] H[aviland and Augustine Mathewes] for William Lee, 1626 [i.e. 1627]
Folger STC 1168 c. 1
Sig. G3

Francis Bacon, viscount St. Alban and Lord Chancellor, was a prolific writer and influential philosopher, who argued for a method of investigation based on active observation. In *Sylua Syluarum*, a posthumous collection of one thousand observations organized as ten centuries, he rejected traditional scholastic approaches as "*Yeelding* of the *Causes* of the *Practique* very weakly; being reduced unto certain Mysticall Subtleties, of no use, and not much Truth." Instead, working from Porta's *Magia Naturalis*, he presented a series of observations about sound, its causes and properties. His work stands at the beginning of the development of acoustics as a field of investigation.[70]

Detail, cat. 80.

78. Francis North, first baron Guilford (1637–1685)
A philosophical essay of musick directed to a friend. Feb. 3d 1676/7. Imprimatur, Guil. Sill.
London: for John Martyn, printer to the Royal Society, 1677
Private collection
Table 1

Francis North was a judge and politician, serving as chief justice of common pleas and then as lord keeper of the great seal. He published this essay anonymously for an unidentified friend, possibly his brother John.[71] Not a member of the Royal Society, North nonetheless communicated with members, and his synopsis was published in the *Transactions* of the Society. The treatise deals with the causes of musical sound, the effects of sensory perception, and the implications for musical cognition.[72] North defines a tone as "the repetition of cracks or pulses in equal spaces of time so quick that the interstices or intervals are not perceptible to sense." Consonance is explained in terms of patterns of coincidence, known as coincidence theory. In the diagram, North illustrates the patterns of coincidence of pulses for seven consonant intervals; the shorter the distance between coincidences (shown on the horizontal axis), the more consonant the interval.

79. René Descartes (1596–1650)
William Brouncker, viscount (1620 or 1621–1684), translator
Renatus Des-Cartes excellent compendium of musick: with necessary and judicious animadversions thereupon. By a person of honour
London: Thomas Harper, for Humphrey Moseley, 1653
Folger D1132
Sig. I2

William Brouncker, second viscount Brouncker of Lyons, served as president of the Royal Society from its founding in 1663 until 1677. A mathematician, he translated Descartes's youthful treatise on music (*Compendium Musicae*, written in 1618 but not published until 1650), publishing it anonymously ("By a Person of Honour"). He added an essay challenging Descartes in which he employed logarithms to calculate musical intervals. The diagram shows the older syntonic diatonic scale with three different ways of calculating equal semitones.[73]

80. Claudius Ptolemy (after 83–161 CE)
John Wallis (1616–1703), editor and translator
ΚΛΑΥΔΙΟΥ ΠΤΟΛΕΜΑΙΟΥ ΑΡΜΟΝΙΚΩΝ ΒΙΒΛΙΑ Γʹ
Claudii Ptolemæi harmonicorum libri tres. Ex Codd. MSS. undecim, nunc primum Græce editus. Johannes Wallis, SS. Th. D. Geometriæ Professor Savilianus Oxoniæ, Regiæ Societatis Londini Sodalis, Regiæque Majestati à Sacris; recensuit, edidit, versione & notis illustravit, & auctarium adjecit
Oxford: The Sheldonian Theatre, 1682
184– 262q
Title page, frontispiece signed "J. Sauage sculp." (John Savage, fl. 1680, engraver)

Savilian Professor of Geometry at Oxford and member of the Royal Society, Wallis edited and translated Ptolemy's *Harmonics*, a major treatise setting forth a quantitative approach to musical scales and intervals, part of the on-going project of recovering and interpreting the learning that survived from antiquity. Wallis added a lengthy appendix to his translation ("Appendix de veterum harmonica ad hodiernam comparata") in which he attempted a comparison between Greek musical practices and those of his own time. The rather fanciful frontispiece portrays Ptolemy seated in a landscape with seventeenth-century interpretations of ancient Greek musical instruments at his feet. He holds a string to measure the musical scale, inscribed on a tablet beside him. This is an early engraving by John Savage, who made engravings for the Royal Society from 1683; he was also the engraver of cat. 11. The Sheldonian Theatre appears on the opposite page not as the venue for music recitals it is today, but simply as the title page image of the publisher, housed in the building and better known by its later name, Oxford University Press.

81. Robert Fludd (1574–1637)
Anatomiae amphiteatrvm effigie triplici, more et conditione varia, designatvm Authore Roberto Fludd alias de Fluctibus Armigero & in Medicina D. Ox.
Oppenheim: Johann Theodore de Bry, 1623
Folger QM21.F6 1623 Cage
Plate after p. 314

Educated at Oxford, Robert Fludd was a physician and philosopher. A prolific writer who also served for a time as a music tutor, he wrote a lengthy treatise about practical music while he was at Oxford. He included it in his monumental *Utriusque Cosmi Maioris*, published in Oppenheim between 1617 and 1624 at the expense of the publisher, Johann Theodore de Bry, with extraordinary engravings. A Neoplatonist deeply interested in the occult, Fludd viewed music as the connection between the macrocosm (the universe) and the microcosm (man). The monochord, an age-old device for illustrating the musical scale, here stretches between the alpha and omega. Above the scale are the celestial hierarchy, the seven planets, the four elements, and above that the nine orders of angels, the nine spheres of the ethereal heaven, and the nine regions of the elemental world. This version of the divine monochord appeared as part of his 1621 reply to Johann Kepler, *Monochordum Mundi Symphoniacum*, published in this volume.[74]

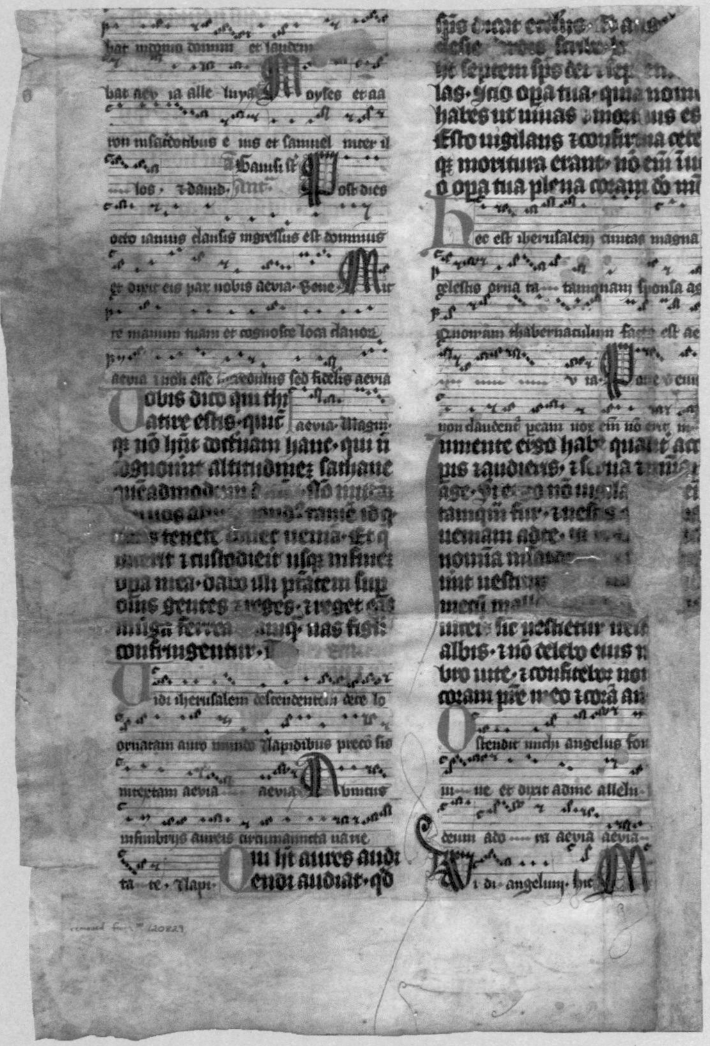

Cat. 82.

"O sing unto the Lord a new song": Worship in Times of Religious Strife

The changes begun during the time of Henry VIII, initially more concerned with economics and politics than with theology, turned during Edward VI's reign into a wholesale assault on the Old Religion, marked by iconoclasm and destruction of the entire apparatus of the liturgy, including music books, and the institutions that had supported the clerics who performed it. Mary I's reign witnessed a return to Catholic observance, while the Protestant exiles were absorbing practices of Calvin's Geneva. Elizabeth I re-established the *Book of Common Prayer*, and composers began to create new music for an English church that would offer a distinctive blend of traditional and reformed practices. The objects associated with worship tell the story of the rapid changes in religious practice.

• \brē-və-rē\ [L summary] book containg the prayers/hymns/readings/psalms for the canonical hours
• The night office forming with lauds the first of the canonical hours • a prescribed form/service of worship • an office of solem praise to God
• an eight day period of observance beginning with a festival ~~observance~~ day
• a musical part of worship sung responsively
• ?

82. Breviary (fragment), ca. 1375–1425, probably from western Germany
Office for Matins on the Octave of Easter (rite and provenance unknown)
Folger MS Z.d.30

This folio leaf, which is from a liturgical manuscript dating from the late-fourteenth or early-fifteenth century, served as part of a binding for a later book—probably one dating from the late-sixteenth century. Such re-use of materials from outdated liturgical books was common all over Europe, but the practice is especially significant for the history of liturgical music in England. Following the dissolution of monasteries and the subsequent adoption of a reformed liturgy, pre-Reformation books were systematically destroyed; remnants from such books are regarded as especially precious since they preserve English chant and occasionally polyphony from earlier liturgical practices.

The fragment here, however, stems from another tradition entirely. It originates from a notated breviary that probably dates from the last quarter of the fourteenth century or the first quarter of the fifteenth. Its notation is of the mixed Messine-German type prevalent in eastern and southern Germany, Austria, and Switzerland, though the decoration of its initials is consistent with that of West German manuscripts. The contents consist of antiphons, lessons, and responsories for Matins on the Octave of Easter. The texts of these works are drawn from the books of *Revelation* and *1 John*, and their order appears to vary substantially from that of the standard monastic cursus, a possible key to determining this leaf's as yet unknown provenance. (Eric Rice)

83. *Hore beatissime virginis Marie ad legitimum Sarisburiensis ecclesie ritum, cum quindecim orationibus beate Brigitte, ac multis alijs orationibus pulcherrimis, et indulgentijs, cum tabula aptissima iam vltimo adiectis. 1530*
Paris: François Regnault, 1530
Folger STC 15968
Fol. 54

Books of Hours, also known as primers, contain liturgies and prayers for lay devotion. "Bestsellers" in late medieval and early modern times, printed Books of Hours retain some of the conventions followed in luxury illuminated manuscripts, such as the use of marginal decorations and images as well as black letter. This edition was printed in France for an English market; it uses the Sarum rite and is written in English as well as Latin.[75] This opening, from a section devoted to the suffrages (brief services including prayers to specific saints), contains the conclusion of *Ave mundi spes Maria*, a medieval French sequence (rhymed poem for the Mass) in honor of the Virgin Mary. The reader is encouraged "every day in the mornynge after thre tollynges of the aue bell [to] say .iii. times the hoole salutacyon of our lady. Ave Maria gratia plena"; each recitation earns three hundred days of pardon. The reader who defaced this page and other references to the Pope reveals the anti-papist and iconoclastic fury of religious reformation in England. The system of buying indulgences or acquiring them through devotional practice came in for particular attack.

De beata Maria. Fo.liiii.

semper tecum sim mãsurus: a te nunq̃ recessu-
rus per infinita secula. Audi nos: quia filius
nichil negans te honorat: salua nos iesu pro
quibus virgo mater te exorat. Amẽ. Pater no
ster qui es in celis. Aue maria gratia plena do
minus tecum. ¶ Our holy father the pope
Sixtus hath graunted at the instaunce of the
hyghe moost and excellent princesse elizabeth
late qwene of englonde and wyf to our soue-
rayne lyege lorde kynge Heri the seuenth. god
haue mercy on her swete soule and all cristen
soules that euery day in the mornynge after
thre tollynges of the aue bell say.iii.times the
hoole salutacyon of our lady. Aue maria gratia plena. that is to say at.vi. the clocke in the
mornyng.iii. Aue maria. at.xii. the clocke at
none.iii. Aue maria. & at.vi. the clocke at euen
for euery tyme so doynge is graunted of the
spirituall tresour of holy chyrche.iii. C. dayes
of pardon totiens quotiens. And also our holy father the archebysshop of cantorbery and
yorke wit other.ix. bysshoppes of this reame
haue graunted.iii. times in the day.xl. dayes
of pardon to all them that be in the state of gra
ce able to receue pardon/the whyche begonne
the.xxvi. day of marche. Anno. M.cccc.xcii.
anno henrici.vii. And the somme of the indul
gence & pardon for euery. Aue maria.viii. hon
dred dayes & .lx. totiẽs quotiẽs. This prayer
shall be sayde at the tollynge of the aue bell.

Persecutus est draco mulierẽ q̃ peperit mas.12.

Misit serpens ex ore suo post mulierẽ. 12.ca.

Cat. 83.

84. Antiphoner (fragment), ca. late 14th/ early 15th century, provenance and rite unknown
Office for Matins for the Common of Several Martyrs
used as binding for
Valentine Leigh (fl. 1562)
The moste profitable and commendable science, of surueying of lands, tenementes, and hereditamentes: drawen and collected by the industrie of Valentin Ligh
London: Iohn Windet for Robart Dexter, 1592.
Folger STC 15419 c. 2
Inside front cover

The folium from this destroyed liturgical manuscript contains chants for the Office of the Common of Several Martyrs.[76] The cue to the psalm, "Deus venerunt gentes," is followed by the antiphon, "Jerusalem ciuitas sancta," which begins on the inside back cover (not shown) and continues on the second staff of the page on display, "ornamentis martirum decorata." Next come another psalm and antiphon, and on the fourth staff of the inside cover the responsory, "Adorauerunt uiuentem," with its calligraphic initial. "Deus venerunt gentes"—"O God, the heathen are come into thine inheritance; thy holy temple haue they defiled: they haue layd Ierusalem on heapes. The dead bodies of thy seruants haue they given to bee meate unto the foules of the heauen: the flesh of thy Saints unto the beasts of the earth" (King James version, Psalm 79)—can stand as a universal song of despair, used by every confessional group and encountered several times in this exhibition (cat. 91, 92).

85. *Manuale ad vsum per celebris ecclesie Sarisburiensis. Londini recenter impressu[m], necno[n] multis mendis tersum atq[ue] emu[n]datum*
London: [J. Kingston and H. Sutton], 1554
Folger STC 16154
Sig. L (fol. 81)

The accession of Queen Mary I in 1553 and the restoration of Catholic worship required a massive project of producing liturgical books for the Catholic rite to replace those destroyed during the reign of Edward VI.[77] A *manuale* contains instructions to clergy for the proper conduct of services such as baptisms, weddings, and funerals. This explanation of how to conduct the Canon of the Mass—the consecration of bread and wine—is described in the table of contents as "Canon cum rubrica a nouo incipientibus commodissima" (The Canon, with rubrics [the instructions printed in red] from the beginning that are very suitable for beginners). At the end of the prayer of consecration the priest sings "per omnia secula seculorum. Amen." A rubric explains, "here the priest raises his hands saying" and then follows the music for the "Pater noster" (Lord's Prayer).

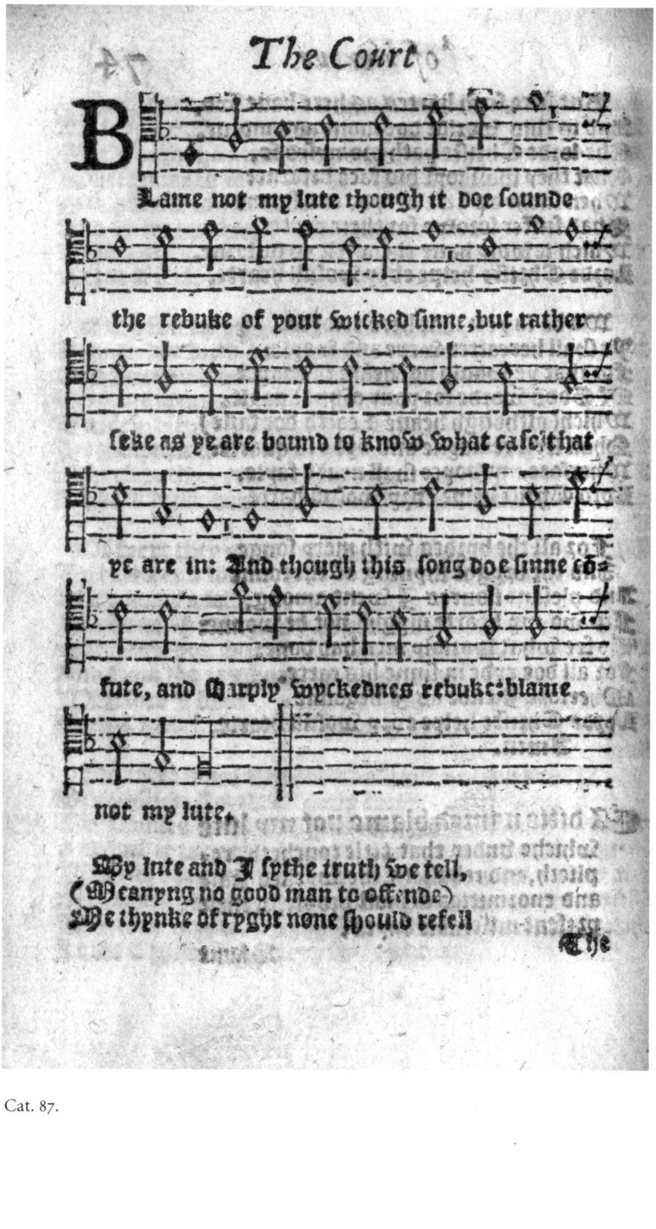
The Court
Blame not my lute though it doe sounde
the rebuke of your wicked sinne, but rather
seke as ye are bound to know what case that
ye are in: And though this song doe sinne sō-
sute, and sharply wyckednes rebuke: blame
not my lute.
My lute and I sythe truth we tell,
(Meanyng no good man to offende)
Me thynke of ryght none should refell
The

Cat. 87.

86. *The forme of prayers and ministration of the sacraments, &c. vsed in the Englishe congregation at Geneua: and approued, by the famous and godly learned man, Iohn Caluyn*
Geneva: Iohn Crespin, 1556
Folger STC 16561
Sig. E8

This "book of common order" presents the manner of worship by English exiles in Calvin's Geneva during the reign of Queen Mary I; it also contains revised versions of Sternhold's metrical translation of the psalms, as well as an English translation of Calvin's catechism. The liturgy is that of the reform faction (rather than the prayerbook faction), devised by John Knox and others.[78] This introduction to the prayer of institution shows the stark contrast with the actions of the Mass, shown in cat. 85: "The exhortation ended, the minister commeth doune from the pulpet, and sitteth at the Table, euery man and woman in likewise takinge their place as occasion best serueth, then he taketh bread and geueth thankes, either in these woordes followinge, or like in effect" (p. 75). The opening shows the administration of the Lord's Supper, in which members of the congregation, gathered around the table, partake of both bread and wine.

87. John Hall (1529/30–1568/9)
[*The courte of vertue*]
[London: Thomas Marshe, 1565]
Folger STC 12632
Fol. 75: "Blame not my lute though it doe sounde the rebuke of your wicked sinne"

This volume was listed in the Stationers' Register as "The couurte of vertu contaynynge many holy or spretuall songes sonettes psalmes ballettes shorte sentences as well of holy scriptures as others &c." Created by surgeon and author John Hall to counteract the *Court of Venus* and "other bokes of lecherous Ballades," it includes a number of sacred songs or hymns, some of them to tunes familiar from ballads. This parody of Thomas Wyatt's "Blame not my lute" (cat. 61) is introduced as "A ditie named blame not my lute whiche under that title toucheth, replieth, and rebuketh, the wycked state and enormities of most people, in these present miserable dayes."[79]

88. *The mornyng and euenyng prayer and communion, set forthe in foure partes, to be song in churches, both for men and children, wyth dyuers other godly prayers & anthems, of sundry mens doynges*
London: Iohn Day, 1565
Folger STC 16443 c. 1 vol. 1
Tenor, sig. R2

John Day (1522–1584), the prominent printer who held the valuable patent for printing psalms, also published this collection of four-voice service music for the reformed English liturgy. Thomas Causton (ca. 1520–1569), a gentleman of the Chapel Royal, was the composer of half of the music in this collection and possibly its compiler. This opening contains an anthem by Robert Johnson (ca. 1500–ca. 1560), "I geue you a new commaundement," Thomas Tallis's (ca. 1505–1585) well-known "Yff ye loue me kepe my commaundements," and Robert Okeland's (fl. 1532–1550) "Prayse we the father, the son and holy ghost." The printing of this collection began in 1560, under the title *Certaine notes set forth in foure and three parts to be song at the morning communion, and evening praier*; it was not published until 1565.[80] The music was probably composed during the time of Edward VI, using a simple chordal style that made the text audible.

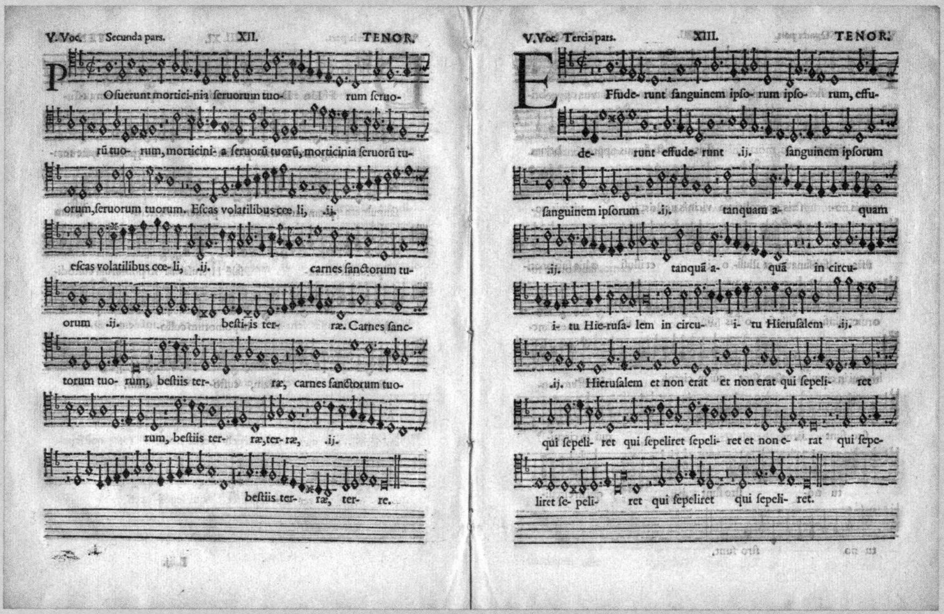
V. Voc. Secunda pars. XII. TENOR.
POsuerunt mortici-nia seruorum tuo- rum seruo-
rũ tuo- rum, morticini- a seruorũ tuorũ, morticinia seruorũ tuorum, seruorum tuorum. Escas volatilibus coe li, .ij.
escas volatilibus coe- li, .ij. carnes sanctorum tuorum .ij. besti-is ter- ræ. Carnes sanctorum tuo- rum, bestiis ter- ræ, carnes sanctorum tuorum, bestiis ter- ræ, ter- ræ, .ij.
bestiis ter- ræ, ter- re.
V. Voc. Tercia pars. XIII. TENOR.
EFfude- runt sanguinem ipso- rum ipso- rum, effu-
de- runt effude- runt .ij. sanguinem ipsorum
sanguinem ipsorum .ij. tanquam a- quam
.ij. tanquã a- quã in circu-
i- tu Hie-rusa- lem in circu- i- tu Hierusalem .ij.
.ij. Hierusalem et non erat et non erat qui sepeli- ret
qui sepeli- ret qui sepeliret sepeli- ret et non e- rat qui sepeliret se- peli- ret qui sepeliret qui sepeli- ret.

Cat. 91.

"Thy holy temple haue they defiled: they haue layd Ierusalem on heapes": Religious Persecution

In the continuing conflicts over religious beliefs and practices, composers wrote music to serve the needs of their communities. The compositions by William Byrd intended for the use of recusants are a case in point. The grisly executions, suffered at various times by all of the religious persuasions, were recorded in images and texts but also in musical settings. In a time of censorship, a multivalent text like Psalm 79 (78 in the Vulgate)—"O God, the heathen are come into thine inheritance, thy holy temple haue they defiled: they haue layd Iersusalem on heapes."—could register in turn the despair of each confessional group. Biblical texts were safe from censorship and yet profoundly expressive.[81]

89. Richard Verstegan (ca. 1550–1640)
Theatrum crudelitatum haereticorum nostri temporis
Antwerp: Adrian Hubert, 1587
Folger BR1605.V4 1592 Cage
Sig. L2

Images such as this one, depicting the "persecution of Catholics by Protestant Calvinists in England," were designed to inflame, functioning as a Catholic counterpart of Foxe's *Actes and Monuments.*[82] Martyrs were drawn on hurdles to the place of execution, hanged, drawn and quartered, and burned; their heads were displayed on Bridge Gate, at the south entrance to the city (see cat. 7).

90. Thomas Alfield (1552–1582)
A true reporte of the death & martyrdome of M. Campion Iesuite and preiste, & M. Sherwin, & M. Bryan preistes, at Tiborne the first of December 1581 observid and written by a Catholike preist, which was present therat wheruuto [sic] is annexid certayne verses made by sundrie persons
[London: Verstegan, 1582]
Folger STC 4537
Sig. E2: "Why do I use my paper inke, and penne"

Entitled "Vpon the death of M Edmund Campion, one of the societie of the holy name of Iesus," this long poem, attributed to Henry Walpole (1558–1595), who would later himself become a Jesuit martyr, captures the horror of Campion's execution, a verbal counterpart to the images that circulated soon after his death (see, for example, Verstegan's *Theatrum Crudelitatum*, cat. 89).[83] Being in possession of this poem was grounds for imprisonment. Byrd's setting and publication of a sanitized version (cat. 107) was audacious.

91. William Byrd (between 1540 and 1543–1623)
Liber primus sacrarvm cantionum quinque vocum. Autore Guilielmo Byrd organista regio, Anglo
[London]: Thomas Est, the assigne of William Byrd, 1589
Folger STC 4247 c. 2
Tenor, sig. B4, nos. XII–XIII: secunda pars, "Posuerunt morticinia"; and tertia pars, "Effuderunt sanguinem"

Byrd's setting of "Deus venerunt gentes," a grisly psalm whose words can be taken as a description of the martyrdom suffered by Campion and other Jesuits, employs the same text that the reformer Bishop Ridley uttered as he was burned by order of Queen Mary. Byrd published this motet in his first book of "sacred songs" (his 1575 *Cantiones, qvae ab argvmento sacrae vocantvr* was a joint enterprise with his teacher Tallis), a collection replete with themes of Babylonian captivity, martyrdom, and liberation. The pope had granted an indulgence for those who prayed for the conversion of England by saying this text.

92. Nicholas Ridley (1500?–1555)
John Foxe (1516–1587), editor
A frendly farewel, which Master Doctor Ridley, late Bishop of London did write beinge prisoner in Oxforde, vnto all his true louers and frendes in God, a litle before that he suffred for the testimony of the truthe of Christ his Gospell. Newly setforth and

allowed according to the order apoynted in the Quenes Maiesties iniunctions
London: Ihon Day, 1559
Folger STC 21051 bd. w. STC 6152
Sig. B2

Bishop of London and ardent reformer, Nicholas Ridley drew on the words of Psalm 79, "Deus venerunt gentes in hereditatem tuam," as he neared death: "O Lord God the gentiles, heathen nations are come into thy heritage, they haue defiled thy holye Temple, and made Ierusalem an heape of stones." His "frendly farewell," described by its editor, John Foxe, as "this litell treatis of Doct. Nicholas Ridley, late Byshoppe of London," would subsequently be included in *Actes and Monuments.* Ridley's theology is clear: "In the steade of the Lordes holy table, they geue the people with muche solemne disgisinge a thinge they call it their masse, but in dead and in truthe it is a uery maskinge and a mockery of the true Supper of the Lord."

93. William Byrd (between 1540 and 1543–1623)
[*Mass for three voices*]
[London: Thomas East, ca. 1599–1600]
Folger STC 4249.2
Cantus, sig. A1: "Kyrie eleison" and "[Gloria] Et in terra pax"

This is one of Byrd's three settings of the Ordinary of the Mass, for three voices (the other two are for four and five voices), a second edition of a work first published in 1593 or 1594.[84] Each of the three voice parts was printed as a single gathering in upright quarto format (one sheet printed on two sides, containing eight pages). Because Catholic observance was illegal, it is printed with no title page or indication of the name of the printer, city, and date, though with the composer's name—"W. Byrd." Printing of this hidden edition may have coincided with a meeting of recusants at East's house in April 1600; two of East's apprentices informed the authorities, and the Catholics were arrested. This set of parts, now bound in a single volume, once belonged to a binder's copy.

94. William Byrd (between 1540 and 1543–1623)
Gradvalia; seu cantionvm sacrarum: quarum aliæ ad quatuor, aliæ verò ad quinque et sex voces editæ sunt. Lib. secvndvs. Authore Gulielmo Byrde, organista Regio, Anglo. Ex noua & accuratissima eiusdem authoris recognitione
[London]: H. L[ownes] for Richardi Redmeri, 1610
Folger STC 4243.2
Sextus, sig. A3: In festo S.S. Petri & Pauli, "Nunc scio vere"

Byrd's *Gradualia* (1605 and 1607; reissued with a cancel title page in 1610) is a two-volume collection of polyphony, 109 pieces in all, for various feasts and observances of the Catholic liturgical year. It was the last of his Latin publications, the end of a three-decade journey which began in the inner circle of the Elizabethan court and ended among a disenfranchised Catholic community reeling from the aftermath of the 1605 Gunpowder Plot. His music for SS. Peter and Paul is the most opulently scored in the *Gradualia*: as the only six-voice Mass in the cycle, it appears as a bright splash of Counter-Reformation triumphalism in a collection

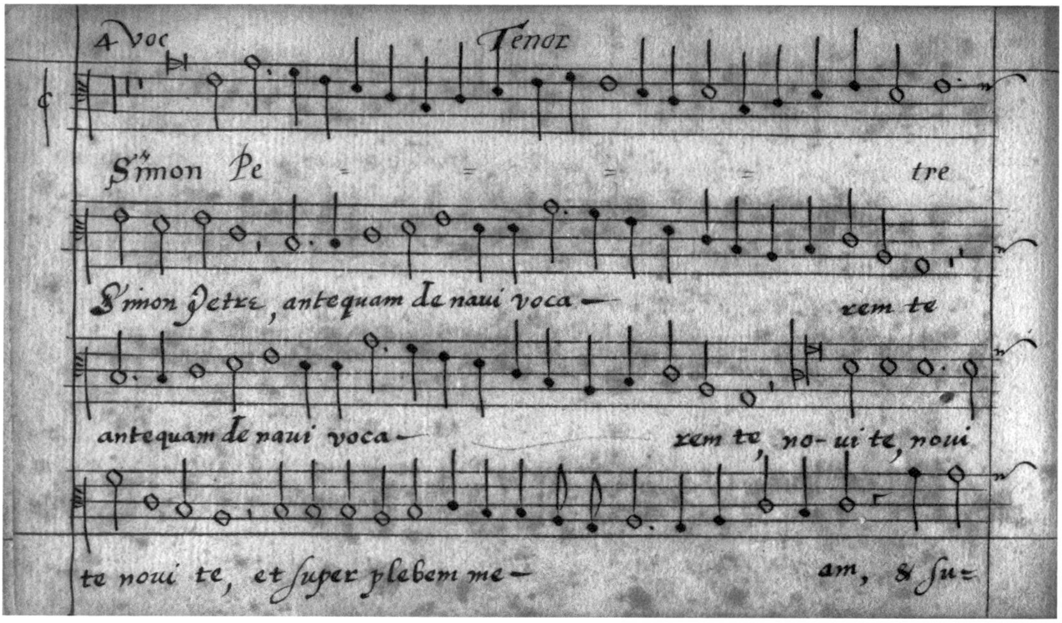
4 Voc
Tenor
Simon Pe tre
Simon Petre, antequam de naui voca- rem te
antequam de naui voca- rem te, no- ui te, noui
te noui te, et super plebem me- am, & su-

Cat. 95.

dominated by spare and often dark sonorities. With the ongoing debate in England over the claims of the papacy, it was also some of the most controversial music Byrd ever published. Either he or his printer acted in self-defense by censoring all non-biblical texts referring to the authority of Peter. He left the well-informed musician to fill them in again. Nothing certain is known about the identity of "G. Ga.," author of the poetic tribute to Byrd on the back of the dedication page. The Folger exemplar, with ink foliation on the music pages beginning "17," was once part of a binder's copy.
(Kerry McCarthy)

95. Tenor partbook containing Latin sacred music (primarily motets, with several hymns and a Kyrie) and two instrumental fantasias (catalogued as "A collection of anonymous non-liturgical motets, mass-movements, and hymns"), ca. 1600–1630
Folger MS V.a.406
Fol. 18: Anonymous, "Simon Petre"

This manuscript is one of a set of three surviving partbooks (a cantus book is missing) originally owned by the English Catholic recusant Edward Paston (1550–1630). Paston compiled one of the largest manuscript collections of music in England in his time: over forty sets of partbooks and lute-books have been identified as written by scribes in his employ at his manor houses in Norfolk. The large number of works by William Byrd in these manuscripts as well as Paston's acquaintance with Sir William Petre, a close friend and patron of Byrd's, makes it likely that Paston knew Byrd personally. Their common faith and interest in music is also suggestive. Byrd for his part set a number of poems by Paston, some referring to mutual acquaintances and daily life in Paston's home.[85]

The text of the motet "Simon Petre" describes Jesus's call of the apostle Peter, to whom he gives the "keys of the kingdom of heaven" ("claves regni caelorum"); it is drawn from the liturgy for Matins on the Feast of SS. Peter and Paul (responds 1 and 2). This feast, suppressed in the liturgy of the established English church, naturally would have had deep resonance for the Catholic recusant community in England, celebrating as it does the office of the papacy. The text may also have been chosen by Paston as a tribute to the Petre family; Byrd included settings of the Mass propers for the Feast of SS. Peter and Paul in his *Gradualia* (cat. 94), also perhaps as a tribute to his patron. The unidentified composer writes in an imitative style long established in continental European sacred music.[86]
(Samuel A. Schmitt)

Cat. 101.

“If any of you be mery let hym synge psalmes”: Psalms in Church and at Home

It is hard to overestimate the importance of the Psalms of David in early modern England. Chanted Latin psalms played an essential part in Roman Catholic worship. The Reformation introduced metrical psalms in the vernacular for congregational singing in the translations of Sternhold, Hopkins, and others. These became a treasured possession of the common people, and were also used in family prayers, sometimes in elaborate settings. They were published in more than 1,450 editions over 300 years. In addition the daily chanting of the prose psalms in English was a staple of the cathedral service.[87]
(Nicholas Temperley)

96. Thomas Ravenscroft (ca. 1590–ca. 1635), compiler
The whole booke of psalmes: with the hymnes evangelicall, and songs spiritvall. Composed into 4. parts by sundry authors, to such seuerall tunes, as haue beene, and are vsually sung in England, Scotland, Wales, Germany, Italy, France, and the Nether-lands: neuer as yet before in one volumne published. Also: 1. A briefe abstract of the prayse, efficacie, and vertue of the Psalmes. 2. That all clarkes of churches, and the auditory, may know what tune each proper Psalme may be sung vnto. Newly corrected and enlarged by Tho: Rauenscroft bachelar of musicke
London: [Thomas Snodham] for the Company of Stationers, 1621
Folger STC 2575.2
Sig. M7 (pages 180–81)

This is a revision of East's book (cat. 97), with many new tunes. As before, the settings are in four parts with the tune in the tenor. The magnificent tune for Psalm 104, still in common use, was probably created and certainly harmonized by Ravenscroft himself; its anapestic meter (based on a foot consisting of two unstressed syllables followed by a stressed syllable) and the irregular rhythm of its last phrase are distinctive.
(Nicholas Temperley)

97. Thomas East (ca. 1540–1608), compiler
The whole booke of psalmes: with their wonted tunes, as they are sung in churches, composed into foure parts: being so placed, that foure may sing each one a seueral part in this booke. VVherin the church tunes are carefully corrected, & thervnto added other short tunes vsually sung in London and most places of this realme. VVith a table in the beginning of this booke, of such tunes as are nevvly added, vvith the number of each Psalme placed to the sayd tune. Compiled by x. sondry authors, vvho haue so laboured heerein, that the vnskilful vvith small practice may attaine to sing that part, vvhich is fittest for their voyce
London: Thomas Est, the assigne of William Byrd, 1594
Folger STC 2488
Sig. B

This is a complete edition of the "Old Version" with a tune for every psalm and hymn, harmonized by a leading composer. It could be carried in the pocket, and the vocal parts were "so placed, that foure may sing each one a seueral part." The table of contents shows East's innovation of tune names, dating from the first edition of 1592, and his statement (1594 onward) that only four tunes were in use in "most churches of this Realme."
(Nicholas Temperley)

98. John Playford (1623–1686/7)
An introduction to the skill of musick. In two books. The first: the grounds and rules of musick, according to the gam-vt, and other principles thereof. The second: instructions & lessons for the bass-viol: and instruments & lessons for the treble-violin. By John Playford. To which is added, the art of descant, or composing musick in parts. By Dr. Tho. Campion. With annotations thereon, by Mr. Chr. Simpson
London: W. Godbid for J. Playford, 1674
Folger P2480
Sig. F5 (pages 72–73)

In 1658 Playford started adding a section of the most popular psalm tunes, with basses, to his highly successful music tutor. The early (1564) tune OXFORD, possibly derived from a psalm tone, spawned several other tunes as descants. One of them was LITCHFIELD, included here with an independent bass. On the opposite page Playford offers advice to parish clerks on choosing tunes and setting the pitch; organs, even after the Restoration, were extremely rare in parish churches.
(Nicholas Temperley)

99. John Cosyn (d. 1609)
Musike of six, and fiue partes. Made vpon the common tunes vsed in singing of the psalmes. By Iohn Cosyn
London: Iohn Wolfe, 1585
Folger STC 5828
Altus, sig. A2 dedication

This very rare collection, in six partbooks, contains forty-three settings of the common psalm tunes. No surviving set includes the cantus part, which has been supplied editorially in the recording of Sternhold's Psalm 130. Tunes may be carried by any part, or may migrate between several parts: here the tune is in the altus. The dedication shows that the book's function was to provide for devout singing in aristocratic homes rather than in church.
(Nicholas Temperley)

100. John Playford (1623–1686/7)
Psalms & hymns in solemn musick of foure parts on the common tunes to the psalms in metre: used in parish-churches. Also six hymns for one voyce to the organ. By John Playford
London: W. Godbid for J. Playford, 1671
Folger P2498
Sig. O

This handsome volume is Playford's quixotic effort to restore due dignity to the singing of psalms in church. The male-voice harmony was meant for the Company of Parish Clerks of London, whose weekly practices he directed. Black letter distinguishes the "Old Version" translations from the alternate texts supplied by Playford. The "Hymn to this Tune" is by the Catholic John Austin. The tune, WINCHESTER (1592), had already won its enduring place in English affections. Now it is chiefly associated, in England, with the Christmas hymn "While shepherds watched their flocks by night."
(Nicholas Temperley)

101. Thomas Sternhold (d. 1549) and others
The whole booke of psalmes: collected into English meeter by T. Sternhold, I. Hopkins, W. Whittingham, and others, conferred with the Hebrew, with apt notes to sing them withall. Newly set foorth, and allowed to be sung in all churches, of all the people together, before and after morning and euening prayer, as also before and after sermons. Moreouer in priuate houses, for their godly solace and comfort, laying apart all vngodly songs and ballads, which tend onely to the nourishing of vice, and corrupting of youth.
London: for the Companie of Stationers, 1610
Folger STC 2535.2 bd. w. STC 2907
English embroidered dos-à-dos binding

202

The "Old Version" appeared in over 450 editions with tunes between 1562 and 1688, in sizes from folio to 32mo; many were bound with bibles or prayer books. The 24mo dos-à-dos binding reflected the Puritan principle that women as well as men should sing. It could be easily carried in the purse, and was often adorned with embroidery.
(Nicholas Temperley)

102. Henry Lawes (1596–1662) and others
Choice psalmes put into musick, for three voices. The most of which may properly enough be sung by any three, with a thorough base. Compos'd by Henry and William Lawes, brothers; and servants to His Majestie. With divers elegies, set in musick by sev'rall friends, upon the death of William Lawes. And at the end of the thorough base are added nine canons of three and foure voices, made by William Lawes
London: James Young for Humphrey Moseley and Richard Wodenothe, 1648
Folger L640 pt. 2
Title page, verso

This partbook is one of five forming a collection of original polyphonic settings by Henry Lawes and his late brother William, who was killed fighting for the king at the siege of Chester in 1645. The texts are psalm paraphrases by George Sandys, set as vocal chamber music with continuo. The dedication shows that Lawes, who was one of Charles I's court musicians, was unafraid to advertise his loyalty even at this late date. This book also contains Milton's well-known tribute to its author, as well as Lawes's elegy to his brother.
(Nicholas Temperley)

103. Thomas Sternhold (d. 1549) and others
The whole booke of psalmes, collected into Englishe metre by Thom. Sternh. Iohn Hopkins and others, conferred with the Ebrue, with apt notes to sing them withall. Set forth and allowed to be song in all churches, of all the people together before and after morning and euening prayer: as also before and after sermons, & moreouer in priuate houses, for their godly solace and comfort, laying apart all vngodly songs and balades, which tend onely to the nourishing of vice, & corrupting of youth
London: Iohn Daye, 1573
Folger STC 2443 bd. w. STC 2108
Sig. A2

In this edition of the "Old Version," Day placed solmization letters before each note in an effort to teach "all sortes of people" how to sing the psalms from the music. The device was a French invention, first used in English psalmbooks in 1569. The first page of music shows two of the hymns that preceded and followed the 150 psalms: a translation of the "Veni Creator" and John Markant's original hymn, "The humble sute of a Sinner."
(Nicholas Temperley)

The binding is English, in imitation of earlier French work. A rose and crown flanked by the initials "E R" (Elizabeth Regina), plus "D F" (Defensor Fidei) is worked on the head-edge; and a painted vellum inlay of a crown and shield bears the Royal Arms ensigned by the Garter and motto "Honi. Soit. Qui. Mal. Y. Pense." This may have been a presentation copy given to Queen Elizabeth.[88]

Regi, Regis, &c.
Regum Ar- ca- na cano.
Henricus Lawes
Regiæ Majestatis à sacra Musica.

Cat. 102.

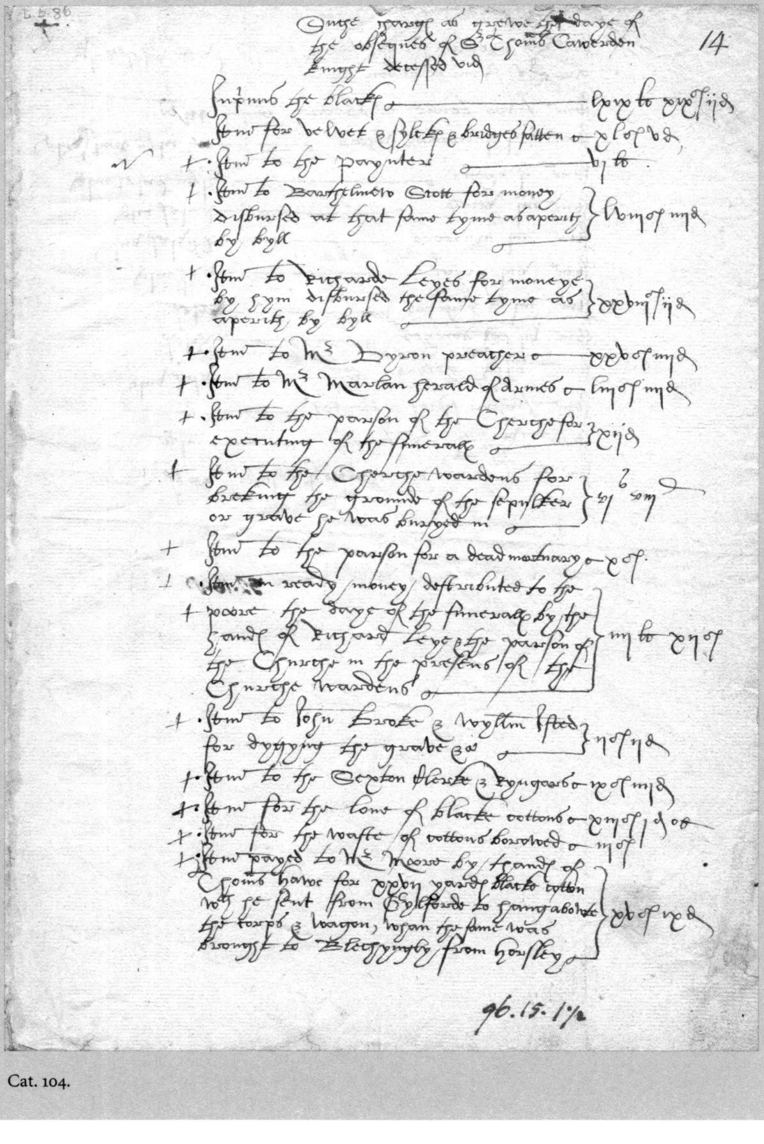

Charges layed out at the tyme of the obsequies of Sr Thomas Cawarden Knight deceased — 14

Inprimis the blacke

Item for velvet silke & bridges satten

Item to the paynter

Item to Bartholomew Scott for money disbursed at that same tyme as apperith by byll

Item to Richarde Leyes for moneye by hym disbursed the same tyme as apperith by byll

Item to Mr Byron preacher

Item to Mr Marten herald of armes

Item to the parson of the churche for [illegible] of the funerall

Item to the churche wardens for breking the grounde of the sepulchre or grave he was buryed in

Item to the parson for a dead mortuary

Item in ready money distributed to the poore the daye of the funerall by the handes of Richard Leye the parson of the churche in the presens of the churche wardens

Item to John Brooke & Willm Sted for digging the grave [illegible]

Item to the Sexton clerke & ryngers

Item for the lone of blacke cottons

Item for the waste of cottons borowed

Item payed to Mr Moore by the handes of Thomas Harve for [illegible] yards blacke cotton wch he sent from Oxforde to hang aboute the corps & wagon, when the same was brought to Bletchingly from Horsley

96.15.1½

Cat. 104.

"For whom the bell tolls": Sounds of Mourning

The sounds of bells are inextricably linked to death and mourning, as many references in the literature of the time make clear.[89] The bell that interrupts Macbeth at the end of his soliloquy (2.1) signals Duncan's murder:

A bell rings.
I go, and it is done. The bell invites me.
Hear it not, Duncan, for it is a knell
That summons thee to heaven or to hell.

A knell is the sound of the slow tolling of a bell rung once for each year of a person's life; known also as a death-bell or passing-bell or soul-bell, it announces a death and calls mourners to the funeral. This is the "sullen" bell about which Shakespeare writes in Sonnet 71 (1609):

No longer mourn for me when I am dead
Than you shall hear the surly sullen bell
Give warning to the world that I am fled
From this vile world with vilest worms to dwell.

So essential were bells to Shakespeare's conception of a funeral that he would anachronistically put bells in ancient Rome. At the end of *Titus Andronicus* (5.3), in denying Tamora proper obsequies, he writes:

No funeral rite, nor man in mourning weed;
No mournful bell shall ring her burial.

In times of plague, funeral knells sounded constantly, as John Taylor, the "Water-Poet," records:

. . . now heare
And marke the mournefull musicke of the Eare,
There doe the brazen Iron tongu'd loud bells
(Deaths clamorous musicke) ring continuall knells,
Some lofty in their notes, some dadly towling,
Whilst fatall dogs made a most dismal howling.[90]

Donne, in his *Devotions*, becomes polemical in his defense of the use of bells at funerals in their function of creating community. Hence his famous line: "Therefore, send not to know for whom the bell tolls, it tolls for thee."[91]

The most powerful musical responses to mourning can be found in the rich and highly affective repertories of elegies and laments that composers wrote for their friends and teachers, or for patrons and other worthies. Music gave expression to grief. In the case of Sir Philip Sidney or Henry, prince of Wales, the musical tributes became part of a national period of mourning.

104. Sir William More (1520–1600)
"Suche charges as grewe the daye of the obseques of Sr Thom*as* Cawerdon Knight decessed," ca. 1559
Folger MS L.b.86
Fol. 1

This document records the expenses for the lavish obsequies, or funeral rites, for Sir Thomas Cawarden (ca. 1514–1559) and includes a payment of nine shillings and four pence to the "Sexton Clerke & Ryngars." Cawarden was a gentleman of Henry VIII's privy chamber and master of the Revels, and Sir William More was his friend and executor.

The document illustrates the elements of a funeral appropriate to a knight.[92] Payments for provision of mourning attire—the blacks, velvet, silk, satin—at over 79 pounds, represented more than half of the total expenditure of 129 pounds. The ritual of the funeral and burial—including payments to the "Sexton Clerke & Ryngars" as well as to the preacher, the parson, the herald of arms, the church wardens, the grave diggers, and 4 pounds distributed to the poor—at about 17 pounds, amounted to less than a quarter of what was spent on cloth. The funeral banquet, which included ox, pig, mutton, rabbit, pigeon, chicken, and veal, cost 32 pounds.

Just what tasks the "ryngars" performed is not specified. Rules established shortly after Cawarden's death "provided that bells were to be rung for the dying, and that there was to be 'but one short peal' after a person's death, and two others before and after the burial."[93] As Peter Marshall explains, "The passing-bell urged hearers to pray for the sick person in their last moment, and after they were dead the ringing served first to announce the departure of the soul, and at the funeral to 'gather the people together to hear the word of God and the thanksgiving." But it would not be unusual, even with committed Protestants like both More and Cawarden, to find practices associated with Catholic beliefs. One example is the dole—money given to the poor—that can be viewed as an attempt to buy prayers for the dead. Another may be the practice of ringing a handbell called the "lich bell" as to accompany the corpse in the funeral procession (one church decreed "there shall no bedeman go . . . [ringing] any bell before any cors ne pray in the stretes openly for the deade with a bell tynkynge"). Despite the admonition that the peal be short, Cawarden's status probably merited quite an extended period of ringing.

105. Thomas Weelkes (1576–1623)
Ayeres or phantasticke spirites for three voices, made and newly published by Thomas Weelkes, gentleman of his Maiesties chappell, Batchelar of Musicke, and organest of the Cathedral Church of Chichester
London: [John Windet for] William Barley, 1608
Folger STC 25202
Bassus, sig. E2: "Death hath depriued me of my dearest friend" (bassus and cantus on facing pages)

Composers sometimes saved their best creative efforts for musical tributes to their teachers or friends. Thomas Weelkes published "A remembrance of my friend M. Thomas Morley" in his final publication; this majestic six-voice elegy seems out of context with the frothy three-voice "ayeres." Despite the claim on the title page, there is no record of his having served as a gentleman of the Chapel Royal; he was organist at Chichester and was dismissed for drunkenness.

The text was written by John Davies of Hereford (1565?–1618), best known as author of the *Writing Schoolemaster*, a handbook that went into many editions. The text is a lament for the death in 1601 of Henry Herbert, second earl of Pembroke, husband of Mary Herbert, countess of Pembroke and sister of Sir Philip Sidney. Davies published the lament in *Wittes Pilgrimage*, undated but entered in the Stationer's Company on 27 September 1605. Morley died in early October 1602. Unless the poem circulated in manuscript, Weelkes must have composed it between 1605 and 1608, several years after Morley's death. His revisions, introducing "must" in the final lines and tightening the repetitions (shown in italics), give him a text that brings out the inevitability of death and dust. His setting ends in a mood of triumphant affirmation.

DAVIES
Death, hath depriud me of my deerest friend;
My Deerest friend is dead, and laid in Grave:
In graue He rests vntill the World shall end:
The World shall end, and end shall all things haue:
All Things haue end, on Earth, that nature wrought;
That Nature wrought shall vnto Dust be brought.

WEELKES
Death hath depriued me of *my dearest friend*
my dearest friend is dead and laid *in graue*
in graue he rests vntill *the world shall end*
the world shall end, as end must all things haue,
all thinges must haue an end *that nature wrought*,
that nature wrought, must vnto dust be brought.

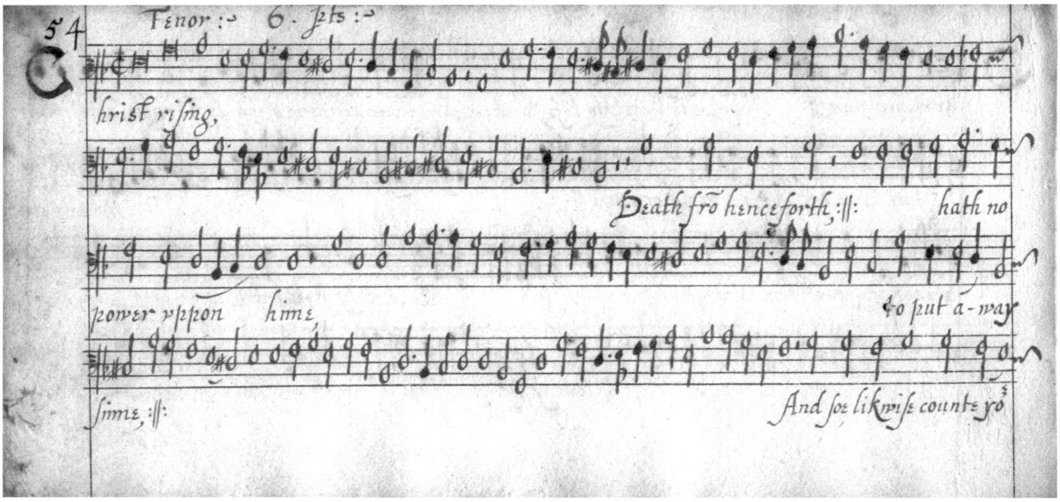
Tenor :- 6. pts :-
Christ rising,
Death fro hence forth, :||: hath no
power vppon hime,
to put a-way
sinne, :||:
And so likewise counte yo

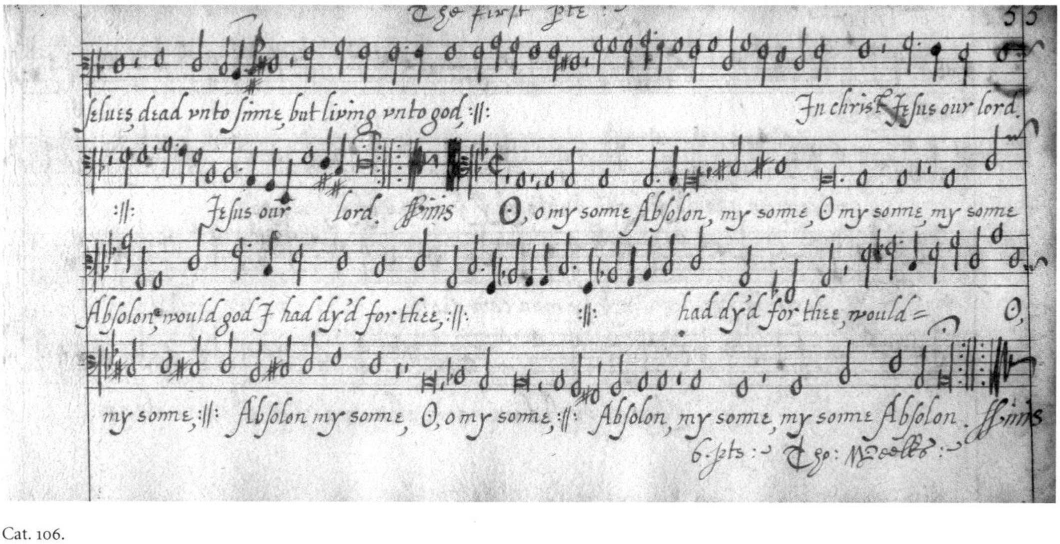
selues dead vnto sinne, but living vnto god, :||:
In christ Jesus our lord.
:||: Jesus our lord. ffinis
O, o my sonne Absolon, my sonne, O my sonne, my sonne
Absolon, would god I had dy'd for thee, :||:
:||:
had dy'd for thee, would=
O,
my sonne, :||: Absolon my sonne, O, o my sonne, :||: Absolon, my sonne, my sonne Absolon. ffinis
6. pts :- Tho: Weelkes :-

Cat. 106.

106. Benjamin Cosyn (ca. 1580–1653), compiler and copyist
Tenor partbook containing English madrigals and "englished" Italian madrigals, Latin settings, instrumental fantasias, and English sacred works (catalogued as "A commonplace book of English madrigals and sacred motets"), ca. 1620–1630
Folger MS V.a.412
Pp. 54–55: William Byrd, "Christ rising" (part 1); Thomas Weelkes, "O my sonne Absolon" (part 2 of "When David heard")

When the Folger Shakespeare Library acquired MS V.a.412 from Rosenbach & Co. in 1941, the bookseller's catalogue described the manuscript as "An Extremely Important Inedited Collection of Elizabethan Songs, Written by Thomas Weelkes." The scribal hand in the manuscript does not agree with known Weelkes autographs, however. But two Jacobean keyboard manuscripts that are in the same hand (one residing in Paris, Conservatoire, Rés. 1185, and the other in London, British Library, R.M.23.l.4, known as the Cosyn Virginal Book) allow identification of the compiler of Folger MS V.a.412 as London organist and composer Benjamin Cosyn.[94]

The sole survivor from an original set of five or six partbooks, Folger MS V.a.412 contains chiefly English madrigals and "englished" Italian madrigals, copied from sixteenth- and seventeenth-century printed sources, as well as a few Latin settings (from Thomas Morley's *Plaine and Easie Introduction to Practicall Musick*, cat. 31), instrumental fantasias, and English sacred works. The manuscripts, which probably date from ca. 1620–1630, may have been used at Dulwich College or Charterhouse, where Cosyn served as organist.

The most striking feature of the source is its inclusion of no fewer than five settings of texts based on 2 *Samuel*. These lamentations by King David on the death of Absalom or Jonathan form part of a larger tradition of musical settings, composed between 1612 and 1620, in which David appears to stand in for King James I and Absalom or Jonathan for Prince Henry, whose death in 1612 provoked comparable, stylized outpourings of grief in literature. Two of the settings Cosyn chose to copy, the highly expressive "O Jonathan, woe is me for thee" and "O my son Absalom" (part 2 of "When David heard that Absalom was slain"), both by Thomas Weelkes, were among the most widely copied David laments in seventeenth-century England and are still among Weelkes's most popular settings of sacred texts.
(Craig Monson)

107. William Byrd (between 1540 and 1543–1623)
Psalmes, sonets, & songs of sadnes and pietie, made into musicke of fiue parts: whereof, some of them going abroad among diuers, in vntrue coppies, are heere truely corrected, and th' other being songs very rare and newly composed, are heere published, for the recreation of all such as delight in musicke: by William Byrd, one of the Gent. of the Queenes Maiesties honorable chappell
[London]: Thomas East, the assigne of VV Byrd, 1588
Folger STC 4253 pt. 2 medius
Medius, sig. G: "Why do I vse" (first singing part) and "Come to me grief"

This is a curious juxtaposition of two elegies, one for the Jesuit Edmund Campion, executed in 1581, and the other for Sir Philip Sidney, who died in 1586. Byrd's decision to publish his setting of Walpole's poem about Campion was daring; to satisfy the censors, he removed specific details and references to Campion, but sympathetic readers would surely have been thinking about the original version, circulating in manuscript as well as print (cat. 91).[95] Might the juxtaposition be a comment by Byrd about Sidney's failure to intervene on behalf of his friend? Jeremy Smith argues that this collection, the first in the period when Byrd was actively employing his monopoly on music printing (1588–1591), was designed as a plea for re-instatement at court following a period when he was placed under house arrest for political purposes.[96]

108. John Coprario (ca. 1570–1626)
Songs of mourning: bevvailing the vntimely death of Prince Henry. VVorded by Tho. Campion. And set forth to bee sung with one voyce to the lute, or violl: by Iohn Coprario
London: [Thomas Snodham] for Iohn Browne, 1613
Folger STC 4546
Title page

John Coprario, possibly known as Cooper or Cowper until he assumed the Italianate form of his name, composed consort music as well as vocal music. The account book of William, second Lord Petre (1575–1637), Folger MS V.a.334, records a 1601 payment for "Lessons hee brought mee while still in London." He entered the service of Robert Cecil, first earl of Salisbury, in 1603 and later served the future Charles I. These settings of poems by Thomas Campion reflect the outpouring of grief at the death of Prince Henry, James I's eldest son and heir apparent. They address the mourners by name—his family (King James, Queen Anne, Prince Charles, Lady Elizabeth, and Frederick Count Palatine) as well as Great Britain and the World.

109. John Coprario (ca. 1570–1626)
Fvneral teares. For the death of the Right Honorable the Earle of Deuonshire. Figvred in seauen songes, whereof sixe are so set forth that the wordes may be exprest by a treble voice alone to the lute and base viole, or else that the meane part may bee added, if any shall affect more fulnesse of parts. The seaventh is made in forme of a dialogue, and can not be sung without two voyces. Inuented by Iohn Coprario
London: Iohn VVindet, the assigne of William Barley, for Iohn Browne, 1606
Folger STC 5679
Sig. D: "In darknesse let me dwel"

Coprario composed these songs on the death of Charles Blount (1563–1606), from 1594 eighth baron Mountjoy and from 1603 earl of Devonshire. Blount, a soldier and courtier, died at a relatively young age in disgrace because of his marriage in 1605 to Lady Penelope Rich, sister of Robert Devereux, the earl of Essex, and Sidney's Stella; Blount had been involved with her for over fifteen years (they had six children) while she was married to Lord Rich. Coprario, possibly the author of this lament, set it in the key of E, unusual in England but common on the Continent. Printed in table layout to facilitate performance, it is scored for canto (soprano), an optional alto, bass viol, and lute. John Dowland would publish his famous setting of this text in 1610.

Notes to the Catalogue

Biographical information is drawn primarily from the *Oxford Dictionary of National Biography* and *Grove Music Online*; references to Samuel Pepys are from *The Diary of Samuel Pepys*, ed. Robert Latham and William Matthews (London, 1971; paperback edition, Berkeley, 2000). Richard Charteris's *An Annotated Catalogue of Music Manuscripts in the Folger Shakespeare Library, Washington, D.C.* (Hillsdale, 2005) appeared after the catalogue was nearly finished; references to his inventories are included but the catalogue entries are largely independent of his work. Citations from Shakespeare follow the Folger Edition. Other texts are given with original spelling and punctuation in the title but normalize capitalization and information concerning place of publication, printer, publisher, and date. Unsigned entries were written by Jessie Ann Owens.

1 See J. J. Raven, *The Bells of England* (London, 1906); H. B. Walters, *Church Bells of England* (London, 1912); Trevor Holloway, "Bells," *Musical Times* 97 (1956); J. Sanderson, ed., *Change Ringing: The History of an English Art* (Cambridge, 1987); David Cressy, *Bonfires and Bells: National Memory and the Protestant Calendar in Elizabethan and Stuart England* (Berkeley, 1989); Judith Maltby, *Prayer Book and People in Elizabethan and Early Stuart England* (Oxford, 1998).

2 Ben Jonson, *Epicoene, or the silent woman A comedie. Acted in the yeare 1609. By the children of her majesties revels* (London, 1620), sig. B4.

3 John Donne, *Deuotions vpon emergent occasions* (London, 1624 [STC 7033]), no. 17.

4 Dorothy L. Sayers offers a vivid account of the customs and techniques of bell-ringing in her mystery novel *The Nine Tailors: Changes Rung on an Old Theme in Two Short Touches and Two Full Peals* (1934).

5 William Stonard (ca. 1575–1631) was an organist and master of the choristers at Christ Church, Oxford. For a modern edition (verse one only), see *The Aldrich Book of Catches* (London, 1989), 87.

6 Ross W. Duffin, "To Entertain a King: Music for James and Henry at the Merchant Taylors Feast of 1607," *Music & Letters* 83 (2002); Linda Phyllis Austern, "Thomas Ravenscroft: Musical Chronicler of an Elizabethan Theater Company," *Journal of the American Musicological Society* 38 (1985).

7 J. A. W. Bennett and H. R. Trevor-Roper, eds., *The Poems of Richard Corbett* (Oxford, 1955), 80–81, 149–52.

8 Julie Spraggon, *Puritan Iconoclasm during the English Civil War* (Woodbridge, 2003).

9 *The Melvill Book of Roundels*, ed. Granville Bantock and H. Orsmond Anderton (London, 1916); Ross W. Duffin, *Shakespeare's Songbook* (New York, 2004), 224.

10 On Stedman and the mathematics behind the changes, see Arthur T. White, "Fabian Stedman: The First Group Theorist?," *The American Mathematical Monthly* 103 (1996); and John Fauvel, Raymond Flood, and Robin Wilson, eds., *Music and Mathematics: From Pythagoras to Fractals* (Oxford, 2003).

11 Eric Wilson, "Plagues, Fairs, and Street Cries: Sounding out Society and Space in Early Modern London," *Modern Language Studies* 25 (1995); Smith, *The Acoustic World*; John Milsom, "Cries of Durham," *Early Music* 17 (1989); *Consort Songs*, ed. Philip Brett, *Musica Britannica* XXII (London, 1967).

12 Eberhard Nehlsen, "Street Musicians of Paris: Evolution of an Image," *Music in Art: International Journal for Music Iconography* 23 (1998); Sean Shesgreen, *Images of the Outcast: The Urban Poor in the Cries of London* (New Brunswick, 2002).

13 John Case, *The Praise of Musicke* (Oxford, 1586), 44.

14 In *Much Ado About Nothing* (2.3); *Mr. William Shakespeares comedies, histories, & tragedies* (London, 1623), 107. Duffin, *Shakespeare's Songbook*, 251, offers a different, conjectural tune for this text. Richard Charteris, *An Annotated Catalogue of the Music Manuscripts in the Folger Shakespeare Library, Washington, D.C.* (Hillsdale, 2005), no. 98, describes the contents of the manuscript before conservation. The scrapbook (formerly in the collections of J. O. Halliwell-Phillipps and the Warwick Castle Library) consists of nine folios with music taken from four leaves that originally belonged to three unrelated manuscripts. Pasting the music into the scrapbook required crossing out and covering up the music on the reverse side; two of the four leaves had to be cut into smaller strips to fit into the quarto format. During conservation, the strips of music were lifted from the scrapbook, and the pages were reconstructed where necessary and photographed. There are five newly visible compositions. Two are by John Wilson: "Deere giue mee a thousand kisses" and "Tell me where ye beauty lye," published in 1659/1660; the two sheets (fol. 1-7) are in the same hand and probably come from the same manuscript. Two (on fol. 8) have concordances in the 1652 *Catch that Catch Can* (cat. 47): John Hilton's "Boy go up and see" and William Webb's "Let me sleepe." See Cyrus L. Day and Eleanore Boswell Murrrie, *English Song-Books, 1651–1702: A Bibliography with a First-Line Index* (London, 1940). The verso of fol. 9 is the second bass viol part for the Alman from Sett no. 6 (D major) of William Lawes's Royal Consort (new version), no. 38 in the 1995 edition by David Pinto. Labeled "21," it is on the back of the Paven labeled "20," (no. 22 from Sett no. 4 in the Pinto edition). This juxtaposition of movements is found in three sources: Oxford, Christ Church 479–83 and London, British Library Add. 31433 and Add. 10445; the writing resembles that identified as Matthew Locke's in the related source Add. 10444. See Andrew Ashbee, Robert Thompson, and Jonathan P. Wainwright, eds. *The Viola Da Gamba Society Index of Manuscripts Containing Consort Music* (Aldershot, 2001).

15 *The Aldrich Book of Catches* (London, 1989).

16 Sean Shesgreen, *The Criers and Hawkers of London: Engravings and Drawings by Marcellus Laroon* (Aldershot, 1990), 100–101; Richard Luckett, ed., *The Cryes of London: The Collection in the Pepys Library at Magdalene College, Cambridge* (Leeds, 1994); Shesgreen, *Images of the Outcast*; Anthony Griffiths, *The Print in Stuart Britain, 1603–1689* (London, 1998), 260.

17 [John Earle], *The Character of a Tavern* (London, 1675), 1–2.

18 John Earle, *Micro-cosmographie* (London, 1628; edition cited, 1664), 85.

19 See, for example, Richard Suggett, "Vagabonds and Minstrels in Sixteenth-Century Wales," in *The Spoken Word: Oral Culture in Britain 1500–1850*, ed. Adam Fox and Daniel Woolf (Manchester, 2002); Emily Cockayne, "Cacophany, or Vile Scrapers on Vile Instruments: Bad Music in Early Modern English Towns," *Urban History* 29 (2002); and *Records of Early English Drama* (Toronto).

20 Stephen Gosson, *The ephemeirides of Phialo* (London, 1586), which contains "An Apologie of the Schoole of Abuse," fol. 87.

21 A. M. Hind, *Engraving in England in the Sixteenth and Seventeenth Centuries*, ed. M. Corbett and M. Norton (Cambridge, 1964), 3:02, 144.

22 See James G. Turner, *Libertines and Radicals in Early Modern London: Sexuality, Politics and Literary Culture, 1630–1685* (Cambridge, 2002).

23 The Folger exemplar seems to be the same as Oxford, Bodleian Library, Firth b.20(145); a facsimile is available at Bodleian Library Broadside Ballads, http://www. bodley.ox.ac.uk/ballads/ballads. A reader has helpfully added "Made upon ye Irish upon Tyrconnells goeing Deputy thither 25 Oct. 1688" and filled in the blanks in the Bodleian copy.

24 Claude M. Simpson, *The British Broadside Ballad and its Music* (New Brunswick, 1966), 449–55.

25 Ibid., 62–64.

26 Duffin, *Shakespeare's Songbook*, 397–400, 152–54; Simpson, *The British Broadside Ballad*, 225–31.

27 Duffin, *Shakespeare's Songbook*, 384–91, 245–47.

28 From the extensive scholarship on this topic, let me cite only a few recent studies: Duffin, *Shakespeare's Songbook*; Smith, *The Acoustic World*; and David Lindley, *Shakespeare and Music* (London, 2006). See the essays by Bruce Smith and Ross Duffin in this volume.

29 See the essay by Bruce Smith in this volume.

30 Duffin, *Shakespeare's Songbook*, 422–24.

31 Andrew J. Sabol, "A Three-Man Song in Fulwell's *Like Will to Like* at the Folger," *Renaissance News* 10 (1957); Charteris, no. 70.

32 It is possible that this frontispiece is from the 1672 edition.

33 Duffin, *Shakespeare's Songbook*, 221–23.

34 Ibid., 433–34. Charteris, no. 93.

35 On the gamut, see Jessie Ann Owens, "Concepts of Pitch in English Music Theory 1560–1640" in *Tonal Structures in Early Music*, ed. Cristle Collins Judd (New York, 1998); on instruction in practical music, see Rebecca Herissone, *Music Theory in Seventeenth-Century England* (Oxford, 2000).

36 One of the many instances of this sort of didactic verse can be found in John Playford, *A breefe introduction to the skill of musick* (London, 1654), 4.

37 *The Folger 'Dowland' Manuscript*, The Lute Society Facsimiles, vol. 3 (Guildford, 2003). Charteris, no. 104.

38 John Milsom, "Songs and Society in Early Tudor London," *Early Music History* 16 (1997).

39 D. W. Krummel, *English Music Printing 1553–1700* (London, 1975); John Milsom, "Music," in *The Cambridge History of the Book in Britain*, vol. 3: 1400–1557, ed. Lotte Hellinga and J. B. Trapp (Cambridge, 1999) and Mary Chan, "Music Books," vol. 4: 1557–1695, ed. John Barnard and D. F. McKenzie (Cambridge, 1999).

40 *The Byrd Edition*, vol. 1 (London, 1977), xxiv.

41 Ibid., viii.

42 Jeremy L. Smith, *Thomas East and Music Publishing in Renaissance England* (Oxford, 2003).

43 Richard Freedman, *The Chansons of Orlando Di Lasso and Their Protestant Listeners: Music, Piety, and Print in Sixteenth-Century France* (Rochester, 2001), 171.

44 Craig Monson, *Voices and Viols in England, 1600–1650* (Ann Arbor, 1982), 77–123.

45 Smith, *Thomas East*, 45–48.

46 Michael G. Brennan, "Sir Charles Somerset's Music Books (1622)," *Music & Letters* 74 (1993). The identification was made by Rachel Doggett.

47 Smith, *Thomas East*, 107–11.

48 See the essay by Stacey Houck in this volume.

49 Charteris, no. 95; Duffin, *Shakespeare's Songbook*, 157–69.

50 Nicholas Barker, ed., *The Great Book of Thomas Trevilian*, 2 vols. (London, 2000); Heather Wolfe, *"The Pen's Excellencie": Treasures from the Manuscript Collection of the Folger Shakespeare Library* (Washington, DC, 2002).

51 Mary Rasmussen, "An Iconography of the Bagpipe 16th Century," http://www.unh.edu/music/Icon/ibpjs.htm. Concerning the print formerly attributed to Galle, see Philips Galle, *The New Hollstein Dutch & Flemish Etchings, Engravings and Woodcuts 1450–1700*, comp. Manfred Sellink, Marjolein Lessberg, ed. Manfred Sellink (Rotterdam, 2001): 4:249.

52 For an interpretation of the significance of this representation of music, see Smith, *The Acoustic World*, 110–12. My thanks to Nicholas Temperley for this information; see his *Hymn Tune Index* (Oxford, 1998).

53 Tobias Hume, *The First Part of Ayres (1605), Captaine Humes Poeticall Musicke (1607)*, ed. Sterling Jones, intro. Veronika Gutmann (Winterthur, 1980). A facsimile of the British Library copy is in *English Lute Songs 1597–1632: A Collection of Facsimile Reprints*, vol. 6, ed. Frank Traficante (Menston, 1969). Lynn Hulse, "'Musique which pleaseth myne eare': Robert Cecil's Musical Patronage," in *Patronage, Culture and Power: The Early Cecils*, ed. Pauline Croft (New Haven, 2002), 143.

54 See the essay by Jeremy Smith in this volume. On the lute and its social context, see Julia Craig-McFeely, "The Signifying Serpent: Seduction by Cultural Stereotype in Seventeenth-Century England," in *Music, Sensation, and Sensuality*, ed. Linda Austern (New York, 2002).

55 Peter Fischer, *Music in Paintings of the Low Countries in the 16th and 17th Centuries* [=*Sonorum Speculum* 50–51] (Amsterdam, 1972), 38–46, observes, "... in the midst between the principal figures playing their instruments so peacefully we see this tree with its fruits: the tree separates the two people who are craving to be united. Underneath the tree, hidden under the joining sleeves of the couple yet plainly visible is the serpentlike body of the Earthly Seducer and destroyer of Harmony, stretching lugubriously upwards." Concerning a similar de Passe allegory, see Linda P. Austern,

"For, Love's a Good Musician": Performance, Audition, and Erotic Disorders in Early Modern Europe," *Musical Quarterly* 82 (1998).

56 Jeremy Smith, "Music and Late Elizabethan Politics: The Identities of Oriana and Diana," *Journal of the American Musicological Society* 58 (2005).

57 A similar document is published in Andrew Ashbee, *Records of English Court Music*, vol. 4: 1603–1625 (Snodland, 1991), 30; British Library Add. MS 31825, "Establishment List." See G. A. Philipps, "Crown Musical Patronage from Elizabeth I to Charles I," *Music & Letters* 58 (1977); Peter Holman, *Four and Twenty Fiddlers* (Oxford, 1993); and Walter L. Woodfill, *Musicians in English Society from Elizabeth to Charles I* (New York, 1969, 1st ed., 1953).

58 Woodfill, *Musicians in English Society.*

59 John Milsom, "Sacred songs in the chamber," in *English Choral Practice 1400–1650*, ed. John Morehen (Cambridge, 1995).

60 The information about this manuscript is drawn from John Ward, *Music for Elizabethan Lutes* (Oxford, 1992), 1:16–21, 84–88, 110–12; editions are give in vol. 2. Charteris, no. 85.

61 Peter Walls, *Music in the English Courtly Masque, 1604–1640* (Oxford, 1996).

62 John R. Elliott, Jr., "The Folger Manuscript of the Triumph of Peace Procession," *English Manuscript Studies 1100–1700* 3 (1992).

63 Warwick Edwards, "The Sources of Elizabethan Consort Music," Ph.D. diss., University of Cambridge, 1974; Matthew Jeffries, *Consort, Full, and Verse Anthems*, ed. John Cannell (Madison, 1998), 119; Charteris, no. 92.

64 Alan Stewart and Heather Wolfe, *Letterwriting in Renaissance England* (Washington, DC, 2004), 100–102.

65 Charteris, no. 84.

66 Lynn Hulse, "The Musical Patronage of Robert Cecil, First Earl of Salisbury," *Journal of the Royal Musical Association* 116 (1991): 34.

67 Thomas Morley, *A plaine and easie introduction to practicall musicke* (London, 1597), 180.

68 Brennan, "Sir Charles Somerset's Music Books," items 10–17; identification of "C. S." made by Rachel Doggett.

69 This case draws heavily on the work of Penelope Gouk, *Music, Science and Natural Magic in Seventeenth-Century England* (New Haven, 1999); Part II, "The Gallery," is a virtual exhibition in itself.

70 Ibid., 157–70.

71 Jamie C. Kassler, *The Beginnings of the Modern Philosophy of Music in England: Francis North's* A Philosophical Essay of Musick *(1677)* (Aldershot, 2004), 30–35.

72 Ibid., 39.

73 Gouk, 142–43.

74 Jocelyn Godwin, *Robert Fludd: Hermetic Philosopher and Surveyor of Two Worlds* (London, 1979), 52.

75 Edgard Hoskins, *Horae Beatae Mariae Virginis; or, Sarum and York Primers, with Kindred Books, and Primers of the Reformed Roman Use* (London, 1901), no. 93; Roger S. Wieck, *Painted Prayers* (New York, 1997); Roger S. Wieck et al., *Time Sanctified: The Book of Hours in Medieval Art and Life* (New York, 1988).

76 Charteris, no. 73.

77 A. Jefferies Collins, *Manuale ad vsum Percelebris Ecclesie Sarisburiensis* (London, 1960).

78 Robin A. Leaver, *"Goostly psalmes and spirituall songes": English and Dutch Metrical Psalms from Coverdale to Utenhove 1536–1566* (Oxford, 1991), 226–37.

79 Ward, *Music for Elizabethan Lutes*, 1:110. Rivkah Zim, *English Metrical Psalms: Poetry as Praise and Prayer, 1535–1601* (Cambridge, 1987), 127–28.

80 H. Nixon, "Day's Service Book, 1560–1565," *British Library Journal* 10 (1984): 1–31. See also John N. King, "John Day: Master Printer of the English Reformation," in *The Beginnings of English Protestantism*, ed. Peter Marshall and Alec Ryrie (Cambridge, 2002).

81 See the essay by Craig Monson in this volume.

82 *Théâtre des cruautés des héretiques de notre temps de Richard Verstegan*, ed. Frank Lestringant (Paris, 1995).

83 Gerard Kilroy, *Edmund Campion: Memory and Transcription* (Aldershot, 2005), 59–88.

84 Smith, *Thomas East*, 103–105.

85 Philip Brett, "Edward Paston (1550–1630): A Norfolk Gentleman and His Musical Collection," *Transactions of the Cambridge Bibliographical Society* 4 (1964).

86 Samuel A. Schmitt, "The Paston Manuscripts in Context: A Study of Folger Shakespeare Library MSS V.a.405–407," Ph.D. diss., Catholic University of America, 2004; Charteris, no. 91.

87 See the essay by Nicholas Temperley in this volume.

88 This description of the binding is taken from "Bindings from the Reign of Queen Elizabeth I," no. 5, in Frederick A. Bearman, Nati H. Krivatsy, J. Franklin Mowery, *Fine and Historic Bookbindings from the Folger Shakespeare Library* (Washington, DC, 1992), 62–63.

89 Ralph Houlbrooke, *Death, Religion, and the Family in England, 1480–1750* (Oxford, 1998); Peter C. Jupp and Clare Gittings, eds., *Death in England: An Illustrated History* (Manchester, 1999); Vanessa Harding, *The Dead and the Living in Paris and London, 1500–1670* (Cambridge, 2002); Peter Marshall, *Beliefs and the Dead in Reformation England* (Oxford, 2002).

90 *The Fearefull Summer: or Londons Calamatie* (London, 1625), 59; cited by Wilson, "Plagues, Fairs," 12.

91 Richard Strier, "Donne and the Politics of Devotion," in *Religion, Literature, and Politics in Post-Reformation England, 1540–1688*, ed. Donna B. Hamilton and Richard Strier (Cambridge, 1996).

92 Marshall, *Beliefs and the Dead in Reformation England*; David Cressy, "Death and the Social Order: The Funerary Preferences of Elizabethan Gentlemen," *Continuity and Change* 5 (1989).

93 Marshall, *Beliefs and the Dead in Reformation England*, 161–68, quotations from 162 and 165.

94 Craig Monson, *Voices and Viols in England, 1600–1650* (Ann Arbor, 1982), 39; Pamela Willetts, "Benjamin Cosyn: Sources and Circumstance," in *Sundry Sorts of Music Books: Essays on the British Library Collection*, ed. Chris Banks, Arthur Searle, and Malcolm Turner (London, 1993); Charteris, no. 96.

95 Kilroy, *Edmund Campion.*

96 *The Byrd Edition*, vol. 12 (London, 2004).

Suggestions for Further Reading

(see also the notes to the essays and to the catalogue)

Ashbee, Andrew. *Records of English Court Music.* Snodland; Aldershot, 1986–1995.

Ashbee, Andrew, and David Lasocki, eds. *A Biographical Dictionary of English Court Musicians 1485–1714.* Aldershot, 1998.

Austern, Linda. "'Alluring the Auditorie to Effeminacie': Music and the Idea of the Feminine in Early Modern England." *Music and Letters* 74 (1993).

———. *Music in English Children's Drama of the Later Renaissance.* New York, 1992.

Baldwin, Elizabeth. *Paying the Piper: Music in Pre-1642 Cheshire.* Kalamazoo, 2002.

Bowers, Roger. *English Church Polyphony: Singers and Sources from the 14th to the 17th Century.* Aldershot; Brookfield, 1999.

Boyd, Morrison Comegys. *Elizabethan Music and Musical Criticism.* Revised edition. Philadelphia, 1974.

Bray, Roger, ed. *The Sixteenth Century.* The Blackwell History of Music in Britain. Oxford, 1995.

Caldwell, John. *The Oxford History of English Music.* Vol. I, *From the Beginnings to c. 1715.* Oxford; New York, 1991.

Charteris, Richard. *An Annotated Catalogue of Music Manuscripts in the Folger Shakespeare Library, Washington, D.C.* Hillsdale, 2005.

Clark, Peter. *The English Alehouse: A Social History, 1200–1830.* London; New York, 1983.

Duffin, Ross. *Shakespeare's Songbook.* New York, 2004.

Finney, Gretchen L. *Musical Backgrounds for English Literature: 1580–1650.* New Brunswick, 1962.

Gouk, Penelope. *Music, Science and Natural Magic in Seventeenth-Century England.* New Haven, 1999.

Harper, John. *The Forms and Orders of Western Liturgy from the Tenth to the Eighteenth Century.* Oxford; New York, 1991.

Hollander, John. *The Untuning of the Sky: Ideas of Music in English Poetry, 1500–1700.* Second edition. New York, 1970.

Holman, Peter. *Four and Twenty Fiddlers: The Violin at the English Court 1540–1690.* Oxford; New York, 1993.

Houck, Stacey Jocoy. "Decoding Music Resistance: Vocal Music in the Service of the King (1625–1660)." Ph.D. diss., University of Illinois, 2005.

Kisby, Fiona, ed. *Music and Musicians in Renaissance Cities and Towns.* Cambridge; New York, 2001.

Krummel, D. W. *English Music Printing 1553–1700.* London, 1975.

Le Huray, Peter. *Music and the Reformation in England, 1549–1660*. Second edition. Cambridge; New York, 1978.

Lindley, David. *Shakespeare and Music*. London, 2006.

McColley, Diane Kelsey. *Poetry and Music in Seventeenth-Century England*. Cambridge; New York, 1997.

Mellers, Wilfrid. "Music: Paradise and Paradox in the Seventeenth Century." In *Seventeenth-Century Britain*, ed. Boris Ford. Cambridge, 1992.

Milsom, John. "Music, Politics, and Society." In *A Companion to Tudor Britain*. Blackwell Companions to British History, ed. Robert Tittler and Norman L. Jones. Malden, 2004.

———. "Sacred Songs in the Chamber." In *English Choral Practice 1400–1650*, ed. John Morehen. Cambridge, 1995.

———. "Songs and Society in Early Tudor London." *Early Music History* 16 (1997).

Monson, Craig. "Byrd, the Catholics, and the Motet: The Hearing Reopened." In *Hearing the Motet: Essays on the Motet of the Middle Ages and Renaissance*, ed. Dolores Pesce. New York, 1997.

———. "Elizabethan London." In *The Renaissance: From the 1470s to the End of the 16th Century*, ed. Iain Fenlon. Englewood Cliffs, 1989.

———. *Voices and Viols in England, 1600–1650: The Sources and the Music*. Ann Arbor, 1982.

Morehen, John, ed. *English Choral Practice 1400–1650*. Cambridge, 1995.

Page, Daniel Bennett. "Uniform and Catholic: Church Music in the Reign of Mary Tudor (1553–1558)." Ph.D. diss., Brandeis University, 1996.

Price, David C. *Patrons and Musicians of the English Renaissance*. Cambridge; New York, 1981.

Schmitt, Samuel Armstrong. "The Paston Manuscripts in Context: A Study of Folger Shakespeare Library MSS V.a.405–407." Ph.D. diss., Catholic University of America, 2004.

Seng, Peter J. *The Vocal Songs in the Plays of Shakespeare, a Critical History*. Cambridge, Mass., 1967.

Shesgreen, Sean, ed. *The Criers and Hawkers of London: Engravings and Drawings by Marcellus Laroon*. Aldershot; Stanford, 1990.

———. *Images of the Outcast: The Urban Poor in the Cries of London*. New Brunswick; Manchester, 2002.

Smith, Jeremy. "Music and Politics in Late Elizabethan England: The Identities of Oriana and Diana." *Journal of the American Musicological Society* 58 (2005).

———. *Thomas East and Music Publishing in Renaissance England.* Oxford; New York, 2003.

Smith, Bruce R. *The Acoustic World of Early Modern England: Attending to the O-Factor.* Chicago, 1999.

Spink, Ian, ed. *The Seventeenth Century.* The Blackwell History of Music in Britain. Oxford, 1992.

———. *English Song: Dowland to Purcell.* Second edition. London; New York, 1986.

Temperley, Nicholas. *The Hymn Tune Index: A Census of English-Language Hymn Tunes in Printed Sources from 1535 to 1820.* 4 vols. Oxford; New York, 1998.

———. *The Music of the English Parish Church.* Cambridge; New York, 1979.

Walls, Peter. *Music in the English Courtly Masque 1604–1640.* Oxford; New York, 1996.

Woodfill, Walter L. *Musicians in English Society from Elizabeth to Charles I.* Revised edition. New York, 1969.

Notes on Contributors

Erin Blake is the Curator of Art and Special Collections at the Folger Shakespeare Library. A specialist in early-modern prints, her current research focuses on the history of book illustration.

Rachel Doggett is Andrew W. Mellon Curator of Books and Exhibitions at the Folger Shakespeare Library where, over the past fifteen years, she has overseen the preparation and mounting of forty exhibitions and the production of numerous exhibition publications.

Ross W. Duffin teaches Music History and directs the Early Music Performance Practice program at Case Western Reserve University in Cleveland. He is the author of *Shakespeare's Songbook* (2004).

Ian Harwood has worked on sixteenth- and early seventeenth-century English music and instruments since the 1960s, as an independent scholar and a maker and player of bowed and plucked stringed instruments. He was co-founder of the Lute Society in 1963 and is currently its president.

Stacey Jocoy Houck teaches music history at Texas Tech University. She is editor of a critical edition of John Playford's *Introduction to the Skill of Musick* (in progress). Her current research is on the role of music in the English Civil Wars.

Lubbock

Kerry McCarthy is Assistant Professor of Musicology at Duke University, where she recently hosted an international conference on the music of William Byrd. Her book on Byrd's *Gradualia* will appear with Routledge in 2006.

John Milsom has taught at Christ Church, Oxford, and Middlebury College, Vermont. He has published widely on sixteenth-century music in general, and Tudor music in particular. His catalogue of the important collection of early printed and manuscript music at Christ Church, Oxford, is available online as an interactive database.

Jessie Ann Owens is Louis, Frances and Jeffrey Sachar Professor of Music at Brandeis University and a former Folger Fellow. She is author of *Composers at Work: The Craft of Musical Composition 1450–1600* (1997) and is currently working on a book about key in early modern England.

Leigh Anne Palmer is Exhibitions Coordinator and Assistant to the Andrew W. Mellon Curator of Books and Exhibitions at the Folger Shakespeare Library.

Eric Rice is Assistant Professor of Music History at the University of Connecticut, Storrs. A specialist in music of the late Middle Ages and Renaissance, his scholarship is focused on music of the Western liturgy and its relationship to architecture, politics, and secular music.

Samuel A. Schmitt recently completed his dissertation on the Paston manuscripts at the Catholic University of America under the guidance of G. Grayson Wagstaff. His current research is on the role of music in the devotional life of the English recusant community.

Bruce Smith is College Distinguished Professor of English and Professor of Theatre at the University of Southern California. His book *The Acoustic World of Early Modern England: Attending to the O-Factor* (1999) has found readers with interests in acoustic ecology, anthropology, history, musicology, sociology, and sound art as well as English and cultural studies. He is completing a book on the color green that includes a chapter on "Hearing Green."

Jeremy Smith (University of Colorado, Boulder) is the author of *Thomas East and Music Publishing in Renaissance England* (2003) and editor of volume 12 of the *Byrd Edition*. His most recent essay, "Music and Late Elizabethan Politics: The Identities of Diana and Oriana," appeared in the Fall 2005 issue of the *Journal of the American Musicological Society.*

Pamela F. Starr is Professor of Music History at the University of Nebraska-Lincoln, and a Fellow of the American Academy in Rome. She has published widely on the Cappella Sistina in the fifteenth century, and is now working on a monograph, *Music at the Margins in Early Modern England.*

Nicholas Temperley taught musicology at the University of Illinois at Urbana-Champaign from 1967 to 1996. He is the author of *The Music of the English Parish Church* (1979) and *The Hymn Tune Index: A Census of English-Language Hymn Tunes in Printed Sources from 1535 to 1820.* He is currently editing, jointly with Sally Drage, a volume of eighteenth-century English psalmody for Musica Britannica.

Andrew Walkling is Dean's Lecturer in Art History, English, and Theatre at the State University of New York at Binghamton. He specializes in the politics of cultural production at the court of Charles II; his publications include studies of Restoration opera and court masque.

Heather Wolfe, Curator of Manuscripts at the Folger Shakespeare Library, has edited *Elizabeth Cary, Lady Falkland: Life and Letters, The Pen's Excellencie: Treasures from the Manuscript Collection of the Folger Shakespeare Library*, and, with Alan Stewart, *Letterwriting in Renaissance England.* She has also written several articles on manuscripts in early modern England.

Georgianna Ziegler is the Louis B. Thalheimer Head of Reference at the Folger Shakespeare Library. She has curated exhibitions on Shakespeare's heroines and on Elizabeth I and has published on early modern women and on Shakespeare in the nineteenth century.

Design:
Studio A, Alexandria, Virginia
www.thestudioa.com

Printing:
HBP, Inc., Hagerstown, Maryland
www.hbp.com

Paper:
Mohawk Options, True White Vellum, 70 text
Lustro Dull, White, 100 cover with matte lamination

Type:
Minion